Authoritarian Capitalism in the Age of Globalization

T0327476

This book is dedicated to my grandmother,
Margaret Hershberger Cowan
(20 October 1926–26 May 2011)
who taught me it is possible to change the world every day

Authoritarian Capitalism in the Age of Globalization

SECOND EDITION

Peter Bloom

Essex Business School, University of Essex, UK

Edward Elgar
PUBLISHING

Cheltenham, UK • Northampton, MA, USA

Published by
Edward Elgar Publishing Limited
The Lypiatts
15 Lansdown Road
Cheltenham
Glos GL50 2JA
UK

Edward Elgar Publishing, Inc.
William Pratt House
9 Dewey Court
Northampton
Massachusetts 01060
USA

Paperback edition 2024

A catalogue record for this book
is available from the British Library

Library of Congress Control Number: 2022950544

This book is available electronically in the **Elgar**online
Business subject collection
http://dx.doi.org/10.4337/9781802204612

ISBN 978 1 80220 460 5 (cased)
ISBN 978 1 80220 461 2 (eBook)
ISBN 978 1 0353 4299 0 (paperback)

Printed and bound by CPI Group (UK) Ltd, Croydon, CR0 4YY

Contents

Preface to the Second Edition

As I am completing this second edition the world once more appears on the verge of war. While military conflicts continue to go on unabated, the Russian invasion of Ukraine by Putin stokes particular fears in many of a potential global conflict. It has dangerous historical resonances with the Second World War in which an autocratic leader seems to be displaying unchecked military aggression against a less powerful but determined foe claiming to fight not just for their own survival but the very preservation of democracy.

Whatever the ultimate outcome of this imperialist assault, it has perhaps never in modern history been so urgent to understand the role of capitalism for ultimately promoting authoritarianism. The half decade since the publication of the first edition has witnessed the resurgence of demagogic leaders fueled by far-Right populist movements worldwide. The once believed permanent triumph of liberal democracies at the end of the Cold War is suddenly in dire peril. Underpinning this resurgence is growing global inequality and an ever more profitable and hi-tech "security" industry.

Not geographically far but seemingly a world away, one of the oldest modern democracies, France, held at the same time a much anticipated national election. It pitted the legitimately dreaded far-Right provocateur Marine Le Pen against the paradigm of respectable Centrism Emmanuel Macron. It seemed the entire international community sighed a breath of victorious relief as Macron won, signaling a temporary but far from secure victory not just for him but for liberal democracy. It is tempting and perhaps comforting for many to take these established narratives at face value. The fact that democracy is presently endangered is, of course, undeniable. Yet, its so-called protectors appear only slightly less authoritarian in practice than those they are meant to be fighting against. Promising to run France as a "start-up" nation, the President has regularly undermined key democratic institutions and threatened individual liberties of those who oppose his regime, styling himself as a modern-day political "boss" straight out of the corporate boardrooms that make up his strongest supporters.

The purpose of this second edition is to directly apply the original insights of the book for understanding this continued rapid explosion of "authoritarian capitalism" across the globe. It will explore how the fantasy of "state-led market progress" has quickly evolved into a dystopian reality where fascism is on the rise and illiberal democracy is the norm. It will critically attempt to see the matrix of our "smart" politics and economy where individuals and groups are regularly monitored by governments and corporations while new "strong" leaders emerge representing "the people."

Importantly, this updated edition is meant to show that the resurgence of fascism and repressive democracies are connected and symptomatic of the fundamental authoritarianism of capitalism. When the book was originally published in 2016, its focus was on how corporate globalization was catalyzing new discourses and associated practices of state-led market progress. In particular, it highlighted the intensification of a hyper-capitalist international marketplace which had given rise to an appealing vision of the need for a strong state actor. Emerging was an appealing fantasy of a government able to best compete in this world market while repressing internal forces that put this victory in danger.

In the proceeding half decade since its publication, authoritarian capitalism has evolved, intensified, and spread. It is now far-Right demagogues who are simultaneously promising to protect "the people" from the continued exploitation of globalization while seeking to eliminate any progressive alternative to capitalism. Challenging them is a political establishment who present themselves as the last beacon of hope for preserving democracy even while expanding new forms of hi-tech surveillance and profiting off lucrative authoritarian industries such as detention centers, weapon making, and "smart" behavioral modification technologies. The first aims, it would appear, to destroy democracy, the other to limit it to within acceptable elite boundaries. Both reflect a contemporary authoritarian capitalist logic and each in its own way puts into jeopardy the very future of popular rule and freedom.

This new edition builds on the original version by trying to succinctly capture this updated form of authoritarian capitalism. It does so mainly through a new chapter alongside a substantially expanded conclusion. The new chapter explores the emergence of "popular authoritarianism" interrogating how repressive discourses of state-led market progress are being weaponized into a mass politics by both the far-Right and the Centre. Specifically, both have taken advantage of the crisis of corporate globalization to forge fresh visions of an empowering market order. Indeed, it explores how the state has become in no small part even more reified as necessary for market progress either as the basis for a conservative ethno-capitalism or the foundation for recovering liberal democracy. What is exceedingly apparent is that, despite their profound differences, both revolve around using the state for protecting the population, whether it be from foreigners and liberal elites on the one hand or "deplorables" and progressives on the other. These politics share a capacity to cover over the deeper authoritarianism at the heart of global capitalism.

Yet this edition will also explore the resistances that have sprouted to directly challenge this growing and increasingly virulent trend of "authoritarian capitalism." Around the world, movements have arisen challenging police brutality and demanding enhanced data protection and rights. The fear that even limited basic liberal democracy is in peril has led to renewed efforts to save it against social media misinformation and updated forms of voter exclusion. More radically, there are fresh ideas for how to reboot democracy against the tyranny of autocracy, illiberalism, and fascism. The prospect of a more emancipated and progressive society is now not only more politically realistic but also technologically sophisticated. At stake is whether it is still possible to imagine and create a politics and world free from the grip of authoritarian capitalism.

Acknowledgments for the Second Edition

This new edition book was inspired by the desire to better understand, and in doing so transform, the current global rise of authoritarian capitalism. I would like to thank the editors at Edward Elgar Publishing for their continuing belief and support for this project and its updated second edition. In addition to all the people I thanked in the first edition I would also like to show my profound gratitude to my partner Sara Gorgoni and our son Tomas Bloom-Gorgoni – to whom all my work is dedicated.

Acknowledgments for the First Edition

I am grateful to all the members of the Department of People and Organisations at the Open University for their encouragement. I would also like to give a special thanks to the former research group People, Organization and Work at Swansea University including Carl Rhodes, Alison Pullen, Pasi Ahonen, Paul White, Sam Dallyn, and Sheena Vachhani. I am also indebted to the members of the Ideology and Discourse program and the Government Department at the University of Essex for its early intellectual stimulation of these ideas – notably David Howarth, Aletta Norval, Jason Glynos, Leonidas Karakatsanis, Cengiz Gunes, Emilio Allier Montaño, Albert Weale, Hugh Ward, David Sanders, Deborah Savage, David Hugh Jones, and Sevasti-Eleni Vezirgiannidou. Finally, I am grateful to Chris Ratke for his excellent copy-editing of the final draft.

Personally, this book could not have been completed without the support of those closest to me. I am grateful to my parents, Martin Bloom and Sarah Cowan Bane, for their lifetime of support, as well as to my sister Jane Bloom. I am also grateful to Frederick Bane, Phyllis Bloom, Mallory Powers, Justin Golden, Meghan Powers, and Jay Bauer. I would like to thank my partner Sara Gorgoni and her family, Marcello Gorgoni, Maria-Rosaria Stabili, and Barbara Gorgoni. Lastly, I am grateful for all my friends and colleagues who helped make this possible, including my "other family", Nikolaos Dipsis, Victoria Sverdlov-Dipsis, Leon Dipsis, and Alex Dipsis along with Gideon Ratke, Angella Bellotta, John Stanbro, Kathleen Stanbro, Luke Stanbro, Mrinalini Greedharry, Nicholas Watts, Jennifer Miller Watts, and Kayla Miller Watts.

1. The rise of authoritarian capitalism in the twenty-first century

As the twenty-first century dawned there was fresh optimism for the triumph of democracy over political authoritarianism. The end of the Cold War supposedly signaled the "end of history" and with it the rise of liberal democracy and the demise of authoritarian regimes worldwide. Associated with this promise was the spread of economic capitalism internationally. It was to be an era of peaceful democratic markets. As one commentator at the time famously declared:

> What we may be witnessing is not just the end of the Cold War, or the passing of a particular period of post-war history, but the end of history as such: that is, the end point of mankind's ideological evolution and the universalization of Western liberal democracy as the final form of human government. (Fukuyama, 1989)

Yet the first decade of the new millennium has belied these optimistic expectations. While it is indeed an age of capitalist globalization, political authoritarianism has not only survived but seems to be gaining new steam. Moreover, it has done so in the name of preserving marketization nationally and transnationally.

This apparent contradiction between economic liberalization and political authoritarianism has raised questions about the contemporary role of capitalism as a positive force for democratization. Rather than transitioning previously totalitarian states toward democracy and deepening it within perceived established liberal states, globalization has instead been theorized as enhancing despotism and repressive policies. Economic liberalization is increasingly viewed as a national "shock" that requires an oppressive sovereign state to implement and maintain its commonly unpopular "reforms" (Klein, 2007). This has also brought to the forefront deeper concerns regarding the fundamental relation of capitalism to authoritarianism. In this regard, economists are pointing to the inherent function of marketization for creating and sustaining political oligarchy (Piketty, 2014). These fears have only been exacerbated following the financial crisis of 2008 alongside the rising power of authoritarian "great powers" internationally.

At stake then is how to account for this paradox, that the more economically liberal a country becomes the greater its reliance on authoritarianism seems to be across contexts. More precisely, to illuminate how the deepening of marketization worldwide is contributing to the strengthening of explicitly dictatorial regimes and the illiberal policies progressively pursued by traditionally democratic states. What are the underlying dynamics driving this diverse "authoritarian capitalism" in the twenty-first century? How to explain the rise of authoritarian capitalism in the age of globalization? What does this reveal about the more fundamental relationship between political authoritarianism and economic capitalism?

AIM

These concerns are especially pressing given the resurgence of political authoritarianism in the twenty-first century. Indeed the new millennium has been witness to the appearance and strengthening of explicitly despotic and non-democratic regimes, notably Russia and China, all extolling their exclusive ability to properly and successfully guide their country's market transition. Just as worrying has been the growth of "illiberal democracies" (Velasco, 2013; Zakaria, 1997) whose authoritarian social policies belie their stated formal democratic institutions and economic commitment to liberalization. Somewhat less explored but in a similar vein have been fears regarding the authoritarian characteristics of established liberal democratic nations within "developed" liberal democratic capitalist economies associated with such policies as the "War on Terror" and "War on Drugs" (Henry et al., 2005; Steger, 2008). Many continue to fear the strengthening of the so-called "imperial executive" within these nominally democratic regimes in the new millennium (O'Hehir, 2014; Schlesinger, 2004; Yuhan, 2004).

What is at the root of this emerging and seemingly universal rise of "authoritarian capitalism"? How, specifically, are contemporary processes of economic globalization not only not diminishing these established forms of authoritarianism but seemingly positively contributing and reinforcing them in the present era? To answer these questions it is necessary to approach anew a more fundamental question – what is the general relationship between economic capitalism and political authoritarianism? In addressing this deeper concern it is then possible to begin addressing how globalization is currently reflective of and evolving this relationship in the making of diverse forms of "authoritarian capitalism." Crucial to such an investigation is to ask in what ways is the structural spread of capitalism internationally giving rise to renewed desires for an authoritarian politics and the legitimization of authoritarian policies. And how has the crisis of authoritarian capitalism, paradoxically, created new fantasies of authoritarian leadership and more repressive forms of democracy?

POLITICAL AUTHORITARIANISM AND GLOBALIZATION

This book explores the relationship of economic capitalism and political authoritarianism within the contemporary era of globalization. The examination of this relationship has taken on increased importance with the rise of authoritarian capitalist states on the one hand and the deployment of authoritarian-style politics by ostensibly liberal democratic countries on the other. The proliferation of such a politics alongside intensified economic policies of marketization across the globe represents the emergence of diverse forms of authoritarian capitalism nationally and internationally. This manuscript illuminates the political legitimization and spread of capitalism through these different but connected authoritarian politics.

This analysis emerges out of these present-day challenges and attempts to contribute to a wide range of existing literature on this topic. Traditionally, marketization has been inexorably linked with processes of democratic transition. More precisely, economic liberalization is meant to be a necessary condition for democratization (see most notably Dahl, 1989; Lipset, 1959; Moore, 1967; Muller, 1995). To this end, economic and political liberalization are theorized to have a complimentary relationship, as the former creates the required conditions for the latter. Here, the emerging bourgeois class, formed in the transformation to a market economy, exists as an independent force challenging dictatorial rule and catalyzing the shift to liberal democracy. It follows logically, from this perspective, that as marketization spreads globally so too will democracy.

Nevertheless, this dominant perspective has long been challenged by critical, especially Marxian, scholarship emphasizing the strong function of the state in maintaining capitalist, and often oligarchic, relations (Jessop, 1990; Plamenatz, 1992; Poulantzas, 1978). Here, governments worked in conjunction with dominant capitalist classes to ensure elite rule, facilitating political authoritarianism both informally and at times formally. Historically, these theories were supported by the persistence of politically authoritarian yet economically capitalist states throughout the developing world during the Cold War period (see, for instance, Canak, 1984; Robison, 1988; Serra, 1979). However, with the fall of the Soviet Union there was a renewed optimism about the positive role of marketization for fostering new democratic regimes (Fukuyama, 1989).

This debate has expanded recently to encompass broader discussions of the relation of democratization with globalization. Scholars increasingly focus on the effect of international factors such as marketization for positively producing democratic governments in replacement of authoritarian regimes (Drake,

1998; Whitehead, 1996). This positive view of economic liberalization as a force for democratization and against authoritarianism conforms to previous modernization theories. Economic globalization, in this sense, serves as a catalyst for a political liberalization globally. These theoretical assumptions, moreover, stand as a strong justification for policies of privatization across contexts in both developing and developed countries.

However, this positive relation has been put into question. By contrast, recent evidence suggests that policies of economic capitalism tend to weaken the prospect for political democracy nationally (O'Neal, 1994). Notably, it is said to incentivize governments to pursue policies, often coercively, favoring foreign investors at the expense of popular opinion and welfare (Cox, 1996; Diamond, 1999; Gray, 1996). This view resonates with broader perspectives setting processes of marketization directly against the prospect for genuine democratic transitions due to its need for oligarchy and a strong government to legitimize such restructuring (Cammack, 1998; Im, 1987; Martin et al., 1997).

These insights resonate with recent literature chronicling the rise of enhanced political authoritarianism coupled with hyper marketization. These studies have been especially prevalent in former communist states. The fall of the Soviet Union brought with it expectations of democratization (Pickel, 1993). While this has occurred in many places nominally, the region has also experienced a preservation, and in many cases enhancement, of authoritarian forms of governance (Bunce, 2003; Heryanto, 1999). Russia is a prime example of this tension. Whereas it has successfully maintained an edifice of parliamentarianism, in practice the country has seen the retention of quite non-democratic features ranging from the presence of a "strong" national leader in Putin to the large influence of new capitalist oligarchs (Ambrosio, 2009; Aslund, 2007; Gavrov, 2007; Hanson, 2007; Sautman, 1995; Schatz, 2009). Similarly inspired studies have concentrated on the proliferation of authoritarianism in East Asia, even as countries across the region have increasingly embraced economic liberalization (Chang, 2002; Gills, 2000; Han and Ling, 1998; Lingle, 1996a; Robison, 1988). China remains the foremost example of this "authoritarian capitalist" state – a government whose monopoly rule not only survives amidst marketization but who in fact uses its non-democratic power to further its capitalist economic agenda (Dirlik, 1997; Ma, 2009; Tsai, 2007; Winfield and Peng, 2005).

Emerging from such country-specific studies have been novel attempts to understand more generally this new combination of political authoritarianism and economic marketization. In particular, this phenomenon has been referred to as "soft authoritarianism." This label has been applied to a wide range of regimes internationally, all of whom have combined authoritarian rule with economic marketization (Pei, 2000; Prizel, 1997; Roy, 1994; So, 2002; Stubbs, 2001). More precisely, it has crystallized, at least in rhetoric, a popular vision of a strong non-democratic state or leader for effectively implementing these changes for the sake of national progress and popular welfare (Gat, 2007; Rodan and Jayasuriya, 2009; Swyngedouw, 2000). Consequently, globalization has produced in its wake not only concrete authoritarian regimes but also a new authoritarian myth of capitalist development and socioeconomic prosperity (Beeson, 2010; Fu and Chu, 1996; So and Chan, 2002; Thompson, 2004).

Somewhat less explored, but in a similar vein, have been examinations of the authoritarian characteristics of established liberal democratic nations within "developed" capitalist economies. Perhaps not surprisingly, these have primarily focused on the "War on Terror" and its adoption of what for many appear to be traditionally authoritarian language and methods (Henry et al., 2005; Steger, 2008). Yet this tacit form of authoritarianism within liberal democratic settings is also witnessed in the quite prohibitive "War on Drugs," the rise of a prison-industrial complex and the marginalization both in rhetoric and practice of groups such as immigrants and "benefit thieves" for explaining the nation's ills (Giroux, 2007; Hetherington and Weiler, 2009). This "liberal authoritarianism" has further been associated with, though problematically only limitedly and often without proper explanations, chronic economic problems such as recession and rising inequality.

These observations have led, in turn, to theoretical discussions explaining the persistence of such explicit and implicit authoritarianism to the global spread of "neoliberalism." According to this perspective, the proliferation of capitalism internationally is part of a broader shift away from democratic forms of rule (Brownlee, 2007; Tickell and Peck, 2003). In its place will be new types of power, prioritizing the authority of corporations and their state allies as well as the ability of individuals to "self-discipline" themselves in line with these market-based values (Giroux, 2004; Ong, 2006, 2007). Present then is the legitimization of political authoritarianism, whether through non-democratic regimes or everyday practices of coercion, in the service of furthering corporate globalization.

NEW APPROACHES FOR UNDERSTANDING "AUTHORITARIAN CAPITALISM"

There is no one explanation for exhaustively investigating or understanding political authoritarianism in relation to capitalism. As the above studies reveal, this is a multifaceted issue that demands a wide array of perspectives and explanations. Globalization only adds to the complexity of this problem. Called for are perspectives that illuminate the deeper structural relation of capitalism to political authoritarianism as well as the historically specific ways such a politics is serving to legitimize and support global capitalism. To do so requires a theoretical framework that ably combines both structural and post-structural approaches. This would enable an investigation, at once general in its explanation and respecting of contextual differences, of simultaneously how economic liberalization catalyzes political authoritarianism and political authoritarianism discursively strengthens economic liberalization.

For this reason, it is imperative to study not only the material economy of globalization but its discursive and psychic economy as well. At stake is illuminating what types of subjects global capitalism is currently producing both in its generalizable practices and its shared identifications. This book draws, therefore, on an ideology and discourse approach for studying the current relation of political authoritarianism and economic liberalization. This perspective focuses on the role of dominant discourses for structuring social relations and identity according to its understandings (Laclau and Mouffe, 1986). Emphasized is the ability for a prevailing set of beliefs, understandings, and values to organize a field of meaning according to its own rationale and logic. Thus, Howarth (2000: 102) describes a hegemonic project as one which strives to "weave together different strands of discourse in an effort to dominate or structure a field of meaning, thus fixing the identities of objects and practices in a particular way."

Hegemony is also reinforced at the affective level, as a dominant discourse psychologically "grips" subjects according to its constructed desires. The Lacanian concept of fantasy, employed by a number of Laclauian commentators (see especially Glynos and Stavrakakis, 2004), is key for understanding this process. Fantasy is defined as "the element which holds together a given community [that] cannot be reduced to the point of symbolic identification" (Žižek, 1993: 201). As such:

> the bonds linking together its members always implies a shared relationship to the Thing, toward enjoyment incarnated … If we are asked how we can recognise the presence of this Thing, the only consistent answer is that the Thing is present in that elusive entity called our "way of life." (Žižek, 1993: 201)

Social identity is consequently formed around common fantasies promising shared wholeness, ideals regarding a potential "way of life" to be captured and strived toward. All social and political identity thus "is supported by a reference to a lost state of harmony, unity and fullness, a reference to a pre-symbolic Real which most political projects aspire to bring back" (Stavrakakis, 1999). Liberal democracy, for example, is not just a set of principles citizens rationally accept as correct. It is, additionally, a fantasy; seizing subjects psychologically in its utopian vision of a perfected and perfectible society based on reified values of freedom, individualism, collective self-determination, and shared prosperity.

Importantly, these fantasies have a dualistic structure. On the one hand they are sustained through reference to a positive "stabilizing" fantasy, as referred to in the examples above. On the other hand, these beatific visions are constantly placed under threat by the presence of a negative "destabilizing" fantasy. Returning to the example of liberal democracy, it is a politics that while often utopian in its sentiment and aims is nonetheless often desperately partisan and antagonistic in its actual politics. Conservatives imagine Liberals maliciously trying to prevent their vision of an idealized Christian market society from materializing while Liberals similarly demonize the evangelical Right for supposedly stopping a secular fairer market economy. Consequently, all hegemony is marked by the appearance of a utopian fantasy promising wholeness linked to a malevolent fantasy trying to prevent such enjoyment from ever coming to pass.

This work examines how a market ideology in a particular historical context – in this case contemporary globalization – is politically supported by cultural fantasies. More precisely, it aims to show how political authoritarianism has arisen as a diverse but nonetheless common political fantasy for legitimizing and strengthening economic capitalism globally. These efforts resonate with the various ways the state has historically attempted to promote itself as a sovereign actor able to effectively "guide" markets. These previous efforts may seem to have become outdated due to the "free market" neoliberal ideologies of the past several decades leading up to and continuing into the twenty-first century. Nevertheless, the goal of this book is to illuminate the ways this sovereign-based fantasy has arisen once again in this era of corporate globalization, attached to particular resurgent authoritarian values politically. A question that must be asked, thus, is how politics is a central and vital element to the contemporary global spread of neoliberalism.

DEFINING ECONOMIC LIBERALIZATION AND POLITICAL AUTHORITARIANISM

In order to set forth this argument it is important to clarify what is meant in the work by the terms political authoritarianism and economic liberalization. The latter will be defined first, as its meaning within the context of this work is more straightforward. The concept of economic liberalization is predominantly defined as the process by which a national economy becomes more market oriented, profit driven, and placed within private hands. It is normally associated with the right of private property, wage labor, reduced state intervention into the economy, and the relatively unregulated buying and selling of goods on the market. Processes of transition toward such a system are referred to as marketization. Of course, there is by no means total agreement as to a universal description of economic liberalization – for instance, some demand no public role in the economy and others a limited one, or some proponents focus on macro considerations of economic growth as an indicator of economic health while others concentrate on the privatization of production and consumption on the micro level. However, there is a relative consensus as to the core tenets of principles, one which espouses a general commitment to capitalism.

The concept of authoritarianism is more ambiguous and therefore deserves greater analytical reflection. Traditionally, authoritarianism connotes a non-democratic regime (Gill, 2000; Vesta, 1999). More precisely, one which has not been legitimized by popular election or who upon election seeks to remain in power indefinitely. Authoritarianism is thus counterposed to democracy, a relationship further transposed onto the opposition between capitalism and its economic competitors. Turning again to modernization theory, it is predominantly assumed that democracy and liberalization are partners in the struggle against authoritarianism and non-market "state-"based economic systems.

Recently, theorists from a wide range of perspectives have associated authoritarianism with themes of ideological openness. The sociologist Howard Gabennesch (1972), for instance, in the early 1970s, linked authoritarianism, both as a politics and a personal framework for action, with ideological reification and the presence of a narrow "world view." Similarly, psychologists Adorno, Frenkel-Brunswik, Levinson, and Sanford (1950) postulated the so-called "authoritarian personality," which resonated strongly with values of conformity and an unquestioned commitment to conventional values. Empirically, illiberal attitudes have been statistically associated with an authoritarian perspective (e.g. a desire for orthodoxy and acceptance of existing beliefs), stressing the need for orthodoxy and acceptance of existing belief – thus Canetti-Nisim (2004) found that the more orthodox one's religious views the more authoritarian, and less democratically oriented, one's political views tended to be.

Within the post-structuralist tradition, a normative and ethical commitment to ideological plurality, "openness" rather than essentialism, is a central component of its overall approach. Howarth (2000: 124) notes in this regard that: "a postfoundational perspective does not give rise to a certain set of political and ethical decisions – though it does rule some positions out – those based on essentialist presuppositions – for example. The assertion and justification of values are thus the result of an articulatory practice, rather than a necessary entailment."

Politically, this has spawned a rethinking of democracy highlighting the contingency, and therefore contestability, of prevailing norms and larger belief systems governing society. Laclau and Mouffe (1986: 149–93), among others, argue accordingly for a project of "radical democracy," which in recognizing the inherently contingent, incomplete nature of the social would render political institutions and identities more open to contestation and differing ideological perspectives. In their words, "This moment of tension, of openness, which gives the social its essentially incomplete and precarious character, is what every project of radical democracy should set out to institutionalize" (1986: 190). Consequently, it is a type of politics "founded not upon dogmatic postulation of any 'essence of the social,' but, on the contrary on affirmation of the contingency and ambiguity of every 'essence,' and on the constitutive character of social division and antagonism" (1986: 193).

As alluded to in the previous discussion of the conception of "illiberal democracies" of a democratic hegemony, it can be seen that such accounts of democracy, and by association authoritarianism, are both structural and subjective in nature. The former speaks to the ways in which a particular entrenched ideology remains unquestioned for guiding individual actions and decisions and the latter refers to how subjects ethically experience and relate to a social belief system – either democratically (e.g. contingent, open to contestation, never complete in its explanatory ability) or authoritarian (e.g. essentialist, unquestioned, and totalizing in its scope). In this respect, political authoritarianism can be judged according to the degree of ideological openness within a given context as well as the affective investment individuals place in political discourses empowering the state to preserve this status quo.

This work accepts, and seeks to unite, these more formal and informal accounts of political authoritarianism. It defines authoritarianism as the presence of a non-democratically elected government as well as a political culture with relatively little ideological debate or possibility of change. Furthermore, it connects such authoritarianism to the legitimized power given to governments to protect this hegemonic system through a range of formal and informal repressive practices. Importantly, these are not always simultaneous in their occurrence. For instance, a formally democratic society may rely on a rather closed set of ideological values, such as the United States and its commitment to economic capitalism. This is, of course, not to assume that there is ever a society, field of meaning, free from any sort of closure. Instead it is a discussion of the degree to which certain dominant norms, beliefs, and subjectivities are available to contestation and possible transformation within an existing political terrain as well as the state and other sovereign institutions' accepted and often desired role for maintaining these entrenched socioeconomic relations.

However, it is the contention of this book that there is a positive and mutually reinforcing relationship between these two forms of political authoritarianism. To this end, the higher degree of ideological closure the greater likelihood for formal political authoritarianism. The way ideological closure can give rise to and legitimize practices of political authoritarianism is important, whether in formal democracies or explicitly authoritarian regimes. Again, looking at the

United States context, the ideologically closed principles underlying the Bush administration's "War on Terror" served to catalyze and justify authoritarian practices such as the curtailing of civil liberties and refusal of habeas corpus to suspected terrorist prisoners.

This research focuses thus on the exact ways official attempts to ideologically objectify, and thus close debate around, capitalism have discursively reinforced political authoritarianism, both formally and informally, in different settings internationally. More precisely, how an unquestioned ideological commitment to economic liberalization linked to discourses of globalization has produced a structurally reinforcing and affectively appealing capitalist fantasy of authoritarian capitalism politically. In doing so, it will also hope to shed light on the reasons why the recent challenges to this dogmatic faith in the free market has led to such authoritarian rather than democratic alternatives.

OUTLINE

This book will hopefully provide a fresh perspective for understanding the relationship of authoritarianism and capitalism both generally and as specific to this current era of globalization. To do so it will explore this diverse authoritarian politics of capitalism within a range of national and international contexts. It will do so by first providing a historical overview revealing the previous linking of capitalism ideologically and in practice with both democratic and authoritarian political discourses. Central to this historical account will be the ways capitalism dealt with ideological challenges, similar to other economic belief systems such as communism, through political fantasies that championed authoritarian governments and policies. It will then update this largely hidden authoritarian history of capitalism to the contemporary period revolving around discourses of globalization.

From this foundation it will examine the proliferation of capitalist fantasies of political authoritarianism in rising despotic "state market" powers such as Russia and China, and "developing countries" like Singapore and Mexico who legitimize formal and informal authoritarian rule through discourses of "modernization" and "democratization," respectively. It will then shift its attention to long-standing liberal democratic regimes who have drawn on globalization discourses, such as the "War on Terror," for granting the state greater power to use "illiberal" measures to protect liberal democracy politically and neoliberalism economically. Following this investigation, it will interrogate the paradoxical way international capitalist institutions, notably the International Monetary Fund and World Bank, have encouraged authoritarian capitalism at the national level in the name of maintaining a "responsible" international financial order. It will conclude by highlighting theoretically and empirically how the global spread of capitalism strengthens political authoritarianism.

Chapter 2 will provide a historical account linking the evolution of economic capitalism to political fantasies of progress. This will explore, in particular, the connection of marketization to affective discourses stressing at different times democracy, colonialism, and political authoritarianism. It will also reveal how leaders attempted to deal with the inability of capitalism to always deliver on its promises of prosperity, especially in bourgeoning liberal democratic countries, with fantasies demonizing social groups involving the deployment of a range of authoritarian rhetoric and concrete methods.

Chapter 3 looks in more depth at how present-day globalization has contributed to these historical trends. The ideologically closed nature of corporate globalization, reflected in popular understandings of it as "inevitable," produces resurgent desires for personal and collective agency. These desires are translated politically into a renewed appeal to the power of the state to recapture this lost sense of freedom and collective self-determination. In particular, it presents the government as effectively able to shape and guide globalization for the needs of its citizens. Consequently, these longings for sovereign protection become channeled into affectively resonant capitalist discourses of political authoritarianism.

Chapter 4 will examine the growth of new national regimes combining traditional authoritarian politics with the promotion of intensified economic marketization. Focusing particularly on the cases of China and Russia, it will trace out the shared legitimization of this form of authoritarian politics and capitalist economics through a fantasy of state-led market progress. It will then reveal how the closed ideological nature of capitalism as a "global" economic project – one where other ideas of economic development are marginalized or repressed – contributes to a matching authoritarian politics revolving around the state's singular ability to popularly guide this "inevitable" marketization against internal and external enemies.

In a similar vein, Chapter 5 looks at how affective authoritarian discourses linked to values of "modernization" and "democratization" are legitimizing neoliberal development. In particular, it will concentrate on how policies of marketization and privatization within "developing" countries have been conjoined with explicit and implicit political fantasies extolling the dominant function of the state for achieving and preserving national development. It will do so through the case studies of Singapore and Mexico, where aspirations for economic and political "modernization" have been strategically deployed to justify authoritarian rule and marketization policies for advancing the country.

Chapter 6 investigates the seemingly paradoxical deployment of authoritarian political rhetoric and practices by established liberal democratic regimes. This can be witnessed, for instance, in the West's ongoing "War on Terror," as well as enhanced policing to deal with internal threats ranging from "terrorists" to "immigrants" to social deviants such as drug users to "benefit thieves." To explain this apparently contradictory phenomenon, the chapter will explore the displacement of social and economic dissatisfaction, structurally related to policies of increased financialization, onto a demonized external or internal "other." More precisely, it champions the ability of a state to extend its power politically to spread liberal democracy abroad and protect it at home, while accepting its dramatically retreating role economically. It will also reveal how this discourse of liberal authoritarianism actively prevents the development of more democratically substantive and empowering forms of politics, as well as geographically confining popular rule to national boundaries.

Chapter 7 surveys the use of authoritarian fantasies to legitimize capitalism globally. It will do so through examining the accepted power of international institutions such as the International Monetary Fund and World Bank to dictate national policy to reflect a narrow neoliberal economic agenda. In particular, it emphasizes its empowering of national governments to police itself and its citizens for the sake of preserving a "responsible" global free market. Such national "self-disciplining" is connected to a broader fantasy of governments using their power, even if necessarily repressively, to ensure that their country can survive and flourish in this international capitalist order. It also reveals how this fantasy empowers international institutions such as the International Monetary Fund to "discipline" fiscally "irresponsible" states.

Chapter 8 will explicitly explore the evolution of authoritarian capitalism into new forms of far-Right populism and increasingly repressive forms of democracy. In particular, it will focus on the transformation of fantasies of "state-led market progress" into political discourses embracing either ethno-capitalism or an illiberal democratic status quo. It explores the emergence of the "global native," reflecting those who feel "left behind" by globalization and are seeking to protect their culture (and ultimately privilege) through investing in demagogic leaders. It also reveals the ways existing political and economic elites have sought to repress the further democratization and possibility of systemic change in the name of protecting democracy against this far-Right resurgence.

The ninth and final chapter concludes with an analysis of the common connection between these various forms of authoritarian capitalism. It will highlight how this analysis reveals the positive and dangerous relationship between economic capitalism and political authoritarianism. It will discuss, in this respect, how corporate globalization is historically, politically, affectively, and structurally producing authoritarian capitalism.

2. Fantasizing authoritarian capitalism: a brief history

There is a long tradition of trying to accurately theorize the relationship between capitalism and authoritarianism. Notably, this reflects fundamental questions linked to the influence of the economy on politics as well as politics on the economy. Is the political sphere merely a deterministic reflection of the economy? Is the economy a byproduct of a prevailing hegemonic politics? These concerns have taken on seemingly new life with the advent of globalization. As noted in Chapter 1, the assumption that liberal democracy would naturally follow from the international spread of marketization has been dramatically put into doubt. Yet it remains unclear how to properly theorize and contextualize the simultaneous growth of economic liberalization and political authoritarianism in the contemporary age.

A still common assumption driving much of the mainstream scholarly literature and public debate is the equating of privatization with economic freedom and, as such, inherently counter to political authoritarianism (Giavazzi and Tabellini, 2005; Haggard and Webb, 1993; Pickel, 1993). Indeed, a central thrust of contemporary political science remains how to effectively conjoin political liberalization with economic marketization (Robinson and White, 1998; Salamé, 1994; Widner, 1994). Private enterprise is viewed by many as the epitome of personal liberty. This idealized perception is captured in the common reference to capitalism as the "free market" or even as a process of economic "liberalization" (Easton and Walker, 1997; Farr et al., 1998; Pitlik, 2002).

Stemming from this association of marketization with economic freedom is the belief that this naturally contributes to political freedom. Put differently, the current era of globalization is marked by a belief that there is a symbiotic relation of personal liberty in the marketplace with the creation and strengthening of liberty politically. Milton Friedman belies such a view in his rather famous declaration:

> Historical evidence speaks with a single voice on the relation between political freedom and a free market. I know of no example in time or place of a society that has been marked by a large measure of political freedom that has not also used something comparable to a free market to organize the bulk of economic activity. (Friedman, 1962: 9)

The modernization theories of the twentieth century have become transformed in the twenty-first century into a new triumphalist discourse of the inevitable victory of the liberal democratic state that combines economic and political "freedom" (Deudney and Ikenberry, 2009).

Nevertheless, perspectives highlighting the inherently authoritarian character of capitalism itself have challenged these ideas. These views directly question the normative legitimization of capitalism as being based upon political "consent" and "free labor." Instead, they stress the exploitation at the core of these "private" economic relations. Capitalism relies on the authoritarian power of managers to profit from the labor of a less powerful workforce. Similarly, twenty-first-century capitalism continues to produce an authoritarian form of managerial-based politics (Amin, 1997; Canterbury, 2005).

These relations certainly fit the beginnings of an industrial economy – one that was marked by quite regulative and hierarchical employment relations. Indeed, counter to much present discourse, the nineteenth and early twentieth centuries witnessed the association of mass economic freedom not only with private enterprise but also with labor rights (Foner, 1999). Here, liberty was encapsulated in the enhanced collective power of the workforce to counteract the domination by owners and management. The economic "freedom" of the market was equated at points with ideas of "slave wages" and even more radically "wage slaves" (Persky, 1998).

Extending into the modern period, critical scholars have sought to illuminate the continued regulative and repressive character of contemporary capitalism. The proliferation of worsening labor conditions internationally, popularly associated with the increased use of "sweatshops" in less-developed economies, highlights, for many, the authoritarianism at the heart of capitalism. Yet, even in developed countries with stronger labor protections and the proliferation of human resource management styles, critical scholars illuminate the authoritarianism that remains central to workplace relations.

"Corporate Culturists commend and legitimise the development of a technology of cultural control that is intended to yoke the power of self determination to the realization of corporate values from which employees are encouraged to derive a sense of autonomy and identity" (Willmott, 1993: 563). This reading of capitalism as authoritarian by nature speaks to and potentially reframes the discussion on the effect of politics and economics on each another. Early theorists critical of capitalism assumed that economic relations were deterministic of political relations. Marx famously envisioned the economy as the fundamental structural driver of the political "super-structure" (Marx, 1977; Williams, 1973). The political sphere, in this regard, was a malleable but nonetheless constant force for legitimizing capitalist economic relations. Liberal democracy was decried noticeably as merely a political mirage of liberty masking the repressive reality of market-based exploitation. Globally, colonialism and imperialism were traced back to an inexhaustible profit motive of capitalist elites and their eternal hunger for new markets (Marx, 1990, 1992).

Recently, though, there has been a recognized need to complicate and possibly go beyond this deterministic model. Rather than economics serving as the foundation for the political, it is now the political that is prioritized as the basis for sustaining entrenched economic practices and values (Söderberg and Netzén, 2010). The economy then is viewed as an outgrowth of existing political relations and dominant ideologies (Laclau and Mouffe, 1986). Capitalism, in this view, can be democratized at both the micro level of the workplace and at the macro level of national as well as transnational politics. Whether or not the market produces an authoritarian politics is completely context dependent. Or more precisely, the economic is continuously able to be politicized and as such transformed.

This book seeks to find a middle ground between these poles of determinism and contingency. On the one hand, it rejects the previous economic determinism of Marxism. It studies political authoritarianism and economic capitalism as contingently formed sets of social practices and value systems. To this end, both are equally formed through historical social movements and ideological struggles. Moreover, while connected, they are not always linked cleanly or compatibly. Rather, formal politics and everyday economic relations are always both negotiated alongside and in uncertain relation with one another.

On the other hand, this analysis does hope to reveal the ways capitalism can positively help to foster and reinforce diverse forms of political authoritarianism. It aims to do so through revealing the various symmetries between the authoritarian characteristics of capitalism economically and the authoritarian politics which this often informs. This may be found in the simple transference of certain market values into the political realm (e.g. the consenting to a powerful manager or leader in exchange for personal wellbeing). Or it may take the form of an authoritarian political response to the chronic problems associated with a capitalist economy (e.g. repressive scapegoating strategies against a minority population deemed publicly "responsible" for a disappointing economy).

This work looks specifically at how economic globalization is helping to produce a similarly globalizing political authoritarianism. What are the specific discourses associated with contemporary globalization that create the conditions for wide-ranging forms of despotism and political repression? Specifically, how are these processes producing rather appealing capitalist fantasies of political authoritarianism nationally? Such an investigation requires a more thorough theoretical and historical overview of this relationship of capitalism to authoritarianism.

APPROACHING THE HISTORY OF AUTHORITARIAN CAPITALISM

The traditional political narrative of capitalism is one of the ongoing triumphs of democracy. The freedom provided by markets goes hand in hand with the liberalization of a society politically. This national discourse is supposedly universal in its scope, as all countries regardless of culture or history can draw upon the forces of marketization to produce a stable and vibrant liberal democracy. However, this triumphant narrative is undercut by the more complex, and at times seemingly explicitly antagonistic, relationship of economic capitalism with the creation of greater political freedom and democracy.

Recent discussions focus on the sheer variety of the political forms capitalism can take. Indeed, it seems to be adaptable to quite progressively regulative social democracies as much as it is at home in explicitly pro-market political environments (Dore et al., 1999; Hall and Soskice, 2004; Rueda and Pontusson, 2000). In the contemporary period of globalization, this variety has come to encompass, as will be shown in Chapter 3, single-party political regimes who are nonetheless economically committed to expanding marketization at all costs. This authoritarian capitalism echoes previous instances where dictators were supported and ruled in the name of implementing a capitalist economic agenda. Repressive measures were legitimized as an important means of fighting communism and providing the stability necessary for capitalist economic growth (Kirkpatrick, 1982).

New historical perspectives are needed to account for the positive interaction between capitalism and authoritarianism. Crucial for such a historical recounting is to move away from deterministic explanations of this relation. Put differently, both Marxists and liberals, despite their differences, have often assumed that there is a necessary and immutable way the economy affects the political sphere. From a so-called "modernization" perspective even up to the present, this outlook is captured in the firm belief of mainstream thinkers and policy-makers that democracy is an organic outgrowth of marketization. By contrast, many Marxists contend that capitalism will necessarily deconstruct due to its own internal contradictions, leading politically to the transition toward socialism (Bullock and Yaffe, 1975; Chesnais, 1984; Clarke, 1994; Grossman, 1992; Mattick, 1981; Yaffe, 1973). Yet this notion has been called into severe question both by the failures of actually existing socialism and the fact that capitalism has remained resilient in the face of multiple historical crises.

Economics and politics are, thus, in a constant, and never predetermined or easily predictable historical negotiation with each other. "Open Marxists" highlight this contingent rather than deterministic history (Bonefeld, 1992;

Burnham, 1994). They stress the role of crisis periods for reconstructing the politics of capitalism. In the words of Bell and Cleaver (1982: 191), "such a 'political reading' of crisis theory eschews reading Marx as philosophy, political economy, or simply as a critique. It insists on reading it from a working-class perspective and as a strategic weapon within the class struggle." This reconstruction can be quite diverse in character. It may mean the expansion or diminishing of the state's involvement in the market, depending on what the political situation demands. Politically, it could entail further repression or caving in to popular pressure for reforms (whatever they may be) to shore up capitalism fundamentally and the authority of elites (Cleaver, 1992).

Such readings gesture toward the compatibility of political authoritarianism for expanding capitalism economically. The state has always played a significant role in supporting and strengthening marketization (Wolfe, 1977). Theoretically, the more representative aspects of liberal democracies are eternally threatened and potentially diminished and limited by the need to protect the rights and power of capitalists (Miliband, 1969; Wright, 1979). Empirically, the state functions to regulate and shape the norms required for the advancement and strengthening of capitalism (Jessop, 1982; Poulantzas, 2000).

From this vantage point, the rise of authoritarian capitalism becomes clearer. Capitalism can politically be more or less authoritarian depending on the broader sociohistorical climate. More to the point, authoritarian capitalism can arise through rendering itself an attractive political discourse. This insight reflects the ideas of neo-Gramscians, who situate the politics of capitalism as inexorably linked to processes of popular legitimization (Cox, 1987; Ruggie, 1982). Quoting from Gramsci himself: "A crisis occurs ... This exceptional duration means that uncurable structural contradictions have revealed themselves ... and that, despite this, the political forces which are struggling to conserve and defend the existing structure itself are making efforts to cure them within certain limits, and to overcome them" (1971: 178). These legitimizations are subject to continual change and evolution in light of political and social events.

Authoritarian capitalism can therefore be seen as a historically specific, though by no means historically unique, dominant political discourse. The previously discussed work of Laclau and Mouffe (1986) is especially instructive in this regard. They emphasize the formation and entrenchment of sociopolitical relations through the hegemonic struggle between discourses for supremacy. Authoritarian discourses and practices are then inexorably associated with broader processes of sociopolitical legitimization and maneuvering. Key is their effectiveness in popularly framing market policies or, conversely, the ability of marketization policies to be strategically directed in support of authoritarian political regimes.

This is not to imply though that the politics of capitalism is completely arbitrary. Rather, it is to show that it evolves out of specific historical and cultural contexts that render certain understandings more sensible and attractive than others. At stake, hence, is to better illuminate the sociohistorical factors that have made authoritarianism politically appealing as a discourse within the present age of expansive global capitalism.

FANTASY, CAPITALISM AND AUTHORITARIANISM

Capitalism is traditionally studied as a largely economic, therefore material, phenomenon. Yet the success of markets and marketization relies upon deep affective commitments (Boltanski and Chiapello, 2007; Hardt, 1999; Kenny et al., 2011). Even at the most basic level, consumption is premised on the emotional appeal of advertisements (Kavka, 2008; Skeggs and Wood, 2012). This affective component extends to all facets of capitalist life, from production to its political legitimization as a socioeconomic system. Employment, for instance, is replete with romanticized workplace identities extolling the virtues of the firm. The search for a job is underpinned by fantasies of personal and professional success (Bloom, 2013). At the broader level, capitalism as an economic system draws on idealized promises of future prosperity and shared socioeconomic development to justify its continued existence, especially during times of crisis (Bloom, 2014).

More than being just a collection of material transactions, capitalism exists, then, as a dynamic and always evolving affective, or psychic, economy. It is composed of a diverse set of emotionally resonant discourses that help to produce social identity and regulate practices. People, in this respect, are psychologically "gripped" by capitalism – constructing and securing their sense of selfhood attached to its appealing promises of psychological fulfillment. Quoting Žižek again:

> [T]he element which holds together a given community cannot be reduced to the point of symbolic identification: the bonds linking together its members always implies a shared relationship to the Thing, toward enjoyment incarnated … If we are asked how we can recognise the presence of this Thing, the only consistent answer is that the Thing is present in that elusive entity called our "way of life." (Žižek, 1993: 201)

Revealed, in turn, is a fresh vantage point from which to understand capitalist reproduction. Its preservation is inexorably linked to its ability to psychologically "seize" subjectivity, and in doing so stand as the exclusive foundation for forming and maintaining identity.

Historically, these fantasies have had a strong connection to authoritarian values. Employment often meant accepting the strictures of a quite hierarchical and regulative workplace. Co-existing alongside political liberalism have been everyday economic institutions largely devoid of democracy and steeped in inequality. Not surprisingly, work fantasies romanticizing the firm were associated with the "seductive" power of managers: "The propeller turning the wheels of 'management by seduction' is hidden in the seduction itself: the future presented is pink and rosy and appears to be full of opportunities. Clearly this seduction process is truly a matter of emotions and feelings rather than rational considerations" (Doorewaard and Benschop, 2003: 279). Indeed, early descriptions of capitalist employment, still characteristic of many workplaces globally, bear much resemblance in spirit to stereotypical authoritarian regimes and the fantasies they deployed.

These authoritarian foundations have survived despite evolutions in workplace culture. New human relations ideas have supposedly revolutionized capitalist employment, emphasizing consensus over coercion. However, underpinning this promise are new justifications for authority and conformity. Human relations paradigms focusing on employee wellbeing as well as their personal and professional fulfillment nonetheless maintain a quite regulative capitalist system. In this respect:

> the person, not the organization, is managing. It consists of all the person's varied experiences in education, training, work in several organizations, changes in occupational field, etc. The protean person's own personal career choices and search for self-fulfillment are the unifying or integrative elements in his or her life. The criterion of success is internal (psychological success) not external. (Hall, 1976: 201)

Such capitalist fantasies have, furthermore, served to directly support the contemporary sovereign power of managers. The contemporary age was meant to spell the end of the authoritarian organization, as there was predicted to be a "crisis of bureaucracy in the age of enterprise" (Courpasson and Reed, 2004: 7). In this new "post-bureaucratic" era, firms would be "structured to increase flexibility, with less formalization and more decentralization than in the traditional bureaucratic organization" (Contu and Grey, 2003: 935). Nevertheless, these established authoritarian structures have persisted, adapting to these new institutional forms. As Courpasson and Clegg (2006: 319) observe, "bureaucracy far from being superseded, is rejuvenating, through complex processes of hybridism in which supposedly opposite political structures and principles, the democratic and oligarchic, intermingle and propagate."

Within these "soft bureaucracies" sovereign power not only remains but is in many ways enhanced. Bosses are invested with a type of transcendental power, able to ensure or prevent an individual's dreams of fulfillment (Rhodes and Bloom, 2012). There is a spiritualized quality, in this regard, granted to managers, linked to employee desires for an "ideal leader" who is perfectly competent and supportive of their professional and personal desires. Tellingly, complex bureaucratic organizations are framed similarly to the "heavenly hierarchies" of the past, where the higher up in the organization one was the closer they were to "God" (Kornberger et al., 2006). As such, these quite administrative and depersonalized firms become identified with and centered upon a strong leader supervising, like God previously, from high above (Parker, 2009). Capitalist identity, then, remains largely transfixed, at least at the level of the workplace, to a rather traditional authoritarian perspective revolving around the "good" or "bad" leader. Stavrakakis (2008), in this regard, directly associates contemporary strategies of organizational control with the affective enjoyment they gain in the "symbolic authority" embodied by the present-day manager. Perhaps even more so, it establishes sovereignty as the primary means to understand and practice power. The "processes of comparison, hierarchization, differentiation, homogenization and exclusion that Foucault observes as the objective mechanisms of discipline have as their necessary correlate similar process 'within' the ego as I seek to fix identity in the essentially competitive space of the mirror of my own and other's objectifications" (Roberts, 2005: 637).

At stake, then, is to understand how these authoritarian fantasies linked to capitalist labor are also present within the political sphere. Illuminated is the compatibility of capitalism economically with authoritarian structures and fantasies generally. There is a long tradition, as shown, for legitimizing and rendering market-based relations attractive and sustainable through appealing to rather strong sovereign-based affective discourses. The "affective economy" of capitalism relies upon authoritarian fantasies for its continued reproduction. This insight opens the space for investigating how it similarly depends on explicitly politically authoritarian fantasies for the same purpose.

FANTASIZING AUTHORITARIAN CAPITALISM

As discussed, despite rhetoric of the "free market," the state has always had an important role within a capitalist economy. From its beginning in the nineteenth-century industrial revolution, private enterprise required huge amounts of public investment. Moving forward into the twentieth century, continued capitalist growth depended on state-funded infrastructure building and tax collection. Socially, a strong government presence was historically necessary to "regulate" employment relations in support of ownership and profit.

The state, hence, has had a significant and arguably necessary structural role in economically and socially reinforcing capitalism. Yet it has also featured prominently in its affective or psychic economy. Capitalist fantasies routinely drew upon the fundamentality of the state and sovereign power politically. Initially this meant, for instance, a Victorian parliamentary government who could properly "morally order" society to reflect new capitalist values (Habermas, 1991; Weber, 1998). However, this soon transformed into competing promises of how the state could guarantee capitalist prosperity. Such phantasmatic claims ranged from conservative appeals to strong national defense abroad and capitalist freedom at home to the liberal championing of an interventionist state able to guide the market toward socially just ends. What these seemingly competing affective discourses share is a belief in the state's role for creating a more perfect market society and citizen.

These sovereign-based capitalist fantasies could and often did turn into explicitly politically authoritarian discourses. Here, the state became a legitimated force for policing society for its own protection. Within established liberal democracies this authoritarian impulse was witnessed in its common need to identify and eliminate an enemy, whether it be "immigrants" (Cacho, 2000; Comaroff and Comaroff, 2002; Demo, 2005), "welfare cheats" (Enck-Wanzer, 2011; Zernike, 2010), "communists" (Epstein, 1994; Heale, 1990), or "Muslim terrorists" (Clarke, 2008; Jackson, 2007; Qureshi and Sells, 2013). Present was a type of authoritarian capitalism, whereby the state had the duty and the right to protect a "free" market society and its people from internal and external threats (Bloom, 2014).

Theoretically, such an authoritarian capitalist politics reflects the dualistic character of fantasy. As mentioned in Chapter 1, fantasies are composed of a positive and negative element. As Žižek explains:

> On the one hand, fantasy has a beatific side, a stabilizing dimension, which is governed by the dream of a state without disturbances, out of reach of human depravity. On the other hand, fantasy has a destabilizing dimension, whose elementary form is envy. It encompasses all that "irritates" me about the Other, images that haunt me about what he or she is doing when out of my sight, about how he or she deceives me and plots against me, about how he or she ignores me and indulges in an enjoyment that is intensive beyond my capacity of representations, etc. (Žižek, 1998: 192)

The demonization of the Jews by the Nazis is a classic example of this construction of a malicious other as part of destabilizing negative fantasy. Returning again to Žižek:

> [f]ar from being the positive cause of social antagonism, the "Jew" is just the embodiment of a certain blockage – of the impossibility which prevents the society from achieving its full identity as a closed, homogenous totality … Society is not prevented from achieving its full identity because of Jews: it is prevented by its own antagonistic nature, by its own immanent blockage, and it "projects" this internal negativity into the figure of the "Jew." In other words, what is excluded from the

symbolic (from the frame of the corporatist sociosymbolic order) returns in the Real as a paranoid construction of the "Jew." (Žižek, 1989: 127)

In this respect, the positive fantasy of capitalism, the appeal to a harmonious and prosperous market society, is challenged by a "malicious" enemy seeking to "rob" individuals of this utopian capitalist promise.

Identity is secured in this ever evolving but stable affective drama between capitalism and its enemies. To this end:

> managerialistic ideology is – unlike many other ideologies – primarily not about a better and promising future, but about a bad and dangerous present. It aims at putting people in a permanent state of fear, alertness, and worries to lose what they have got. The "enemy outside" becomes an "enemy in people's heads." Since the proponents of managerialism and new public management obviously put a lot of effort into "scaring people into it" it seems that even they are not very convinced of the attractiveness of their ideology. (Diefenbach, 2007: 129)

This ongoing phantasmatic struggle produces the conditions for political authoritarianism, granting the state an ongoing legitimization to assume the power necessary to combat these "evil" forces.

By contrast, capitalism has commonly relied on a positive fantasy emphasizing simultaneously shared prosperity and values of individual freedom. Tellingly, a central feature of these beatific visions is the reification of sovereign power. Indeed, this positive fantasy has historically appealed to ideals of personal and national sovereignty. An enduring contradiction of capitalism is that while it usually demands conformity in practice – seen in the regulation of individuals to be, for instance, a "model employee" – at the level of discourse it extols the values of personal freedom and autonomy. To this end, it constructs each individual as their own sovereign, at least rhetorically, personally responsible for their own destinies. Analogously, it highlights the power of sovereignty for influencing and at points ultimately guiding a complex market economy in order to realize desired social and political goals.

This affective capitalist identification is commonly translated into shared desires for an "ideal leader." Within the workplace, this desire for a perfect sovereign is captured in ongoing parodies of "bad bosses" and the underlying wish by employees to be managed competently. Similarly, the continual depiction of the "bumbling" public leader – for example, George W. Bush – demonstrates a deep wish for a powerful sovereign who can effectively navigate global dangers and economic uncertainties for the good of the country (Bloom, 2014). At the base of these longings is a positive fantasy of a strong sovereign, able to shape and guide an often complex and seemingly inhuman capitalist society. These feelings of disempowerment help to produce and strengthen an appealing fantasy of authoritarian capitalism.

CONTEMPORARY FANTASIES OF AUTHORITARIAN CAPITALISM

How then has this fantasy of authoritarian capitalism been manifested, if at all, in the contemporary age of globalization? This would seem a perhaps strange question in a time at the supposed "end of history," where "liberal democracies" are supposed to reign unchallenged as an ideal and concrete form of government, and in which a globalizing market is meant to create economic, social, and political liberalization worldwide. Yet, as discussed, traditional forms of political authoritarianism persist, just as, if not more troubling, the increasingly "illiberal" character of established and emerging national democracies. At stake is how each is drawing on, though in diverse ways, a common present-day affective discourse of authoritarian capitalism.

To answer the question in the previous paragraph, it is worth first looking to the past, specifically at the affective legitimization of authoritarian regimes and policies historically, capitalist or otherwise. Notably, any and all fantasies have a certain "totalitarian" character, in their attempt to form an exclusive identity around a specific affective structuring of "reality." Moreover, this "totalitarian" aspect is very much connected to sovereign discourses associated with a "master":

> What psychoanalysis can do to help the critique of ideology is precisely to clarify the status of this paradoxical jouissance as the payment the exploited, the served received for serving the master. This jouissance of course, always emerges within a certain phantasmic field; crucial precondition for breaking the chains of servitude is thus to "transverse the fantasy" which structures our jouissance in a way which keeps us attached to the Master – makes us accept the framework of the social relationship of domination. (Žižek, 1997: 48)

However, Žižek (2006: 88) noticeably differentiates between the general "totalitarianism of fantasy" and an explicitly "totalitarian fantasy."

Turning his attention to communist discourses, Žižek highlights the explicitly totalitarian fantasy associated with Bolshevism, particularly during its Stalinist period. It was not just that a fantasy exclusively promised psychic wholeness. Rather, it was that this fulfillment could only be achieved through the auspices of a strong sovereign. Here, "The party functions as the miraculous immediate incarnation of an Objective neutral knowledge ... the paradoxical intersection between the subjective will and the laws" (Žižek, 2006: 67–8). What is particularly relevant to the current era is the relation between a closed ideology of progress to the construction of a totalitarian fantasy connected to supreme sovereign power. Likewise, as will be explored throughout this book, a key function of this supreme sovereign is to protect this "correct" ideology from internal and external enemies.

While the contemporary "psychic economy" of capitalism does not trade, at least usually if ever, in such an all-encompassing "cult of personality," the totalitarianism of the past does resonate with the rather closed ideological character of current globalization discourses. As will be investigated in greater detail in Chapter 3, economic liberalization is extolled as the exclusive path to national and international prosperity. Accordingly, its positive fantasy of progress is quite narrow in terms of underlying economic ideals. Similar to the ways communism was an unquestioned ideology for structuring present society and achieving future development, global capitalism has largely monopolized ideological discussions as to the "right way" to realize socioeconomic progress now and going forward. The primary contemporary question is not what type of socioeconomic system we desire, but rather what is the "right" market society both for ourselves and globally.

This closed ideological fantasy of globalized capitalism has, in turn, legitimated the increasing power of political sovereigns. More precisely, it dramatically increases the affective appeal of enhanced political power. The primary objective of modern politics is to "correctly" guide the market for attaining national prosperity. In its most positive envisioning, the capitalist sovereign is one who is uniquely able to understand and implement marketization for the benefit of those they rule. Crucial, in this respect, is having an intimate knowledge of the best ways to maximize the effects of the market given a specific country's particular culture and economic needs. The fantasy of authoritarian capitalism in the present era thus is one of a benevolent sovereign "governing" the market in the service of the general population.

Intimately associated with this idealization of sovereignty is the appeal to a sense of freedom ironically attached to such authoritarianism. There is a natural feeling of disempowerment, an experience of lacking agency, in the face of "inevitable historical processes." In other words, if there is only one correct path toward progress, and, moreover, it is already in motion, then what agency is left to individuals? This is a common problem historically for many totalitarian regimes, perhaps most notably international communism and fascist regimes. Yet it also rings true for current affective discourses of globalization.

Indeed, as Žižek points out, authoritarian regimes are "supplemented" by an accompanying and reinforcing affective identification with the sovereign granting them "an enjoyment which serves as the unacknowledged support of meaning" (1994: 56–7). Thus, in the face of what Žižek (1994: 81–2) refers to as "traditional" forms of sovereignty premised on the legal "rights" of the ruler and ruled, individuals reify the non-legal agency found for instance in vigilantes. Their enjoyment here stems from the ability to imagine and invest in an identity that is counter to their "legal status" as sovereign subjects. Conversely, in a totalitarian regime, where the sovereign is granted unlimited power and employs quite arbitrary and brutal methods for maintaining rule, an affective public image of a "caring" and "personable" ruler emerges (also see Tie, 2004: 163).

The extolling of sovereign power, hence, reinvests individuals, even if only by proxy, with the power to shape history and their destinies. This can be captured positively in the investment in a manager for granting individuals the opportunity to achieve their "dreams" (Bloom, 2013). It is also found in economic fantasies extolling the ability to become like a powerful corporate executive, thus having the freedom to live and act as one pleases (Bloom and Cederstrom, 2009). At the political level, the promise of future "market progress" serves as a potentially unifying social force for organizing society and identity. This beatific political identification often revolves around the ability of a strong sovereign (in the form of a person, party, or elected representative) to "correctly" realize this capitalist dream.

A crucial means for experiencing such freedom, furthermore, is via the identification and elimination of enemies. Here, the negative aspect of fantasy unites with its positive component. The idealization of a "good capitalist leader" is translated into the justified task of confronting enemies to this national progress linked to the proper implementation of a market economy. This malevolent force, as will be discussed throughout the book, can be quite heterogeneous. It may be a direct economic threat (e.g. immigrants, leftist populists, or even bankers), it may be foreign dangers (e.g. terrorists), or it may be international "capitalist" enemies (e.g. the Washington Consensus). Connecting all these forms of demonization is the need to eradicate this enemy who is putting at constant risk capitalist prosperity, a task uniquely suited to a powerful sovereign. In this call to protect "market progress" there emerges a reinvigorated contemporary global fantasy of authoritarian capitalism. And it is precisely from these affective roots that the threat of far-Right demagogues promising to protect "real" people from external and internal threats has grown.

CONCLUSION

This chapter has provided a brief historical overview of the relationship between economic capitalism and political authoritarianism. It highlighted the "affective economy" fundamental to the survival and reproduction of capitalism both in the past and present. To this end, capitalism, as with all socioeconomic systems, relies in part on the construction of an affective fantasy for its evolving legitimization. This chapter, furthermore, sought to illuminate the historic compatibility of capitalist fantasies with politically authoritarian values. It concluded by gesturing toward how this fantasy of authoritarian capitalism remains a vital sociopolitical affective discourse. Chapter 3 will expand on these conceptual insights, examining authoritarianism as specifically associated with present-day globalization.

3. Globalization and the desire for authoritarianism

With the demise of the Soviet Union, there seemed to be no barrier to the spread of liberal democracy and global economic prosperity. Globalization promised greater international cooperation and national democracy. In practice, the last two decades have witnessed a resurgence of authoritarianism and quite virulent forms of nationalism. The question is why this is the case. Or more precisely, what is it about globalization that breeds this type of political authoritarianism and parochialism?

This reflects the supposed paradoxical character of present-day globalization. At the dawn of this millennium, United States (US) labor leader John J. Sweeney (2000) stated, "In its current form globalization cannot be sustained. Democratic societies will not support it. Authoritarian leaders will fear to impose it." Such sentiments seem naïve in light of contemporary circumstances whereby democracies and dictatorships alike have fervently embraced marketization and an international "free market." At stake, then, is a perceived choice between popular, specifically national, sovereignty on the one hand and a growing economic international financial regime on the other. According to the President of the Council on Foreign Relations, Richard Haas (2006), "states must be prepared to cede some sovereignty to world bodies if the international system is to function."

To put it more bluntly, the stronger globalization is the weaker national, and perhaps democratic, self-determination appears to become. Such insights may be accurate, but they fail to get to the core of the issue at hand – it speaks to the results, not the cause of this problem. A common perspective for understanding this dynamic is to attribute it to structural problems of corporate globalization (Scholte, 2000). According to Ohmae (1995: vii), corporate globalization spells the "end of the nation state" as it has "raised troubling questions about the relevance – and effectiveness – of nation states as meaningful aggregates in terms of which to think about, much less manage, economic activity." There is much to recommend from this reading. It is undeniably true that rising political and economic inequality is a historically fertile breeding ground for populism of both right- and left-wing varieties.

Further, the harmful social effects of this marketization, or "shocks," as Naomi Klein (2007) aptly refers to them, necessitates a strong state to ensure the implementation of these "reforms" in the face of often widespread popular dissent. Yet this explanation does little to explain why such authoritarianism remains so attractive to individuals across contexts. It is not just that the implementation of hyper capitalism commonly requires the iron fist of a willing government. It is that this authoritarianism is also often demanded, or at least supported, from the bottom up. The appeal to either hard or soft authoritarian rule – with all its traditional accompaniments of a reified leader and civil repression – is gaining in popularity politically in exact relation to the spread of globalization economically. The globalization paradox can, therefore, be restated: as corporate globalization grows so too does the desire for authoritarian state power.

This chapter looks more in depth at how economic discourses of globalization are catalyzing popular desires for political authoritarianism. Specifically, it contends that the portrayal of corporate globalization as "inevitable" and "necessary" creates an intensified desire for individual and collective sovereignty. Rather than simply being a "subjectless" part of an inexorable and unavoidable spread of an international financial regime, people affectively embrace their right and ability to shape this process to their own advantage – to be, in this sense, a subject of globalization instead of merely being subjected to it. As will be shown, this fantasy of sovereignty associated with globalization is quite conducive to conventional authoritarianism, and ironically serves to provide a popular legitimacy to capitalism's ongoing structural necessity of a regulative state for its survival and growth.

THE POWERFUL DISCOURSE OF GLOBALIZATION

Globalization is a term that is used so widely and so often it is commonly assumed that its meaning must be clear. It is usually a short-hand way to refer to "free trade," growing international interdependence between countries, and, more critically, the political, economic, and cultural hegemony of the West over the rest of the world. While these characteristics all have their truths, they do not constitute a singular definition of globalization by any account. It may be said that finding such a definition is not altogether necessary considering the fact that it is already a known part of daily speech across the globe. However, the discourse of globalization does not just reflect reality but is also instrumental in shaping it.

There is a certain tension involved in trying to pin down what exactly "globalization" is. Specifically, it is simultaneously both ambiguous in its meaning and quite socially meaningful (Perkmann and Sum, 2002; Spich, 1995). A dominant account of this phenomenon is one that emphasizes increased international, social, political, and economic integration and interdependence. Globalization is depicted "as a process (or sort of processes) which embodies

a transformation in the spatial organization of social relations and transactions
... generating transcontinental or interregional flows and networks of activity,
interaction and the exercise of power" (Held et al., 1999).

Significantly, such attempts at a definition also represent the underlying
power politics at the core of globalization. It is not just that diverse perspectives of globalization differ, but that their differences perhaps represent competing visions of what globalization is and should be. The meaning granted to
globalization at once reflects and helps to actively reinforce the direction and
instantiation of this phenomenon. It is perhaps not surprising that the dominant
understanding of globalization remains primarily the expansion of a market
economy internationally (Robertson and Khondker, 1998: 25).

It is necessary, therefore, to view globalization as a dynamic and influential
discourse (Rosamond, 2003). Discourse here is considerably more than just the
language used to describe globalization. Rather, it speaks to the multileveled
effect that a given social understanding can have for impacting upon and
constructing social relations. Discourse refers, in this sense, to "the structured
collection of texts embodied in the practices of talking and writing (as well as
a wide variety of visual representation and cultural artifacts) that brings organizationally related objects into being as these texts are produced, disseminated
and consumed" (Grant et al., 2004: 3). According to Fairclough (2007), there
are three particular ways in which globalization currently operates as a discourse in relation to power: (1) the role of discourses for supporting and reproducing growing international networks and relationships of power; (2) the use
of the word "globalization" and associated "global" values such as "democracy" or the "free market" in legitimizing concrete changes to the world's
economy and politics; and (3) the mutually influencing relationship between
"actual processes of globalization and representations of globalization."

Globalization discourses then are fundamental to the creation and ongoing
recreation of globalization in practice. They demand an understanding of the
influence of cultural representations for "generating institutional structures
for the 'global,' mediated through policies and techniques of necessary adap-
tion" (Cameron and Palan, 1999: 270). At perhaps the simplest level, this
relationship between discourse and practice can be said to be self-fulfilling.
Indeed, "the very discourse and rhetoric of globalization may serve to summon
precisely the effects that such a discourse attributes to globalization itself"
(Hay and Marsh, 2000: 9). Popular assumptions of this phenomenon, then,
strengthen and naturalize existing concrete processes, which, in turn, bolster
these commonly held beliefs regarding what globalization actually "is" and
can be. Importantly, this discursive function of globalization can have a strong
ideological dimension (Robertson and Khondker, 1998: 37). More precisely,
the dominant perception of globalization is underpinned by and serves to
bolster a certain worldview and set of beliefs. Politically, this use of discourse

for ideological promotion is witnessed in forms of "rhetoricism" or the intentional use of discourse for strategic purposes (Hay and Rosamond, 2002). When politicians champion the need for "free trade" they are doing more than just advocating international trade agreements. They are also often tactically deploying this phrase to support an agenda of greater marketization globally, commonly at the expense of environmental and labor concerns domestically, for instance. The discourse of globalization is thus "facilitating" in its social effects.

It fosters and helps to culturally embed certain identifications and understandings (Brenner, 1997, 1999). It can be seen in this light as a type of "normative re-ordering," where particular ideals, norms, and practices are prioritized and granted social legitimacy over others. This process of normative reordering, significantly, can be used to justify a dominant ideology – such as those associated with colonialism and Euro-centrism (Banerjee and Linstead, 2001).

Specifically, the mainstream rhetoric of globalization, as well as the deeper discourses surrounding it, represents an elite commitment to a "neoliberal ideology" (Steger, 2005). The objective is to entrench values of privatization and marketization within and across nations (see, for instance, Hill and Kumar, 2008; Mensah, 2008; Passas, 2000). In policy terms it has meant:

> New forms of globalized production relations and financial systems are forcing governments to abandon their commitment to the welfare state. Rather than formulating policies to ensure full neoliberalism employment and an inclusive social welfare system, governments are now focused on enhancing economic efficiency and international competitiveness. One consequence is the "rolling back" of welfare state activities, and a new emphasis on market provisioning of formerly "public" goods and services. (Larner, 2000: 6–7)

Such a project is accomplished, in no small part, by the association of globalization discursively with these neoliberal ideals.

To this end, discourses of globalization reflect the subjective element underpinning the structural and concrete spread of capitalism internationally. In this regard, an underexplored but crucial component of the study of globalization is the affective "grip" it has on individuals. In what ways do discourses of globalization emotionally and psychologically appeal to individuals, and in doing so lead them to invest in these capitalist ideologies, often in quite unexpected ways? And, particularly relevant to this study, how is this creating a common "subject of globalization" across contexts, a subject that displays similar desires for and legitimizations of political authoritarianism?

IN THE AFFECTIVE GRIP OF GLOBALIZATION

Importantly, globalization does not just effect individuals at a purely rational or meaningful level. It also impacts them affectively. Discourses surrounding globalization contain a strong emotional component. Indeed, different interpretations of this phenomenon are necessarily associated with contrasting feelings about its consequences (Kellner, 1998). For those who support corporate globalization, their rhetoric has an almost uniformly optimistic ring to it. Conversely, its critics infuse their disagreement with pessimism over the future and the urgent need for a change in political and economic direction.

Globalization discourses, then, produce certain socialized affective responses. They represent more than just policy prescriptions for a rapidly interconnected world. Instead, they are almost "mythical" in their impact, romanticized visions that play on our deepest hopes and fears. Indeed, globalization has been described precisely in these terms, as a modern myth. According to Spich there exists currently a "hyper enthusiastic version of the globalization folklore myth" encapsulated in the triumphant capitalist story that:

> The world is changing rapidly and really getting smaller. The internationalization of domestic economies, the interdependence of issues and nations, the opportunity to think and act globally have forced us all to note that new political-economic regime is at hand … The way to get the most out of this new world context is to foster free-market institutions and practices while simultaneously limiting government to the important role of protecting and guaranteeing free-market activity. (Spich, 1995: 8)

This mythical account of globalization allows it to be seen in a different light. Rather than discourses merely describing what is "objectively" happening, they instead create the very ground upon which individuals understand and invest in this new sociopolitical reality. To this effect, globalization discourses create what Hay and Rosamond (2002) call "ideational structures." Significantly, these ideational structures influence and are to an extent determinative of these globalizing processes. They culturally delimit for individuals and communities what is perceived to be politically and economically realistic and imaginable. In this respect, individuals and communities thus "become institutionalized and normalized and thereby socially construct conceptions of 'the possible' amongst political actors" (Hay and Rosamond, 2002: 147).

Consequently, globalization discourses help "frame" the world for individuals. According to Fiss and Hirsch (2005: 46): "In the case of globalization, a varied and discursive landscape emerged in which the structural and discursive factors combined to create assorted domains of meaning, with actors in some discursive fields supporting a positive framing, while others emphasized a negative or neutral framing." Such framing is especially crucial, given the uncertain and often quite dislocating effects caused by the spread of market-ization internationally. Discourses of globalization help individuals "make sense" of these profound shifts. More precisely, they become part and parcel of a broader romanticized narrative of individual and collective progress.

The discursive support for corporate globalization involves, moreover, an entire construction of a "globalization" politics. The "normative reordering" linked to globalization, discussed in the previous section, is made possible by situating individuals within a broader hegemonic politics in support, either directly or indirectly, of this neoliberal ideology. Steger (2005) lists "6 claims of globalization":

1. Globalization is about the liberalization and global integration of markets.
2. Globalization is inevitable and irreversible.
3. Nobody is in charge of globalization.
4. Globalization benefits everyone.
5. Globalization furthers the spread of democracy in the world.
6. Globalization requires a "War on Terror".

Globalization, in this way, affectively "grips" individuals through its cultur-ally provided discourses. In doing so, it helps provide them with a deeper ontological security, producing and maintaining them as social subjects. The affective "grip" of globalization goes beyond emotion to the very heart of how individuals identify and understand themselves.

THE FANTASY OF AN "INEVITABLE" GLOBALIZATION

Globalization is therefore more than a concrete set of economic processes or even a completely rational set of political principles. It is a psychologically "gripping" discourse that shapes aspirations and identity. Globalization stands, in this respect, as a modern cultural fantasy, promising economic prosperity and social development. Even in the wake of the disastrous 2008 financial crisis, US President Obama continued to extoll an idealized vision of glo-balization and its positive effects: "a crisis like this reminds us that we just have to put in some common-sense rules of the road, without throwing out the enormous benefits that globalization has brought in terms of improving living standards, reducing the cost of goods, and bringing the world closer together" (Obama, 2009). The appeal of corporate globalization, and thus its strength, lies in no small part in its capacity to continually inspire individuals, affec-tively "seizing" them in its discourses of present and future progress.

Globalization commonly is portrayed, however, in exactly the opposite terms. It is presented as being "inevitable" (Spicer and Fleming, 2007). This view of the international free market is captured, for instance, in then US Undersecretary of State Stuart Eizenstat's declaration that, "Globalization is an inevitable element of our lives. We cannot stop it any more than we can stop the waves from crashing on the shore" (cited in Fairclough, 2007). Its existence and survival, hence, seemingly have little to do with popular desires. The ideological hegemony of corporate globalization is inexorably linked to its depiction as being patently non-political. Tellingly, its social naturalization is manifested in its being made comparable to an actual natural force. According to former United Nations Secretary General Kofi Annan, "It has been said that arguing against globalization is like arguing against the laws of gravity" (Crossette, 2000). Here, the spread of capitalism internationally is an unstoppable phenomenon that humans can neither halt nor contain.

Such a depiction of marketization and change is, of course, quite political, despite its protestations to the contrary. Put differently, the offering up of globalization as inevitable is itself a strategic discourse. Its representation as "natural" and "law like" is a prime means for legitimizing policies and measures associated with enhanced privatization and financial power both locally and globally. In examining the case of the Australian Broadcasting Company, Spicer and Fleming (2007: 533), note that: "senior management made strategic use of globalization discourse to legitimate managerial initiatives such as the introduction of competitive contracting and commercialization. The discourse of globalization around which these practices were couched relied upon a trope of inevitability, external pressure and organizational survival." While the picture of globalization may at times be effective, it is hardly the most inspiring. For this reason, it has often been supplemented with a more emotionally attractive discourse.

These "inevitable" structural changes will supposedly bring with them international wellbeing, eliminating poverty and delivering even the most "backward" nation into modernity. It is a historical force that will usher in an age of universal democracy, grow the middle classes and create mass prosperity, against all odds and setbacks. The G20 exemplified this resilient capitalist fantasy of globalization in the aftermath of the 2008 financial crash, declaring that they remained committed to an "Open Global Economy ... that through continued partnership, cooperation, and multilateralism, we will overcome the challenges before us and restore stability and prosperity to the world economy" (G20, 2008). Former President George W. Bush was even more explicit, maintaining that "[t]he answer ... is to fix the problems we face, make the reforms we need, and move forward with the free-market principles that have delivered prosperity and hope to people all across the globe" (BBC News, 2008).

Reflected, then, is the affective fantasy of globalization underpinning its structural transformations and strategic political maneuverings. The marketization of the world is made possible and justified vis-à-vis an ongoing vision of the better future it will provide. However, any such fantasy requires an enemy for its continued survival. There must be some reason that such a future has yet to arrive. The presence of all those who oppose globalization then becomes a threat to progress and collective civilization itself. This rendering of globalization into a global fantasy enhances its social resilience. Its promise of prosperity becomes translated into a deeper framework for framing and securing one's very sense of self. It constitutes a stable part of an individual's "boundaries of understanding" that, as Giddens (2020: 47) observes, seems to "possess ... answers to fundamental existential questions which all human life in some way addresses." These discourses, in turn, act to "exclude, or reinterpret, potentially distributing knowledge ... avoidance of dissonance forms part of the protective cocoon which helps maintain ontological security" (2020: 188).

Ironically, the more it is threatened or appears to be under siege, the more individuals will cling to its survival and desire its strengthening. As Bloom (2013: 2) notes: "Threats to this affective narrative, this story which not only is rationally meaningful and emotionally resonant but also impacts individuals at the deeper psychic level ... then symbolize a threat to one's very future and as such one's identity."

For this reason, it is precisely when such globalization seems at its weakest and vulnerable that fantasies of its resurrection are most attractive. In this respect, "as revealed in the current economic crisis, capitalism therefore has the potential to remain paradoxically stronger in the face of its own crisis, ensnaring aspirations for change within the past confines of its own idealized future" (Bloom, 2013: 17).

Importantly, it is exactly this disappointment with globalization, the constant non-fulfillment of its utopian claims, from which it draws its most potent social strength. It provides the opportunity to continually redirect attention from its own failures and toward its struggle for survival. Moreover, it entrenches identity even further in a narrative of its eventual triumph (Cremin, 2011). Hence, a crisis becomes co-opted into a romanticized story of global capitalist progress.

LOOKING FOR SOVEREIGNTY IN THE FACE OF GLOBALIZATION

The fantasy of corporate globalization traditionally centers on a romantic vision of market-driven prosperity. This vision is undercut though by existing economic inequalities and continued sociopolitical domination. For this reason, the power of this fantasy emanates not from its realization but from its ongoing struggle to be realized. Present sacrifices and structural imbalances are justified in the name of future progress. Enemies are found and highlighted who must be perpetually fought in the name of achieving this capitalist utopia to come.

This fantastical element addresses a profound tension in the contemporary spread of capitalism globally. Namely, markets are championed as a force for individual liberty and collective self-determination. Yet, globalization is primarily portrayed as existing outside human control. The Finnish President Tarja Halonen (2003) stated this point explicitly: "It is people who are the objects of globalization and at the same time its subjects. What also follows logically from this is that globalization is not a law of nature, but rather a process set in train by people." Consequently, questions emerge as to who and what exactly is the actual "subject" of globalization. Indeed, globalization is strategically legitimatized as "inevitable." As such, it is a force of "subjection" even for those who may support it for ideological or material reasons. It enlists individuals into its beliefs and processes regardless of their wishes. It is economically necessary and people must simply accept its growing prevalence and hegemony.

This speaks to a broader theoretical distinction between "subjection" and "subjectivation." Namely, it reflects the lack of and subsequent longing for a sense of selfhood and identity within regulative and disciplining social systems. Quoting Judith Butler (1997: 102), "how are we to understand not merely the disciplinary production of the subject but the disciplinary cultivation of an attachment to subjection?" For this reason, it is necessary to investigate not only the concrete ways an existing set of social relations dominates subjects, but also the identities that support these prevailing material regimes. Consequently, a "subject's complicity in their subjectivation cannot be understood as being purely the effect of their positioning within discourse. Rather, their complicity has an affective dimension. Where a regime of power is able to incite that dimension, it has an increased capacity to become totalising in its effects" (Tie, 2004: 161).

Neoliberalism has, to this end, produced fantasies of the powerful individual; one who can seemingly transgress and shape entrenched social norms and values at will. It is no surprise then that popular culture increasingly celebrates the anti-hero – whether in its most nihilistic form (e.g. Tony Soprano, Walter White) or those who "break the rules" in the quixotic pursuit of justice (e.g. Jimmy McNulty, Rustin Cohle). Such veneration is borne out of a concrete subjection to social systems demanding individuals be "self-disciplined," a regime over which they appear to have little control or ability to substantially alter.

However, it also is witnessed in the renewed investment individuals place in national or business leaders to "solve the problems" of the economy, even amidst being told repeatedly that marketization and globalization are "naturalized laws" beyond the reach of human interference. Similarly, Rhodes and Bloom (2012) link the post-bureaucracy characterizing much of contemporary capitalism to an enhanced desire for a "competent" and just sovereign manager. They point to the growing appeal of a "fantasy of hierarchy" in which individuals long for the spiritual power of a wise leader to rule over them. This fantasy is especially appealing in the present age marked by the lack of sovereign agency in a world defined by depersonalized economic and organizational processes. The ideal political leader or manager, in this regard, represents the possibility of regaining this sense of lost sovereign power. Both the anti-hero and ideal "leader" reflect a desire to experience personal autonomy, to exhibit a sense of power in a cultural context otherwise defined by powerlessness and subjection. Related specifically to globalization, the forced march of marketization produces similar longings for greater sovereignty. Here, the perceived lack of agency in controlling our economic present and future creates an acute desire for collective self-determination. Significantly, globalization engenders in its wake a need to influence and drive forward this process, not simply be driven by it. In theoretical terms, individuals and groups wish to not only be "subjected to" but also be active "subjects of" corporate globalization. Thus, in the midst of an international capitalism that appears to be a "force of nature" and immune to human control, the desire for sovereignty and the power to shape such globalization grows even more intense.

RECONCEIVING THE GLOBALIZATION PARADOX

The increasing appeal for sovereignty is perhaps not surprising in light of the perceived "inevitability" of globalization. In the absence of agency, the desire for it will undoubtedly grow. This dynamic, nevertheless, opens new ways to conceive of the tension-filled and paradoxical character of contemporary globalization. It is one where the longing for freedom and collective self-determination is transformed into a call for greater sovereign power.

Traditionally, the contradictions of globalization are phrased rather differently. In fact, in the past they were often ignored altogether. Marketization was a cure-all for the world's economic underdevelopment and political tyranny. It would provide not only for material growth but also liberal democracy across the globe. Yet the realities of the twenty-first century have severely tested this rosy picture of corporate globalization. The 2008 financial crisis dramatically challenged the narrative linking international free markets and privatization policies with mass economic prosperity or security. No longer was it possible to simply spout romanticized rhetoric of the benefits of global capitalism.

Politically, the nation-state and national rule was viewed as progressively disintegrating as a result of this new economic world order. As Sassen (1996: 33–4) observed even in the 1990s:

> economic globalization has contributed to the denationalizing of national territory ... sovereignty, until now largely concentrated in the national state, had become somewhat decentered; there are other locations for the particular form of power and legitimacy we call sovereignty; now it is also located in supranational organizations like the European Economic Union, the new emergent transnational legal regime, and international covenants proclaiming the universality of human rights. All of these constrain the autonomy of any state operating under the rule of law ... the processes of economic globalization have played a critical role in these developments.

Just as significantly, the dream of the universal ascent of liberal democracy was crumbling in light of continued authoritarianism and illiberalism in states both formally democratic and dictatorial. The "inevitability" of globalization has, in turn, produced distinctive and enhanced desires for a sovereignty that appears to be increasingly lost.

Emerging from these new challenges, Rodrik introduced the "globalization paradox." At its crux, he argued that corporate globalization simply could not co-exist with nationalism or democracy. He notes: "The intellectual consensus that sustains our current model of globalization had already begun to evaporate before the world economy became engulfed in the great financial crisis of 2008. Today the selfassured attitude of globalization's cheerleaders has all but disappeared, replaced by doubts, questions and skepticism" (2011: xvi–xvii). Speaking with the fervor of a former true believer, he argues that there now exists a fundamental "trilemma" at the core of globalization, whereby it is currently impossible to "simultaneously pursue democracy, national self-determination and economic globalization."

This reading highlights, at the very least, a number of certain contradictory features of present-day globalization. Notably, while it literally refers to something geographic in character – the "globe" – it is not always clear where globalization is occurring or where exactly its power lies. Kelly (1999: 380) observes "the popularity of globalization as a concept is to be found in its own global circulation as an idea – a way of constructing a particular geography of the world." The geography of globalization is, in this sense, quite ill-defined. On the one hand, it appears to be an all-pervasive force for guiding and transforming social relations. On the other, it seems to be devoid of any specific cultural foundations or context. Importantly, it locates individuals concretely within global economic processes but leaves them progressively feeling as if they have no concrete or unique place in this changing capitalist world, particularly as previous identifications, such as with their nation, appear to be rapidly disintegrating due to the inevitable onslaught of globalization.

It is this "decenteredness" that defines modern politics in the age of corporate globalization. The deterioration of "national selfdetermination" and the pining for "democracy" put in sharp relief shared broader concerns over the rise of an international free market that is at once "everywhere" but is increasingly leaving individuals feeling as if they exist "nowhere" – taking away their previous social geographies and groundedness as a social subject. In turn, this creates a fresh and impassioned longing for such an identity, a renewal of one's traditional and secure sense of self. Benjamin Barber (1992: 53) refers to this as the conflict of "Jihad vs. McWorld":

> The tendencies of what I am here calling the forces of Jihad and the forces of McWorld operate with equal strength in opposite directions, the one driven by parochial hatreds, the other by universalizing markets, the one re-creating ancient subnational and ethnic borders from within, the other making national borders porous from without. They have one thing in common: neither offers much hope to citizens looking for practical ways to govern themselves democratically.

However, examining globalization as a fantasy, its geography begins to become better illuminated. It is precisely in its contradictory state of being "everywhere" and "nowhere" at once that makes it so politically durable and vital. This contradiction produces the ground for an affective discourse whereby international processes can be made palatable to local conditions. To this extent, Rosamond (1999: 657) argues "that the deployment of ideas about globalization has been central to the development of a particular notion of European identity among élite policy actors." In this respect, the very frustration over the seemingly amorphous and universal nature of globalization permits for the emergence of new custom-made "localized" fantasies of corporate globalization.

Structurally, this echoes Naisbitt's early identification of a "global paradox" in which "the bigger the world economy, the more powerful its smallest players" (1994: 12). He argues that the greater the international market expands, the stronger "localized" actors – such as indigenous entrepreneurs and confederations of corporate networks – will become. He prophesized that "economies of scale are giving way to economies of scope, finding the right size for synergy, market flexibility, and above all, speed" (1994: 14). While this prediction has not necessarily been completely borne out by contemporary developments, it does point to the continuing longing to combine global capitalism with local control and innovation. The paradox Naisbitt refers to has perhaps ironically revived the political and economic national power found in the "continuing purchase and relevance of nation-state institutions to shape and define the regulatory context for these 'local wonders'" (Gertler, 1997: 24).

There is a similar dynamic at work related to time and corporate globalization. The utopian justifications of international marketization continually place its value in the future. To reiterate a previous point made above, present concerns over inequality and material conditions for the majority of the world's population are pushed aside in favor of idealized claims about the prosperity capitalism will soon provide. Globalization is therefore happening "any time and no time." Again, though, it is this tension in its temporality that creates fertile soil for globalization's mass appeal. The forward-looking character of this discourse renders it easily adaptable to individual and collective desires for future prosperity. As with localization, it provides the sturdy foundations for constructing an affective discourse tailored to the culturally specific desires of a wide range of individuals and contexts. In this regard, there is not one but many co-existing "futures" of globalization.

Reflected, in turn, is the deeper paradox of twenty-first-century global capitalism. The more foreign and alienating corporate globalization appears to individuals and communities, the more they seek to "make it their own." In this respect, the particularist visions of marketization provide individuals with an ontological security that universalist discourses fail to do. Accordingly, the paradox of globalization is not that it destroys nations but that it enhances our subjective attachment to them. Established values of national sovereignty dovetail almost perfectly with these localized fantasies of modern capitalism. They represent a desire to "rule" globalization and not be "ruled by it." To craft it to the specific wishes of those it is affecting rather than subject them to its capricious "one-size-fits-all" agenda. If it is the global aspect of corporate globalization that is "subjecting" present-day individuals, it is the possibility for it to be made local that ironically produces inspired subjects of globalization. And it is upon these foundations, the combining of the economic inevitability of capitalism and the desire for political sovereignty, that authoritarian globalization is born and thrives. Further, this move to combine global capital with local sovereignty plays into emerging political fantasies of ethno-capitalism and repressive democracy.

CONCLUSION: TOWARD A FANTASY OF AUTHORITARIAN CAPITALISM

This chapter has introduced globalization as a contemporary social fantasy. It is an affectively appealing discourse that shapes present-day identity. Its power is not simply regulative or coercive. Nor is it primarily normative – a rational embrace of its ideological principles. The strength of globalization instead flows in no small part from its psychic appeal to modern subjects, more precisely, in its forming and maintaining of individuals as subjects, shaping their desires and very sense of self.

To this end, structural transformations in the material economy are inexorably linked to the construction and reproduction of an associated psychic economy. This concrete, multiple, and evolving spread of capitalism globally depends upon, and is to an extent continually influenced by, a supportive social fantasy. The inscription of individuals in a deepening and expanding market system is made possible and sustained by its ongoing and dynamic "affective" grip upon them.

In the present era, regimes of capitalism are met by desires for greater sovereignty. The "law" of corporate globalization and its presented "inevitability" produces in its wake a subjective lack of perceived human agency. What is longed for then is a renewed ability to shape these "law-like" forces, to place these "natural" forces under social control. In this respect, making globalization subject to human determination rather than making humans mere subjects to global capitalism.

Emerging is a fruitful and rich tension fueling the continued growth of marketization internationally. On the one hand, the utopian future supposedly produced by contemporary globalization offers contemporary subjects a precarious yet continual ontological security. It provides for them a clear narrative of progress and mass prosperity. On the other hand, it leaves individuals feeling as if they are "subjectless," mere cogs without the power or freedom to change an unstoppable capitalist history. Consequently, granted to them in this triumphant twenty-first-century capitalist narrative is not so much a foundation for identity but a promise of a better tomorrow that will arrive regardless of one's wishes.

The success and legitimacy of corporate globalization is found in its capacity to combine the existence of economic capitalism as "inevitable" with a political identity that, nevertheless, celebrates human freedom and collective self-determination. This potent mixture produces the conditions for the rise of a new social fantasy that prioritizes local sovereignty while entrenching global capitalism. It reveals a process of marketization that is international in its reach while being specific to its context. The spread of the "free market" is thus underpinned, as will be shown, by a growing and diverse fantasy of authoritarianism.

4. The market despots: the global capitalist fantasy of authoritarian nationalism

On September 2, 2005, Chinese Communist Party (CCP) leader Li Junru announced the "Chinese will not dream an 'American Dream' but a Chinese one" (People's Daily, 2005b). This declaration symbolized a new vision not just for China but capitalism in general. But what is this "Chinese Dream"? How is it different from the "American Dream"? It illuminates specifically how the CCP, from Deng onward, has attempted to create a new "dream" of capitalism compatible with established revolutionary values of single-party rule, national progress, and Chinese exceptionalism. More precisely, they have done so according to a worryingly similar authoritarian governing paradigm used by Mao to champion socialism in the early revolutionary period.

The notion of a "Chinese Dream" represents a larger, more dangerous political trend arising alongside and from globalization; one based on a potent mix of virulent political nationalism and strident economic marketization. Globalization is transformed into a national project. Emphasized is the ability of the country to shape marketization to fit "local conditions." In this respect, "We are still far from even mapping out the kind of global culture and cosmopolitan ideals that can truly supersede the world of nations" (Smith, 1990: 188). The preceding decades have only heightened this reality, as globalization has ironically transformed contemporary capitalism from a global to a national fantasy.

As the above quote suggests, central to this shift is the revitalization of the importance of the state. Traditionally it was assumed that corporate globalization would weaken national sovereignty and its associated actors (Ohmae, 1990). The significance of national governments was said to be on the wane – a relic of a past age before the rise of an international "free market." Many theorists at the time had even gone so far as to predict that global forces, by which they usually mean transnational corporations and other global economic institutions, global culture or globalizing belief systems/ideologies of various types, or a combination of all of these, are becoming so powerful that the continuing existence of the nation-state is in serious doubt (Sklair, 1999: 144).

Indeed, a crucial attraction of globalization was its proposed doing away with nationalist rivalries and parochial allegiances. The state was to "wither away," to be replaced by a more cooperative and interdependent capitalist global order. Nevertheless, as Jones (2000: 268) observes, despite these optimistic views, "The State will persist because the need for the State has grown, but also because the local resource pools and socioeconomic problems on which States are based are undiminished." Of course, such utopian visions were always unrealistic. The state was not going to be discarded so quickly or easily. However, these romanticized assumptions did seem to point to, at the very least, a relative decline in the importance of the nation and national governments. In its place, supposedly, would be a more integrated economic and therefore political international system and culture.

In the face of such lofty predictions, the twenty-first century has witnessed nationalism return with a vengeance, figuratively and at times quite literally. Ethnic strife linked to the disintegration of the Soviet Union (USSR) has given way to virulent patriotism across the world. This new era is marked by renewed popular longings for national progress and power coupled with novel powers granted to state actors for achieving these goals.

At a deeper level, this represents the revival of desires for agency increasingly linked to established ideas of national sovereignty. It reflects the paradox discussed in Chapter 3, whereby the greater the perceived power of globalization, the stronger the feeling of powerlessness and wish to exert human control over it. State governments, thus, once again emerge as the key figures for exerting such control and recovering the lack of agency attributed to corporate globalization.

Obviously, such longings stand in an almost schizophrenic relation with the reigning economic orthodoxy rejecting "big government" and the "welfare state." Further, the ideological impulse to simply dismiss capitalism runs counter to the historical reality of the death of communism in the twentieth century. To this effect, the rejection of markets appears apocalyptic – impossible to even conceive – while the blind embrace of globalization feels exploitative and the akin to the surrendering of freedom. Into this void, governments have regained their appeal as forces for shaping marketization for the national population's specific benefit. They are the intermediaries for guiding a potentially oppressive and invasive international market into a liberating and prosperous national economic policy.

Crucial politically, in this respect, is the rise of a new and increasingly attractive form of authoritarian capitalism. The demand for national sovereignty, intimately associated with a lack of individual agency, is transposed onto a strong state actor. The personal dictator or the "Party" resonates with a yearning to feel once more in control. They are unbound by strictures of globalization while still secure in its promise of future progress. Such longings are readily witnessed in rising powers such as Russia and China. In each, an economics of marketization is matched by a politics of explicit and implicit authoritarianism. Reflected is the broader appeal and rise of market despots.

THE RISE OF THE MARKET DESPOTS

The twenty-first century has witnessed a pronounced rise of explicitly authoritarian regimes. However, in the face of mainstream expectations, these dictatorial regimes have also embraced marketization (see, for instance, Bunce, 2003; Carothers, 2002; Diamond, 2002; McFaul, 2002; Ottaway, 2003). Countries such as China and Russia have adopted a market system while still maintaining the necessity of a strong, and at times intervening, government presence. The state socialism of the twentieth century has morphed into the state capitalism of the twenty-first century (Lane, 2008; Levitsky and Way, 2010). As one liberal commentator opined:

> [T]he free-market tide has now receded. In its place has come state capitalism, a system in which the state functions as the leading economic actor and uses markets primarily for political gain. This trend has stoked a new global competition, not between rival political ideologies but between competing economic models. And with the injection of politics into economic decisionmaking, an entirely different set of winners and losers is emerging. (Bremmer, 2009: 41)

Whereas this has sparked widespread fears among some mainstream thinkers of the "end of the free market," it can also be seen as an attempt to politically preserve and sustain this transition to a market economy within a volatile global economic and political climate.

Indeed, this resurgent "statism" has had a resounding, and not all together unexpected, political effect. Notably, it has legitimated the continued, and at times enhanced, policing and repressing of the population by the government. Scholars have referred to this phenomenon as "soft authoritarianism," a form of "political control in which a combination of formal and informal mechanisms ensure the dominance of a ruling group or dominant party, despite the existence of some forms of political competition" (Kesselman et al., 2009: 340). It acts, in this regard, as "a type of paternalist authoritarianism that persuades rather than coerces" while often "emphasizing conformity to group interests over individual rights" (Fukuyama, 1992: 60–1). Yet there is often very little that is "soft" about such regimes and their practices. While relying less on such practices they still exhibit the traditional characteristics of "hard" authoritarian governments of the past. They are replete with political prisoners, state censorship, and the formal and informal suppression of internal opposition (see, for example, Moss, 2014; Nasir and Turner, 2013; Slater, 2003; Svolik, 2012).

Further, they are commonly constructed around the cult of a strong leader or leadership, able to singularly guide the country in the right direction for its present and future prosperity. Here, "The manipulation of the electoral process, undermining of democratic institutions, frontal attacks on the rival opposition parties as well as democratic civil society, and the promotion of the personality cult of the leader are usual practices under soft authoritarianism" (Uyangoda, 2015). Perhaps the most famous exemplar of this new "cult of personality" is found in Russia with the rise of Putinism (Cassiday and Johnson, 2010). While certainly not all instances of state capitalism are marked by a charismatic leader, as in the past with fascism or totalitarian communism, they nonetheless exhibit a strong commitment to the ability of an autocratic government to "guide" development. They are, therefore, despotic both in their championing of a strong state actor and in their willingness to engage in a range of repressive measures for defending this central leadership.

This continuation and growth of despotism flies in the face of previous assumptions following the end of the Cold War. It was widely believed, as previously discussed, that the spread of the market economically would go hand in hand with the spread of democracy politically. Yet, if anything, the reverse has occurred. The long march of capitalism globally has been met and, as will be shown, politically aided by a turn to authoritarianism nationally on both a large and small scale. Previous predictions of liberal democracy as the "end of history" are being replaced for some by a new vision of "blurring borders between democracies and authoritarian capitalism, rather than the triumph of democracy or the resurgence of authoritarianism, that defines the global political landscape" (Krastev, 2012).

There is, of course, a traditional story to somewhat explain this continued presence of authoritarianism at the beginning stages of capitalism's "end of history." During the Cold War, the support for right-wing dictatorships was defended on the grounds that they would transition into liberal democracies (Kirkpatrick, 1982). The reasons for this optimistic view were twofold. Politically, it was argued that a conservative despot was closer to the ideals of liberty than their left-wing communist counterparts. If they were not democratic at least they supported "economic freedom." Economically, it was said that these repressive regimes were by nature temporary, as the development of a market economy inherently leads politically to liberal democracy.

Nevertheless, the persistence of authoritarianism directly undermines the underlying logic of these optimistic liberal understandings. Instead, it points to the deeper and more intimate linkages between marketization and despotism. Far from transitioning or withering away to the "ash heap" of history, these authoritarian regimes are thriving. Tellingly, they are doing so not in opposition to capitalism but firmly in support of it, even as they appear to pose a threat to their liberal democratic counterparts (whether real or perceived). "Today's global liberal democratic order faces a significant challenge from the rise of nondemocratic great powers," argues Professor Azir Gat in a 2007 *New York Times* editorial, "the West's old Cold War rivals, China and Russia, are now operating under 'authoritarian capitalist' rather than Communist regimes."

Present then is a political authoritarianism that does more than simply co-exist alongside marketization. It actually appears to maintain, bolster, and reproduce the deepening of capitalism economically. For this reason, these modern regimes can be termed "market despots" – as they simultaneously advocate for greater privatization while also promoting a strengthened right to exclusive rule. There appears then to be competing economic and political logics at work; the shrinkage of the state from the private sphere and its enhancement in the sociopolitical one.

For those familiar with the historical evolution of capitalist political economy, this is not a particularly surprising contradiction. The presence of a strong and supportive state has always been crucial for the implementation and spread of a market economy (Wolfe, 1977). Yet that does not mean that in each context or era this structural support is completely identical. It is imperative, therefore, to illuminate how and in what ways a stronger state is being legitimized and how this legitimization is uniquely justifying capitalism and political authoritarianism within its current era.

The rise of globalization as a modern phenomenon is then central for comprehending this current proliferation of market despotism. Beyond the concrete processes of marketization, the discourse of globalization also creates its own political conditions. Put differently, it frames the contemporary climate in specific ways, directing political desires and identities in quite particular directions. At stake is how globalization is producing desires for authoritarian rule in such a way that reinforces capitalism economically.

THE GLOBAL CAPITALIST FANTASY OF AUTHORITARIAN NATIONALISM

Crucial for addressing this concern is to better understand the contemporary appeal of authoritarianism. It is perhaps an easy and all too understandable perspective to view these regimes as merely unpopular; as repressive governments that simply retain their power through fear against a cowed population. Yet, this is a rather narrow view, ignoring the widespread popular support enjoyed by many of these regimes. The Pew Research Center reports, for instance, that 87 percent of China's population supported the government in 2010, a figure consistent with the 80 percent approval ratings the regime had been experiencing in recent years (Bell, 2011). Moreover, the solution is not solely, or even primarily, reducible to charismatic leaders. Indeed, in the same poll, 66 percent of Chinese citizens thought progress had occurred in their lifetime, while a full 74 percent are optimistic about the future.

Thus, while established authoritarian factors such as fear or personality cults certainly have an effect, they far from fully explain either the persistence or fundamental appeal of market despotism. Historically, the popularity of state capitalism has been aided by the 2008 financial crisis that "discredited free market capitalism for many in the developing world" (Bremmer, 2010: 46). Moreover, the discourse surrounding such authoritarianism reveals much of its attraction. It tellingly centers on the need to recapture and preserve a national identity against the encroachment of a faceless and exploitive globalization. To this effect, it plays on a quite resonant and timely "us versus the world" politics (Bloom, 2011).

Driving this sentiment is the feeling of lost agency caused by the seem-ingly uninterrupted and unstoppable spread of corporate globalization. The attraction of nationalism is a renewed attempt to invest in an identity in which marketization is not directed at but works for a twenty-first-century popula-tion. Accordingly, "the duty of the passive citizenry is merely to recognise the legitimacy of the regime; the duty of the state is to provide security by weeding out citizens who are troublesome" (Nasir and Turner, 2013: 340). Key to such a dynamic is the ability of the state to deliver a "compressed modernity," sacri-ficing the need of individual rights for the broader goal of achieving collective prosperity through state-led marketization (Kyung-Sup, 1999).

Authoritarian governments, whether in the figure of a single person or a party, come to represent (both literally and figuratively) this struggle for freedom, contra globalization. The state stands in stark contrast to faceless marketization processes that appear irrepressible and, at first impression, outside the grasp of human management. If globalization threatens to rob indi-viduals of the enjoyment of their freedom, despotic regimes promise ironically to restore to them this agency.

Reflected is a quite distinct authoritarian fantasy borne out of the discur-sive political conditions of present-day global capitalism. Žižek (2006), for instance, depicts a "totalitarian" fantasy as the embrace of a ruling figure or party that can singularly realize and implement an unchangeable social law. In such a case, "the law has lost all formal neutrality" and the correctness of all norms and practices is ultimately determined by the judgment of an authoritarian ruler. The predominant example, in this sense, is that of Stalin, who pronounced his exclusive ability to put in place the "unmovable laws of history" toward the coming of communism. Here:

> The fetishist functioning of the Party guarantees the position of a neutral knowledge
> ... The Stalinist discourse is presented as a pure metalanguage, as the knowledge
> of "objective laws," applied "on" the "pure" object, (representing) the descriptive

[*constatif*] discourse of objective knowledge. The very engagement of theory on the side of the proletariat, its "hold over the party," is not "internal" – Marxism does not speak of the position of the proletariat; it "is oriented to" the proletariat from an external, neutral, "objective" position. (Žižek, 2006: 33)

The political fantasy underpinning market despotism similarly fetishizes the party, often in quite totalitarian ways – though in practice they rarely reach the totalitarian extremes of their historical predecessors. Present is the ability of a government to link its rule to a positive fantasy, in doing so, affectively associating their regime with the realization of the country's future prosperity and, more fundamentally, psychic wholeness. As Tie (2004: 163), drawing on the work of Žižek, observes, "Totalitarian orders emerge, alternatively, where this sequence reverses, where the unconscious supplement resonates with popular, pleasurable fantasies, and underpins an authoritarian regime." Consequently, "the civilised, even charitable nature of this unconscious underpinning enables authoritarian rule to gain a level of authority unavailable to 'traditional' sovereignty. Brutality embraces affection." Returning to the "soft authoritarianism" of state capitalism, it is the ability of the government to apply its "correct knowledge" to local conditions that reinforces the "popular, pleasurable, fantasies" of state-led capitalism and, thus, justifies repression in its name.

Nonetheless, this resurgent capitalist fantasy of authoritarian nationalism has added a new dimension to the established totalitarian trope. Significantly, it reflects the "traditional" fantasy of authority at work within globalization generally. In this respect, non-totalitarian authority is underpinned by an affective discourse that simultaneously expounds the "non-violent" and procedural nature of its power while having to "supplement" this rule with "excessive" practices that while illegal are fundamental to the survival of the underlying power relations upheld by this sovereign order (Žižek, 1994). Examples, historically, can be found ranging from the creation of the Ku Klux Klan as an extra-governmental force for maintaining racial segregation within an ostensibly democratic American state to modern practices of police brutality to deal with marginalized communities within contemporary liberal nations (Tie, 2004).

Returning to the context of contemporary globalization, the authoritarian excesses of the state capitalists illuminates an analogous need for an actor able to, if necessary, coercively protect and maintain corporate globalization. The post-Cold War fantasies of an integrated "free market" economy characterized by universal democracy is supplemented by a strong national actor who can "do what needs to be done," even if it does not always conform to international standards of human rights, in order to ensure structurally that marketization continues unabated and discursively that it serves the needs of the population as opposed to foreign and domestic elites. Illustrated is the requirement of a strong state actor, whose actions may or may not be always officially sanctioned or accepted, to do the "dirty work" of implementing capitalism globally amidst a regime of global governance that rhetorically stakes its legitimacy to values of "non-coercion" and "fairness" in support of continued national and transnational inequality economically and politically.

In this respect, the rise of the market despots is a virulent combination of traditional and totalitarian fantasies. These authoritarian capitalists represent both the "illegal" but necessary supplement to the liberal hegemony of the "free market" while also the fetishized rulers who uniquely and "objectively" know how to deliver progress to their citizens. They embody, to this effect, the appeal of the anti-hero – the affective investment in an individual or group who directly contravenes and intentionally breaks entrenched social norms and laws when necessary. Market despots of the twenty-first century are modern-day political "bad boys," unafraid to sneer at universally accepted "truths" of market globalization for the sake of their country and subjects.

Importantly, their resistance is not aimed at capitalism itself but an "exploitive" capitalism being imposed on them by sinister global forces. Revealed, therefore, is a new fantasy of "national authoritarian capitalism" whereby a leader or regime is solely able to direct marketization for the "good of the people" based on their specific and unique cultural conditions.

THE "CHINESE DREAM" OF AUTHORITARIAN CAPITALISM

The idea of a "Chinese Dream" that introduced this chapter exemplifies current global capitalist fantasies of authoritarian nationalism. It is a politics that explicitly struggles against the colonizing effects of globalization in order to realize a perfect market economy uniquely tailored to Chinese conditions. The party is championed as the only actor able to fully fend off this "global" menace and implement this Chinese-specific market utopia. Moreover, its hegemony and enhanced power resonates with the deeper desires of the population to shape and not be shaped by global capital.

The New Maoist Fantasy of Capitalism

The politics of Maoism and marketization are on the surface complete opposites. Indeed, they are strictly speaking antagonists – each explicitly committed to the destruction and replacement of the other. Yet, amidst these ideological differences lies a common authoritarian political logic. One premised on the ability of the party to singularly conceive and realize progress, the exclusive actor to properly adopt a universal ideology – communism and the free market, respectively – successfully to the Chinese context. Each reproduces authoritarianism, in this regard, by trumpeting the sole capacity and, therefore, legitimacy of the party to lead the Chinese population "correctly" toward future prosperity.

The two-decade rule of Mao Zedong was marked throughout by repression and single-party rule. Coming to power in 1949, by the early 1950s Mao and the CCP had fully consolidated their rule of the country. Over the next 30 years Mao would go to great lengths to retain this hegemony – against foreign threats, internal enemies, and even those who opposed him within his own party. During this time, he would attempt to sustain this hold on power through a range of dramatic and ultimately disastrous social and economic initiatives – starting with the ill-conceived and collectively fatal Great Leap Forward and culminating in the genocidal anarchy of the Cultural Revolution.

Indeed, the effects of this authoritarianism were and are appalling. The Maoist regime was characterized by harsh repression of dissidents, the use of forced labor "re-education camps," the organization of mass campaigns to stifle dissent against "impure elements," and the deployment of a wide-ranging secret spy network among the populace. The human cost of these authoritarian practices is perhaps even more staggering. Upwards of 30 million Chinese died in the Great Leap Forward alone (Peng, 1987; Yang, 1998), with many more needlessly suffering in the Cultural Revolution (see MacFarquhar and Schoenhals, 2006; White, 2014). Yet, while it is imperative not to minimize these acts through comparison or overly rational analysis, it is just as important to illuminate the motivating and legitimating logic of this authoritarian discourse in order to better view its continued influence in the present day.

Primarily, Mao framed the exclusive rule of the party as necessary for ensuring "ideological correctness." Initially, this correctness conformed to existing universalist interpretations of Leninism-Communism as approved by the USSR, yet for political reasons – notably an increasing rivalry with Soviet Russia – this took on a more culturally specific dimension. Indeed, as early as the 1930s Mao called for the "Sinification of Marxism," whose goal in the words of Chinese scholar Nick Knight (1986: 18) was to "establish a formula by which a universal theory such as Marxism could be utilized in a national context and culture *without abandoning the universality of that theory*" (emphasis in original). Mao himself argued for the need to unite those parts of Leninism representing "a universal truth for all times and all countries, which admits of no exception" with China's realities that "exists conditionally and temporarily and hence is relative" (see Wylie, 1979: 456). However, as the political relationship and the situation between the USSR and China changed in the mid-1950s this discourse began to evolve. It was now the sole responsibility of the party to properly implement communism to meet Chinese conditions. By the summer of 1956 Mao was already in the formative stages of using this as the basis for defining the party's ideology. Speaking of art he declared "the art of the various socialist countries each has socialism as its content, but each has its own national character" (Mao Zedong, 1956). To this end, in 1955 he internally ordered that the party should be the dominant power at the local level while publicly distinguishing between "advanced" and "backward" opinion:

> In any society and at any time, there are always two kinds of people and views, the advanced and the backward, that exist as opposites struggling with each other, with the advanced views invariably prevailing over the backward ones; it is neither possible nor right to have "uniformity of public opinion." Society can progress only if what is advanced is given full play and prevails over what is backward. But in an era in which classes and class struggle still exist both at home and abroad, the working class and the masses who have seized state power must suppress the resistance to the revolution put up by all counter-revolutionary classes, groups and individuals, thwart their activities aimed at restoration and prohibit them from exploiting freedom of speech for counter-revolutionary purposes. (Mao Zedong, 1955)

In place were all the elements of an authoritarian fantasy of communist nationalism: one promising the romanticized vision of a "perfected" communist Chinese society on the horizon; the requirement of single-party rule to correctly put in place this culturally specific nationalist vision; and, finally, the need of the state to repress any and all enemies to the achievement of this Chinese "dream" of communism. Even more so, it associated the repressive agency of the government, in this case the party, with individual and collective desires for greater power to control their own and their nation's destiny, respectively. It responded to the very real previous efforts of the West and Japan to colonize and exploit the Chinese people with an affective authoritarian discourse in which freedom was found in a powerful state able to effectively put at bay foreign threats and do as they wish domestically.

The death of Mao and the rise of Deng Xiaoping represented a seismic shift in the country's political, social, and economic landscape. The rigid ideological orthodoxy and worst political excesses were replaced by a greater flexibility in terms of policy and less oppressive state regime. Soon after ascending to power, in a 1978 speech entitled "Emancipate the mind and seek truth from facts and united as one in looking to the future," the new leader warned against people whose "thinking has become rigid" and therefore were "not guided by Party spirit and Party principles, but go along with whatever has the backing of the authorities" (Deng Xiaoping, 1978). Indeed, Deng would soon become known throughout the world for starting the country down the path of marketization, and in doing so to economic revitalization. The famines and chaos of the preceding decades were giving way to a new communist China that embraced the market and, if not democratic, was at least much more restrained in its repressive practices.

Underlying this transformation, however, was a similar authoritarian logic and fantasy initially espoused by Mao and his supporters. The guiding ideas of what was soon referred to as "Dengism" reveals the continued stressing of the exclusive right of the party to interpret national policy and its state apparatuses for enforcing these decisions. Deng declared in June 1984 that since introducing reforms the regime had "formulated correct ideological, political and organizational lines" that "seek truth from facts, as advocated by Comrade Mao Zedong, and uphold his basic ideas" (Deng Xiaoping, 1984a).

This appeal to pragmatism was, thus, strategically deployed in order to reinforce the correctness of the CCP's reform program and not to enhance democratic debate. It also continued to promote the need for the party to adapt communism (now including certain market principles) to Chinese realities. Deng framed his reform program according to a similar authoritarian governing paradigm to the one first championed by Mao. More precisely, he based his agenda on a proffered objective ideology of socialism properly interpreted by the party to produce the correct policies necessary for the country's national development. This analogous strategy was reflected clearly in 1980 when Deng declared that:

> We believe the socialist road is the correct one. While carrying out reforms, we still adhere to the Four Cardinal Principles, one of which is to keep to the socialist road. In building socialism, each country should adopt policies commensurate with its particular conditions ... The greatest contribution Chairman Mao Zedong made in building socialism was his integration of the universal truth of Marxism with the concrete practice of the Chinese revolution. (Deng Xiaoping, 1980)

By 1984 Deng was promoting a culturally specific reform-oriented discourse of "socialism with Chinese characteristic[s]." Specifically, he linked these desires to past narratives of revolutionary utopianism, as evidenced in his October 1984 remarks at the 35th anniversary celebration of the CCP's revolutionary victory:

> In the past 35 years not only have we ended for all time a dark period of our past and created a socialist society in China, but we have changed the course of human history. On a foundation of national stability, unity, democracy and the rule of law, we have given socialist modernization the highest priority in our work. Our economy has grown more vigorously than ever before, and achievements in all other fields are widely acknowledged. Today, all our people are full of joy and pride. (Deng Xiaoping, 1984b)

The tragedy of Tiananmen would indelibly darken the reign of Deng and the widespread optimism that the country was moving in a more open and democratic direction. The stark image of CCP troops putting down protestors shocked the world and internally led the party to become even more reactionary in safeguarding its exclusive authority. Yet it also revealed how Deng had created the foundations for a new Maoist fantasy of capitalism. One that effectively jettisoned established liberal rights or even more radical socialist ideals of emancipation for an appealing discourse that combined political authoritarianism and an economic ideology of marketization. In doing so, he and his predecessors would champion a discourse where globalization and its Western puppet master were the enemies, while capitalism, as conceived and implemented by the CCP at whatever cost, was the country's sole path to salvation.

The Beijing versus the Washington Consensus

The shift from communism to the market in China was both profound and gradual. It represented the transformation of the nation's direction and economic ordering. It also potentially raised a more existential threat to the single-party rule of the CCP. If the country was no longer socialist, at least in practice, why did it still need to be led by a communist party? More to the point, why were the extreme measures of this government still required?

An immediate, and perhaps somewhat obvious, way the party attempted to address these issues was to situate its strategic adoption of market policies into a broader and well-known narrative of ultimately realizing socialism. Here, rather ironically, for the goals of communism to be achieved the country first needed to take the road of marketization. In a March 1985 speech Deng defended the "development of an individual economy," specifically "joint ventures with both Chinese and foreign investment and of enterprises wholly owned by foreign businessmen." He argued, thus, that "all our policies for carrying out reform, opening to the outside world and invigorating the domestic economy are designed to develop the socialist economy" (Den Xiaoping, 1985).

However, as Deng's leadership gave way to Jiang Zemin and then later Hu Jintao, this promise seemed progressively empty. Far from moving toward deeper socialist relations or values, China was embracing the market ever more strongly, both economically and socially. In the wake of Tiananmen, Deng explicitly and firmly linked the values of protecting the nation through authoritarian measures with creating a stable environment for continued market reforms and development:

> This turmoil has been a lesson to us. We are more keenly aware that first priority should always be given to national sovereignty and security ... This turmoil has also made us more aware of the importance of stability ... We can accomplish nothing without a stable environment. So we had to quell the turmoil by imposing martial law. (Deng Xiaoping, 1989)

Such justification would only be enhanced by his successors. Labeled a "neo-conservative," Jiang emphasized the need to maintain public order and social unity through strengthening the party's rule. This prioritization of stability was reflected in his motto *wending yadao yiqie* ("stability overrides everything"). In 1993 Jiang would declare the advent of a "socialist Market economy," or as popularly termed in the foreign press, a "Leninist Market." This move publicly reinforced capitalist transformation as a permanent and core element of the country's future.

Yet, while this slogan reaffirmed the CCP's monopoly on power, it did little to reassert its ideological authority for leading the country. It was imperative, therefore, to craft a new capitalist fantasy that would effectively, and affectively, combine economic capitalism with the continuing authoritarian rule of the CCP. To do so the party turned to a familiar political discourse – positioning the party as the sole actor capable of defending the nation against the threatening intrusions of an imperialist global order that would seek to exploit it.

Such rhetoric soon transformed into a more entrenched discourse pitting the so-called "Beijing Consensus" against an insidious "Washington Consensus." The regime introduced the concept of a "Beijing Consensus" in May 2004, declaring that "China's unique development experience of 'coordinated development' has been called by experts as (the) 'Beijing Consensus' to differ it from 'Washington Consensus.'" This alternative did not imply a retreat from marketization toward orthodox communism. Instead, the "Beijing Consensus" focused on the need to "reduce the friction losses of reforms," in the words of Western policy analyst Joshua Ramo (2004: 12), credited with coining the term. Moreover, he notes: "The arrival of China's fourth-generation leaders Hu Jintao and Wen Jiabao in the fall of 2003 brought with it an end to the agonizing left–right intellectual debate about whether or not to marketise China's economy" (2004: 22).

Importantly, this struggle served to entrench capitalism as a dominant social ideology. Whereas before marketization was officially considered inherently exploitive and "incorrect," the new emphasis promoted by the party and other elites was on fighting off the wrong type of capitalism. In an official June 2005 article the party explicitly framed debate around a "Beijing Consensus" against the "Washington Consensus," describing this campaign as "the central leadership's proposal to research and criticize neo-liberalism" due to the way it unquestionably "advocates privatization, blazons the perpetual role of the 'private ownership myth' and opposes public ownership" (People's Daily, 2005a). In doing so, it explicitly and implicitly championed the existence of a correct form of marketization.

Apparent then was the promoting of capitalism domestically, ironically through the negative popular portrayal of globalization internationally. The regime was critical of how the United States (US) employed its perceived neoliberal orthodoxy to spread its hegemony, declaring "global liberalization protects the liberal economy under the US's dominance and opposes establishing a new international economic order" (People's Daily, 2005a). For these reasons it contended that "the global economy is in urgent need of vigorous growth and sound development in reflection on and transcending the conservative neo-liberalism economic thought" (People's Daily, 2005a). By contrast, the Beijing Consensus "was brought forward spontaneously by international opinions against the background of China's fast economic development since the reform and opening up and considerable raise in people's living standard" (People's Daily, 2005a).

In its place would be the campaign for a Chinese market that conformed to the nation's unique cultural and historical realities and that would supposedly benefit the wider population and not foreign elites. Reflected is the development of a new Chinese fantasy of capitalism. Like all such affective discourses, it revolves fundamentally around a dual structure of a negative and positive fantasy. It presents a romanticized vision of capitalism that is forever imperiled by the threats of insidious enemies trying to maliciously prevent the achievement of this longed for perfect future. What is significant is that this fantasy, this continual antagonism between a Chinese and Western market, between the CCP and globalization, between the "Beijing Consensus" and "Washington Consensus," creates a new foundation for individuals to construct a secure and appealing capitalist identity. The key, in this regard, is not simply the future attainment of this utopian Chinese market, nor the ultimate defeat of its enemies. Instead, it is also the present ontological security that this unending political struggle provides subjects individually and collectively as capitalist Chinese citizens under the sole and correct leadership of the party.

The Authoritarian Dream of Chinese Capitalism

This fantasy, thus, creates the seeds for bolstering the party's continued authoritarian rule as well as legitimizing its use of authoritarian practices to safeguard this capitalist "Chinese Dream." In the space of three decades, the CCP had once again solidified its position as the protector of the Chinese Revolution. Yet this time, it was being done in the name of capitalism and not communism.

The current regime has embraced a Maoist-like fantasy of party-led progress. The new General Secretary Xi Jinping has said continually that future prosperity depends on the correct leadership of the party. In the evolution from its communist beginnings to its market-inspired present, the sole authority of the party to rule has remained constant. In his first speech as leader in 2012, Xi Jinping made these priorities clear, maintaining "Our [the CCP's] responsibility is to rally and lead the whole party and all of China's ethnic groups and continue to emancipate our way of thinking, insist on reform and opening up" (Xi Jinping, 2012).

Central, in this regard, is Xi Jinping's continued championing of the CCP's exclusive ability to interpret and implement marketization. In November 2013, Xi established the National Security Commission in order to "perfect the national security system and national security strategy and ensure national security" (see Campbell, 2015: 3). Its scope of activities ranged from traditional security spheres (e.g. policing) to cultural and economic protection, "indicating that the concept of security is now being thought about in a much broader sense" (Mulrooney, 2014: 1). Significantly, here the state is trumpeted as required for not only guiding capitalism to the population's advantage but also protecting these reforms against internal and external threats.

Key in this respect is construction of a new identification that is at once anti-Western hegemony and pro-capitalist. Namely, it involves investing in a dream of "Chinese" capitalism – one where the nation under the party's leadership rejects and protects itself from the dangers of corporate globalization (seen as just the most updated version of the story of Western interference and even older foreign invasion). To this end, Xi remains steadfast in his commitment to "opening up" and embracing a global market. In a May 2014 speech he publicly stated:

> As a Chinese saying goes, "The ocean is vast for it admits hundreds of rivers." China will open itself wider to the world, advance mutually beneficial cooperation with other countries, and promote the development of the economic belt along the Silk Road and the Maritime Silk Road of the 21st century so that countries can create and share development opportunities together. (Xi Jinping, 2014)

Yet he has also consistently challenged any attempts by Western powers (notably the US) to infringe on China's national integrity, territorial or otherwise. Earlier that year in June 2014, he took what the newspaper, the *South Morning China Post*, saw as a direct "dig" at interventionist US foreign policy, contending that "sovereignty is the reliable safeguard and fundamental element of national interest. Sovereignty and territorial integrity should not be infringed upon. This is the hard principle that should not be cast aside at any time" (Ng, 2014).

Underpinning these criticisms is the right of the country to be free to control its own destiny, shaping marketization for the benefit of the Chinese people. This "Chinese Dream" provides the exact rationale for enhancing authoritarianism practically, not just state power in principle, as linked to marketization. Here, the party is imperative for rooting out all enemies who may imperil the future prosperity of a Chinese market. The nation must be constantly on guard against such opposition, whether they be foreign or domestic in character.

The CCP's worsening human rights record under Xi reflects this growing authoritarian capitalism. A 2014 US report found that: "Human rights and rule of law conditions in China overall did not improve this past year, and declined in some of the areas covered by this report. The Chinese government and Communist Party continued to emphasize authoritarian control at the expense of human rights and the rule of law" (Congressional-Executive Commission on China, 2014).

Human Rights Watch echoed this assessment, noting that Xi's regime had overall "struck a conservative tone, opposing constitutional rule, press freedom, and 'western-style' rule of law, and issuing harsher restrictions on dissent, including through two legal documents making it easier to bring criminal charges against activists and Internet critics" (2014a). Demonstrated is the continued and increasing willingness and "right" of the party to impose its authority in the name of preserving the "dream" of a Chinese market.

Xi's recent emphasis on corruption speaks to this authoritarian mindset. The CCP has the correct plan for realizing its vision of Chinese capitalism. Yet to do so, it must be vigilant against those within and without the party who are guilty of corruption. Many commentators felt that this campaign was primarily a tool for Xi to eliminate party rivals (Cohen, 2015), while others directly compared it to Mao's previous use of corruption to root out internal dissent. According to Willy Lam, political analyst at the Chinese University of Hong Kong, "The question remains to be whether Xi is taking a page from Chairman Mao. Starting with Mao, corruption has been used to take down enemies of the more powerful faction" (Jiang, 2015).

Yet, the campaign also represents the persistent, and to some extent, expanding authoritarian logic for implementing and safeguarding capitalism nationally. Here, deeper social problems associated with either economic marketization or political authoritarianism is shifted onto the malicious figure of the "corruptor" whose literal corruption figuratively corrupts and is threatening the entire dream of Chinese progress. Xi promised, with "the people's utmost support," that the party "will win the fierce and protracted war against corruption and build a clean Party and government" (Mu Xuequan, 2015). In this sense, the health of the party is equated with its ability to put in place a healthy capitalism.

Present is a reinvigorated capitalist fantasy of authoritarian nationalism. It reveals the construction of a new capitalist self that is committed to fighting off enemies of both the nation and capitalism – which are increasingly viewed as one and the same. It also speaks to an affective need to recapture a feeling of lost agency attached to processes of global capitalism. The triumph of the state and its ability to "stand up" to international rivals and organizations resonates with the desire to not be controlled by marketization or globalization. Rather, the attractiveness of the CCP, in this context, is its appeal to values of self-determination and the possibilities of a market that serves the needs of the people rather than just elites, foreign or otherwise.

RUSSIA AND PUTINISM: THE RISE OF THE AUTHORITARIAN CAPITALIST ANTI-HERO

China is, of course, not the only country under the spell of an affective capitalist discourse of authoritarian nationalism. Its neighbor to the north, and one-time Cold War ally and then rival, Russia is displaying a similarly oppressive market politics. Under the leadership of Vladimir Putin it has transformed into an oligarchic capitalist state, whose inequality is preserved through a combination of ruthless repression and charismatic despotic leadership. Its facade of democracy masks therefore a status quo that is simultaneously committed to the cause of deepening capitalist "reforms" and sustaining a politics of dictatorship. And just like its Chinese counterpart, it does so through a strident appeal against the threat of globalization.

The Birth of the Capitalist Tsar: An Authoritarian Legacy from Tsarism to the USSR

The roots of Russia's current authoritarianism lie in both its Tsarist and Soviet past. Indeed, the despotism of Putin, while not identical to either of these regimes, draws heavily from both. He simultaneously promotes a triumphalist discourse of Russian exceptionalism while trumpeting his singular ability to properly implement market reforms for the betterment of the population. Further, his legitimacy rests on his resistance to globalization, portrayed as a colonizing force that is trying to destroy the country from the inside and out. He is, in this respect, a capitalist tsar with a distinctly Soviet flavor. More precisely, Putin is the epitome of a capitalist despot whose plutocracy and repression extend to rival oligarchs, foreign competitors, social dissidents, and all those who oppose his state-led market revolution.

The Soviet experiment was given birth in the cauldron of an autocratic Tsarist state. For almost 400 years, starting in 1547, Russia was ruled by tsars – regimes that differed, at times almost wildly, depending on the sovereign. It encompassed the early state building and brutality of Ivan the Terrible to the modernization efforts of Peter the Great. What each shared though was a commitment to top-down control and primacy of the state in the form of the monarch for maintaining social order. They reflected a type of Russian "myth" of a great leader able to unite the people and rule them effectively and into prosperity (Cherniavsky, 1961). The legitimacy of the tsars, therefore, rested on their ability to rise above social cleavages and restore justice when needed. To this end, to the people "The Great Tsar insisted that they were not only serving him personally but something beyond him – the State, the fatherland" (Greenfeld, 1990: 557). This duty to preserve Russia extended beyond economics and into the spiritual and social realms as well. The relationship between ruled and ruler was exemplified in the popular description of Russians as "slaves to the Tsar," which "symbolically elevated the status of the tsar, provided his servitors with a respectful way in which to make claims on the government, and helped resolve tension within the governing class" (Poe, 1998: 587).

In practice, this amounted to a form of authoritarianism that was neither practical nor sustainable in the midst of an industrializing economy within a political environment of early twentieth-century Great Power imperialism. The intricacies of the workings and failures of Tsarism obviously go well beyond the scope of this analysis. What is crucial, however, is its authoritarian politics revolving around the population's affective investment in a strong leader who is expected to preserve the country against the chaos of revolutionary new ideas – ones perceived to be fundamentally "non-Russian" – of liberty and equality. Hence, under the tsar: "[a]fter 1825 nationality was identified with absolutism, of consensual subordination, in contrast to egalitarian Western concepts. The monarchical narrative of nation described the Russian people as voluntarily surrendering power to their Westernized rulers" (Wortman, 2000: 12).

The replacement of this "official nationalism" of the tsars by the Bolsheviks, and the establishment of a Soviet communist regime, was at once revolutionary and built on these autocratic foundations. Under Lenin, the Communist Party of the USSR created the basis for both massive socioeconomic transformations in the direction of socialist central planning and collectivism as well as authoritarian repression characterized by secret police and the silencing of internal dissent (see Figes, 1997). Within a decade the country would descend into a fury of state-led terror, perhaps unseen in scale before or since (Kuromiya, 2014; Thurston, 1998), as well as a dangerous cult of personality centering around its new communist leader, Joseph Stalin (Tucker, 1979).

The following five decades of Soviet power, while lessening the strength and excesses of this fantasy, did nothing to fundamentally alter it. The party remained the pre-eminent actor for guiding the country in the proper historical and ideological direction. It promoted, in this respect, an idea of "partiinost [partyness] with expertise" linked to a general "commitment in a totalitarian society to an ideology of 'politics takes command,' to the control and preferably guidance of the society by a group of dedicated people committed to collective interests and to a utopian vision" (Linz, 2000: 86–7). Yet digging slightly deeper, the remnants of an authoritarian Tsarist rationale survived in the eight decades of communist rule. Notably, the party was transformed from an agent of radical social change to the protector of the nation's territorial, spiritual, and social sanctity. Its success, and the justification for its author-itarianism in practice, was intimately linked to the safeguarding of a "strong Russia" nationally and internationally. "The mobilizing impetus," observes Bialer (1982: 15) "came from the 'truths of the state,' not of the party; from patriotism and nationalism, not from ideology in a communist sense."

It was precisely on this basis that Putin would reinvigorate authoritarianism in the post-Cold War era. Amidst the perceived injustices and anarchy of the "gangster capitalism" characterizing Russia in the 1990s, he would project a sense of state-led justice and order. Central in this regard was the saving of Russia from foreign domination and their home-grown oligarch handmaidens. Emerging from this cauldron of chaos, oligarchy, and the social pain of a rapid market transition was a new capitalist fantasy of Tsarism with the name of Putinism.

The Rise of Putinism

The rule of Vladimir Putin follows in this authoritarian legacy. It has been marked simultaneously by optimistic appeals of national renewal and deep-seated paranoia about foes, both foreign and domestic, imperiling the country. More so, his increasingly iron-fisted and repressive regime has, akin to the Chinese example discussed above, continued to commit to economic marketization. While much of his rhetoric at times can speak to feelings of capitalist dismay experienced by many within the country, his actions and populism are aimed not at moving Russia in a different economic direction but rather combining a strong political state with a relatively regulated market society.

The historical backdrop of Putin's rise to power is crucial, in this respect. The decade following the demise of the USSR represented a difficult transi-tion, to say the very least. It was characterized by dramatic rises in inequality (Ravallion and Lokshin, 2000), declining social mobility (Gerber and Hout, 2004), falling economic growth, and precarious employment (S. Clarke, 1998), to match its substantive gains in liberal political freedom. For this reason, the era is commonly referred to as a time of "gangster capitalism" in which anarchy reigned and rival oligarchs fought, with often violent results, to accumulate as much wealth and influence as they could (Handelman, 1995; Klebnikov, 2000). The seeming disintegration of the nation into chaos sparked anger and insecurity throughout the country. The fall of the USSR had been fueled by widespread hope that a new system would emerge delivering greater freedom and fairer rule of law. Instead, this creaking totalitarian regime was replaced by growing violence, elitism, and the inability of the elected gov-ernment to provide either economic security for its citizens or restore social order. Further, the previous material "safety net" and cultural benefits offered by the Soviet regime – such as free education and healthcare as well as secure employment – were now firmly seen as a thing of the past, lost relics from a bygone era where political liberty may have been in short supply but the state still took care of its people. Amidst this volatile and anxious environment, Putin was appointed as prime minister in 1999 and then ascended to the presidency for the first time in 2000. His background gave pause to many within the country, as he was a former member of the KGB. Yet for others, it signaled the possibilities for a "return to normalcy" – the ascendancy of a strong leader who could properly set things to rights. Politically, Putin initially appeared to tread a middle ground ideologically between those who called for complete liberalization and a rising populist movement seeking to go back to the old ways of Leninist-style communism (Rice-Oxley and Cross, 2012).

His first act reflected this perceived centrism, as he made a deal with the oligarchs that they would be left to their economic devices as long as they paid their taxes and drastically reduced their violence. However, he soon began directly taking on these powerful economic figures, doing so officially in the name of pursuing justice, regardless of wealth or status. Unofficially, however, there appeared a more fundamental but no less psychologically resonant reason for attacking the oligarchs – safeguarding the country from the threat of foreign influence, which the Russian corporate leaders were exacerbating by directly negotiating and partnering with Western firms (Goldman, 2004).

Regardless, of its normative or economic effects, these measures created the foundations for Putin to regularize and extend his authoritarianism. As Sakwa (2008: 879) notes:

> Arriving into the presidency in 2000 Putin declared his goal as the "dictatorship of law," and indeed this principle was exercised in the attempt to overcome the legal fragmentation of the country in the federal system; but when it came to pursuing regime goals, it appeared more often than not that the system ruled by law rather than ensuring the rule of law.

Specifically, he has progressively deployed global discourses of the "War on Terror" to legitimate the repression of internal enemies (Shuster, 2010). Moreover, he has done so while maintaining in principle – and to some degree in practice – the country's commitments to continued market reforms. Indeed, while he has nationalized some industries and been seen by many as "conservative" in the pace in which he has implemented marketization, he nonetheless, even as late as 2012, publicly declared that "state capitalism is not our goal" (Busvine, 2012).

This reversion to authoritarian capitalism – even as it maintains the edifice of representative democracy – has been described as "Putinism" (see Hill and Cappelli, 2013). According to Zakaria (2014):

> The crucial elements of Putinism are nationalism, religion, social conservatism, state capitalism and government domination of the media. They are all, in some way or another, different from and hostile to, modern Western values of individual rights, tolerance, cosmopolitanism and internationalism. It would be a mistake to believe that Putin's ideology created his popularity – he was popular before – but it sustains his popularity.

To this effect, Van Herpern (2013: 8) refers to Putinism as a type of "fascism lite," which "shares with 'classical' fascism its ultra nationalism and its ideas of national rebirth and imperialist revision" but with a distinctly modern twenty-first-century twist. In particular, "it combines internal repression with the adoption of the advanced global capitalist economy."

Putinism, thus, conforms to and borrows from its Tsarist and Soviet predecessors. It justifies the strong arm of the state through reference to foreign enemies and the need to maintain a strong Russia at all costs. It has, further, quite successfully played on "traditional Russian values," extolling this social conservatism to expand the repressive scope of the state's power and distracting attention away from the continuing structural problems of marketization. In this respect, it reflects not only the country's autocratic and totalitarian past but also its authoritarian capitalist present.

Putin and the Capitalist Fantasy of the Authoritarian Anti-Hero

The continuing power of Putin, both in terms of the length and security of his rule as well as his ongoing appeal to large segments of the population, reflects his skill at marshaling an affective capitalist fantasy of authoritarian nationalism. In particular, his support stems, in no small part, from the portrayal of himself and his allies as protectors of Russian sovereignty, even more so, in the public championing of his singular ability to not be confined by the prescriptive dictates of foreign countries and international law. He stands, in this regard, as a capitalist anti-hero; one who is attractive exactly due to his willingness to take on the perceived colonial aspects of globalization even as he expands the scope of political authoritarianism and economic marketization at home.

Crucial to the legitimacy of Putin is his framing of politics around an affective discourse that combines in equal measure patriotism, state-supported capitalism, social traditionalism, and aggressive jingoism against foreign threats. Reflected is, akin to what is found in China, a capitalist fantasy of authoritarian nationalism. It is one that leans on the exclusive capability of a strong sovereign, in this case found not in a party per se but a leader, to preserve the country's prosperity and guide its development contra enemies from without and within. Moreover, it is underpinned by a commitment to maintaining and taking advantage of a global market economy.

This phantasmatic narrative is demonstrated in both the regime's domestic and foreign policies. At home, Putin has castigated internal dissent as "anti-Russian." Not surprisingly, he has coupled such charges by strategically presenting himself and his rule as the leading protector of Russia's conservative culture (Bai, 2015; Kaylan, 2014). In his 2013 State of the Union address he railed against the West's "genderless and infertile" liberalism while trumpeting Russia's "traditional values" (Whitmore, 2013). The incarceration of the punk band Pussy Riot exemplifies this trend, as they were imprisoned for publicly singing a satirical song about Putin and the country's generally orthodox legacy. More broadly, the regime has ramped up its rhetoric and repression against those deemed to endanger Russian culture, namely homosexuals, a situation that the *New York Times* referred to as "Mr. Putin's War on Gays" (*New York Times*, 2013).

Tellingly, Putin has defended this state-sanctioned social repression on the grounds that such practices and identities represent something distinctly "foreign," specifically Western. He regularly railed against a "unipolar" world and the problems of external sociopolitical as well as cultural threats to Russian sovereignty. Specifically, he directed his attacks against the US, arguing that: "One state and, of course, first and foremost the United States, has overstepped its national borders in every way. This is visible in the economic, political, cultural and educational policies it imposes on other nations. Well who likes this? Who is happy about this?" (Sternthal, 2012).

By contrast, he espoused the need to strengthen Russia through his strong leadership to repel these "foreign" enemies. He argued that it is essential to bolster the country's defenses in order to make sure that other countries do not perceive Russia as weak, thus strengthening their international power overall. This condemnation fits within a broader discourse attributing the problems of the country to malicious desires of non-Russian exploiters. It is a fantasy built on centuries-old paranoia, but this time in support of a capitalist autocrat.

And yet, such established despotism has a relatively new twist in the contemporary age under Putin. Notably, it is firmly anti-globalization but pro-capitalist. Or, to put it differently, it focuses attention on the population's fears of the specter of an unstoppable global capitalism backed by and for the benefit of the West. In a September 2013 speech he declared, in rhetoric, that he had mined countless times before and would continue to afterwards, "It is evident that it is impossible to move forward without spiritual, cultural and national self-determination. Without this we will not be able to withstand internal and external challenges, nor will we succeed in global competitions"

(David, 2014). To this effect, it reflects prevailing feelings of powerlessness connected to globalization. Through Putin, the country is able to regain its agency, to fight back and seemingly forge its own destiny rather than merely accept internationally proscribed mandates for how it should conduct its affairs.

In practice, this authoritarian agency is manifested in the ethos of portraying Putin, as previously described, as the capitalist anti-hero. He is a figure who does what he wants while disregarding, indeed even basking in, the condemnation of the global community. He treats the rules of the current order as strictures to be broken when and wherever he sees fit. Tellingly, despite or perhaps more accurately exactly because of Western condemnation, Putin is seen by many global leaders, particularly autocratic ones, as "The New Model Dictator" (Caryl, 2015). His conservative machoism and willingness to challenge US and European hegemony appeals to rulers like Erdoğan in Turkey and Orbán in Hungary. In the words of *Washington Post* reporter Erin Cunningham (2015), "Putin … is therefore seen as a virile strongman who crushes dissent and stands up to the West."

The recent invasion of Ukraine by Russia exemplifies this anti-hero political persona inhabited by Putin. In the leadup to the invasion, it was not so much that he supported the annexing of the eastern part of the country to Russia nor that there is strong evidence that he is continuing to interfere in Ukrainian politics to reflect Russian interests. It is rather that he was so publicly dismissive, at times almost satirically so, when called by the foreign community to defend or account for his actions. *The Economist* (2015) laid out the political calculation, some may cynicism, at the heart of this strategy almost a decade before the invasion:

> Against this background a resolution of the Ukrainian crisis and de-escalation of tensions with the West would push the focus back onto economic and social problems, lowering Mr Putin's ratings, just as happened after Russia's war in Georgia in 2008. A continuation of the war in Ukraine and the stand-off with the West will keep his ratings up for longer.

The consequence of this anti-heroism, thus, is one that detracts from the country's more fundamental social and economic problems, many of which are connected to structural issues of ongoing marketization mixed with oligarchy. In this way, his positioning of himself as a fighter of Western hegemony, and its ideology of corporate globalization, bolsters the nation's market transformation. He is, therefore, a capitalist anti-hero. He is one of international capitalism's most public transgressors – the "bad boy" who refuses to bow down to not only foreign rivals but a new world order prioritizing the legal rights and power of multinational corporations. However, he strategically deploys this subversive persona to ironically entrench marketization and with it authoritarian capitalism at home.

CONCLUSION

This chapter examined the rise of an explicitly authoritarian politics associated with the expansion of economic marketization nationally. Using the cases of China and Russia as prime examples, it highlights how capitalism does not just permit for but can in fact encourage such despotic discourses and practices politically. Namely, it relies upon authoritarian fantasies, trumpeting the need for a strong state to properly guide the country's capitalist development and protect it from ideological threats. This mirrors previous regimes that also justified repression and exclusive sovereign power along similar lines of protecting and implementing a "correct" ideology. It furthermore points to the intimate linkages between the structural advantages of if not authoritarianism then the presence of a strong and supportive state for marketization and the construction of an affective authoritarian political discourse in support of these values. Put differently, revealed is how such despotism is not only perhaps to a degree necessary but also an ironically appealing part of this broader international spread of capitalism. It should not be surprising then that authoritarian capitalism has lent itself so readily to the promotion of far-Right populist demagogues in the present era.

In the age of globalization, these authoritarian capitalist fantasies have taken a perhaps somewhat unexpected turn. It is now paradoxically through a direct appeal against globalization that its underlying market norms are most strongly realized. By framing debate around the poles of national self-determination and global colonialism, deeper considerations of marketization economically and authoritarianism politically are marginalized and to an extent ignored. Indeed, such a fantasy situates all problems with capitalism as part of a broader narrative of national progress ensured and preserved by a strong autocratic regime. It also grants further legitimization to the extension of repression in the name of preserving this national market progress. In this respect, national despots serve the structurally vital but internationally derided role of implementing and sustaining deepening marketization within a global capitalist economy that rhetorically trumpets its commitment to "fairness" while continuing to perpetuate inequality. As such, corporate globalization is bolstered exactly through the construction and promotion of an affective political discourse of authoritarian nationalism.

Chapter 5 will examine similar dynamics in economically developing countries, revealing the broader prevalence of authoritarian capitalist fantasies that extend far beyond simply market despotism and instead encompass the very construction of the modern "development" state.

5. Developing authoritarian capitalism: the global capitalist fantasy of authoritarian modernization

On March 23, 2015, Singapore's founding father and longest-serving prime minister Lee Kuan Yew passed away. Leaders from across the world joined in praise for his leadership over the young "city-state" country's development. President Barack Obama called him a "true giant of history" while United Nations Secretary-General, Ban Ki-Moon, referred to him as a "legendary figure in Asia" (Rawlinson, 2015). These words are perhaps understandable given Singapore's economic record of robust growth, global openness to business, alongside low levels of acute poverty (despite high inequality). Yet they are also somewhat disconcerting when considering the government's now seven decade-long authoritarian rule. Indeed, only a month later, a teenage blogger would be arrested and face up to three years in jail for criticizing this "true giant of history" (Abernethy, 2015).

The death of Lee Kuan Yew highlights growing tensions with optimistic accounts that marketization will inevitably lead to both progressive political and economic development. The global shift toward neoliberalism raises renewed questions over whether policies of privatization and deregulation can provide for concrete development goals linked to health and welfare as well as genuine democratization. At the end of the last century, in the midst of the supposed liberal democratic "end of history," a new mentality for national development emerged, revolving around the "dominance of a market oriented approach to the question of national development and the willingness of governments to follow the policy dictates of international finance organizations based on this perspective" (Portes, 1997: 229). However, in the intervening years, it is increasingly ambiguous whether marketization is indeed a driver of development. Kumi et al. (2014) echo a common refrain when they ask, "Can post-2015 sustainable development goals survive neoliberalism?"

These concerns have extended beyond social and economic critique and into the political sphere. Present is a distinct pessimism about the prospects of democracy in an age defined by global capitalism, when before it was seen as a mere inevitability. "Democracy has retreated in Bangladesh, Nigeria, the Philippines, Russia, Thailand, and Venezuela, and the Bush administration's attempts to establish democracy in Afghanistan and Iraq seem to have left both countries in chaos," bemoan Inglehart and Welzel (2009: 1). "These developments, along with the growing power of China and Russia, have led many observers to argue that democracy has reached its high-water mark and is no longer on the rise." Previous evidence backs up this pessimism regarding the future of democracy globally, as it has been shown empirically that economic "modernization" does not naturally or even necessarily lead to political democracy (Przeworski and Limongi, 1997).

This lack of democracy within modernization is by no means a new phenomenon. Rather, it follows a precedent of past examples of authoritarian modernization existing across the world at the end of the twentieth century. Latin American countries throughout the 1970s, for instance, adopted a "bureaucratic authoritarian model" combining economic capitalism and political repression (Collier, 1979). Here the state's "arbitrary rule over workers, politicians, and students is accompanied by attempts to establish pragmatic and predictable relationships with the private entrepreneurial sector, particularly international business, and to rationalize the advance of the economy as a whole" (Kaufman, 1979: 166). This authoritarian model of development, furthermore, expanded beyond the Americas and came to influence East Asian countries such as South Korea (Im, 1987).

In the present era, this "reform-driven" authoritarianism is mirrored in the rise of "semi-authoritarian" states internationally. These are nations that remain dominated by a single party and are marked by illiberal practices, usually associated with dictatorships despite – and in some cases precisely through – the presence of certain established democratic institutions and practices. Significantly, marketization not only exists alongside this contemporary authoritarianism but in fact strengthens it. As Ottaway observes (2013: 148):

> An additional source of ruling party financing at public expense is provided by the liberal economic reforms undertaken by democratizing regimes or by those that want to appear as if they are democratizing. Privatization programs provide ample opportunities for building up the finances of the dominant party and those associated with it.

At the international level, the power relations characterizing corporate globalization further contribute to this authoritarian trend. The demands of global hegemons require simultaneous political stability and managed processes of economic marketization and (if need be) political reforms. To this end, hegemons such as the United States are often more concerned with a managed form of "opening up to the world" rather than an open and vibrant democratization in these client countries (Hinnebusch, 2006). The global spread of democracy meant to accompany the global spread of capitalism has been in practice one of controlled economic liberalization, creating a fertile ground for the persistence and expansion of modern authoritarian rule.

Less explored, though, is the affective "grip" of this emerging form of authoritarian capitalist development. To be more exact, what popular discourses are being marshaled to justify formal and informal state and international repression in the name of a market-based "modernization"? As will be shown, present is a similar fantasy to that of "market despotism" described in Chapter 4. States are increasingly perpetuating a utopian fantasy of economic and political development, associated with marketization and democratization, respectively, that justifies a monopoly of power and quite oppressive popular rule. They do so, moreover, through drawing on the unique possibilities and challenges they face as "developing countries" in a globalizing world.

THE MARKET AUTHORITARIAN TRANSITION

Marketization is commonly used almost interchangeably with democratization. It is almost "common sense" to consider that for democra to emerge it must do so within a market system. In terms of development, it therefore makes intuitive sense that the greater the marketization the greater the potential for democratic transition. Nevertheless, such assumptions have been dramatically challenged when placed alongside actual processes of neoliberal transformation. Privatization and deregulation have been accompanied by and contributed to less rather than more democratisation in many if not most cases.

In the wake of such mass policies of marketization the world over, scholars have increasingly theorized a "new politics of development" (Carroll and Jarvis, 2014), in which the values of popular representation must be linked to, and, if necessary, constrained by, social forces that will ensure that countries implement long-term "reforms" (Cammack, 2012). Larry Summers, former US Secretary of the Treasury, warned of the "propensity for democracies to be short sighted" and the need "to find politically acceptable ways to … preserve the benefits of democracy without letting popular forces destroy the economy that supports them" (Haggard and Webb, 1994: x–xii). For this reason, the implementation of marketization is often described as a type of "anti-politics" whereby economic change is initiated and made permanent through recourse to a variety of non-democratic methods (Roberts, 2010).

Such insights echo emerging views that neoliberalism actively weakens democracy. Specifically, it is asserted that it relies on a form of "technocratic" political leadership (Gualmini and Schmidt, 2013). Politicians are tasked, in this respect, with simply competently putting in place a market agenda of privatization and deregulation rather than encouraging public consultation and open ideological debate. Regionally in Europe, the financial crisis, which popularly signaled the need for a new "economic paradigm," in fact allowed neoliberalism to become even more entrenched as part of a justified "authoritarianism of emergency" (Giannone, 2015). More generally, the high inequality associated with neoliberal economics and politics has a profoundly negative democratic impact (Wade, 2013).

The detrimental effect of neoliberalism for democracy in practice reflects its theoretical underpinnings as a form of sociopolitical governance. In particular, the advancement of marketization economically prioritizes ideologically complementary political values of efficiency and results over participation and deliberation. Neoliberal governance models such as "New Public Management" threaten substantive democracy due to their overriding ethos of managerialism (Box et al., 2001; Christensen and Lægreid, 2002). Its recent evolution to "Public Value Management" is plagued by the same political concerns. While it ostensibly promotes greater consultation and incorporates certain corporatist features of social democracies (Bryson et al., 2014), their democratic credentials are severely compromised by their ultimate and intractable goal of instituting and expanding neoliberalism, leading consequently to the "downsizing of democracy" (Dahl and Soss, 2014).

Specific to themes of development, scholars have highlighted the perpetuation of neoliberalism internationally with similar political processes of "strategic participation." For this reason, Cook and Kothari (2001) ask critically if participation can be considered "the new tyranny." Such forms of participation are often demanded and serve to make populations complicit to already determined policies of marketization (Mosse, 1994; Stirrat, 1996). More than simply reinforcing the economic hegemony of neoliberal values, such "tyrannical participation" also bolsters political authoritarianism. The inclusion of these consultative measures allows for formally and informally non-democratic regimes to legitimize their own power and reform agenda. Such "participatory planning" permits, in this regard, private and public elites to organizationally "seek to secure the benefits (financial, political and symbolic) but avoid the costs of 'participation'" (Mosse, 2001: 18).

It is perhaps not surprising, then, that authoritarianism has become so resurgent nationally, even in the face of rather massive international and popular pressures on developing countries to democratize. There is a rather contradictory tension between the "anti-politics" and strategic management demanded by marketization and the concurrent expectations for democracy. To deal with this tension, elites have tactically deployed liberal democratic institutions for maintaining what is in fact an authoritarian system. Witnessed is "the rise of competitive authoritarianism," whereby different groups vie for repressive power through elections (Levitsky and Way, 2002). The consequences of such democratically sanctioned authoritarianism can, beyond reinforcing institutionalized repression, be quite violent as incumbents and opposition parties exhibit the "perils of pluralism" in literally fighting over the spoils of governing neoliberalism (Taylor et al., 2013).

This has led many to wonder if neoliberalism is at all compatible with democracy and democratization. Despite certain democratic pretensions, is it at its heart a project of capitalism at any cost? Does it leave open the space to fully engage in substantive democratic debate over its values or a deepening of democracy beyond its most basic liberal forms? Extending these lines of thought, Wendy Brown (2015) associates neoliberalism with "the undoing of the Demos." In her view, it is a time marked by the shift from "homo politicus to homo economicus," symbolizing a modern politics that has been almost completely "economized." "What happens to the constituent elements of democracy – its culture, subjects, principles and institutions," she intones "when neoliberal rationality saturates political life" (Brown, 2015: 27). The current era, for this reason, has been considered as profoundly "post-political" (Wilson and Swyngedouw, 2014).

While these critiques remain undeniable in their force, they nevertheless leave comparatively ignored a just as significant concern. There is more at stake than simply how neoliberalism is anti-political or the adverse relation of marketization to democratization. Instead, it must be asked how such economic transformations are explicitly politicizing individuals in support of them. Further, how is such politicization directly linked to prevailing discourses of corporate globalization? More precisely, how is globalization serving to frame development as a political fantasy of authoritarian capitalism?

THE CAPITALIST FANTASY OF AUTHORITARIAN DEVELOPMENT

The once inviolable link claimed by modernization theorists and spreading out to popular thought between marketization and democratization has been increasingly undone. Both theoretically and in practice neoliberalism produces less democracy and more regulatory, often authoritarian, forms of governance. If globalization was meant to create a universal trend toward democracy, even if only its limited liberal version, it has substantially failed on this account. In its place is a growing authoritarian version of market development that draws its support from economic and political fantasies of state-led modernization.

Despite optimistic claims welcoming the end of the Cold War, there is an established history of authoritarian modernization connected to affective discourses of a strong and repressive state. One of the earliest examples is found in Otto von Bismarck's iron-fisted rule as Chancellor of the German Second Reich. Deploying a mixture of hard and soft authoritarianism, as well as strategic political and social reforms, he helped guide the country's rapid industrialization. Tellingly, his rule and methods for achieving such modernization stand as a forerunner for today's "competitive authoritarianism." According to Bernhard (2011: 150):

> One of the best ways to gain insight into the future paths of these political systems, ironically, is to look backward rather than forward, because the past can be prologue. Wilhelmine Germany is a particularly interesting point of comparison, because it had many similar characteristics. Like many of these regimes, it, too, experienced late, rapid growth and social transformation. It, too, developed a competitive form of politics that fell short of full-blown democracy.

Significantly, this authoritarian variant of capitalist development relied upon the affective appeal of a strong-man leader, able to use his power to ensure social order for the sake of attaining rapid modernization. This central responsibility of the state to guide development, and if necessary in quite heavy-handed ways, became an accepted truth of many non-Western modernists, even those who otherwise held extensive egalitarian and liberal values. Within the context of the Middle East, Atabaki and Zurcher (2004: 4) write:

> the fact that the modernists saw in an enlightened intelligentsia, which availed itself of the power of the state machinery to push through reforms, as the only possible engine of change ... meant that many of them were prone to accept the view that only the ruling institutions coordinated by a potent and persuasive leader were able to instigate the overall needed change and reform in order to modernize society.

This paradigm for development persisted throughout the century, evidenced, for instance, in the role of Latin American dictatorships in pushing through "neoconservative" reforms in the 1970s and 1980s (Schamis, 1991).

These historical precedents have been updated to incorporate contemporary discourses of globalization into a new logic for authoritarian development. Economically, this is perhaps best exemplified in the "developmental model" popularized in the 1980s and 1990s in East Asia. It was characterized by the strong role of the state in instituting and managing the country's marketization (Wade, 1990). Indeed, the success of this market-driven modernization was directly linked to the "autonomy of the state" (Jenkins, 1991). To this extent, they were often considered as socially conservative, productivist, and welfare regimes (Holliday, 2000; Lee and Ku, 2007). Not surprisingly, this usually translated into formal and informal authoritarian regimes created and maintained in order to achieve a "governance that works" in a competitive global business environment.

Just as importantly, globalization provided a rich political resource for legitimizing the continuation of this authoritarianism. It was able to shield itself from domestic criticism, at least to an extent, through shifting attention to the attempts by the international community to impose its Western values on these nations. The release of the Bangkok Declaration in 1993 epitomized such efforts, criticizing the United Nations' promotion of universal human rights as a potential violation of their national sovereignty. While accepting the importance of these rights, they nevertheless warned "that the promotion of human rights should be encouraged by cooperation and consensus, and not through confrontation and the imposition of incompatible values," while emphasizing "the principles of respect for national sovereignty and territorial integrity as well as non-interference in the internal affairs of States, and the non-use of human rights as an instrument of political pressure" (United Nations, 1993). The pronouncement of these so-called "Asian values" simultaneously reaffirmed these Asian countries' commitment to corporate globalization while politically defending their right to do so on their own terms, namely against the "threat" of liberal democracy (Subramaniam, 2000; Thompson, 2001). In its place, they championed their own authoritarian system of "Asian democracy" (Hood, 1998).

In a similar fashion, countries are using the affective discourse of state-guided development to stabilize and entrench neoliberal "reforms." This is especially the case in contemporary Latin America. The fall of the "Washington Consensus" as a model for modernization (Gore, 2000) created a political vacuum demanding novel articulations of the relation between the public and private sectors. Rising inequality and deteriorating social welfare throughout the region linked to policies of privatization and deregulation catalyzed novel approaches for involving the government in development while not sacrificing ideological commitments to marketization. New approaches like "neostructuralism" and "post-neoliberalism" sought to merge social development and "market reforms" through a reinvigorated state (Grugel and Riggirozzi, 2012; Leiva, 2008). The case of Chile illustrates this renewed affective discourse of an enhanced state for moderating the effects of, though not directly challenging or regulating, ongoing processes of marketization. Touted as a global success story, the Chilean government has strategically permitted demands for greater equality to exist at the social margins – for instance with unions in the mining industry – without deviating from the country's overall neoliberal direction (Singh, 2012a, 2012b). The government, in this regard, stands as both the protector of market reforms and of the interests of a wider population often adversely affected by these policies. Nonetheless, the country faced nationwide protests over plans to marketize the education sector (Somma, 2012). These protests were particularly resonant as they directly contradicted the regime's use of education as a promised pathway for social mobility in the face of a weakened social safety net (Avigur-Eshel, 2013). Despite having one of the best human rights records in Latin America, these protests commonly resulted in enhanced police repression (Human Rights Watch, 2014b).

Crucial to this affective politics of authoritarian development is the framing of all those who oppose neoliberal measures as "enemies" of modernization. Specifically, previous left-wing movements and ideologies were castigated as being not only wrongheaded but also dangerous. Jorge Casteñeda, Mexico's foreign minister from 2000 to 2003 and one of the architects of "neostructuralism," distinguished a "good" modern pro-market left versus a "bad" traditional anti-market populist leftism. He described their differences as one "that is modern, open-minded, reformist and internationalist ... and the other, born of the great tradition of Latin American populism, [that] is nationalist, strident and close-minded" (Castañeda, 2006: 29).

Reflected is a present-day capitalist fantasy of authoritarian development. It consists specifically of investing in the state as the primary force for protecting neoliberalism and, as such, the country's modernization efforts. This state-centric view of development translates into an embrace of the need for a strong regime willing to use repressive methods if required to fight the "enemies" of such progress. Globalization has only enhanced this affective commitment to a necessary authoritarianism for the sake of national development. Notably, it demands that states employ whatever means necessary to create a fertile environment to economically and politically take advantage of a dynamic but capricious global "free market."

BUILDING THE AUTHORITARIAN MARKET STATE: THE CASE OF SINGAPORE

A prominent discourse for affectively justifying authoritarianism in the face of globalization is to tout the ongoing need of governments to ensure that the country can effectively compete in the global free market. It is similar, in this regard, to the fantasy perpetuated by "market despots." However, it differs in a crucial respect. It is less focused on the need to sustain national sovereignty (though this is a component) and more on how to use its values and centralized governance to maximize their advantage in this globalizing business environment. Here authoritarianism is intimately connected to a capitalist fantasy of profiting from the international free market. More precisely, single-party rule, commonly marked by oppressive measures against dissent, is made palatable and attractive as a force for national modernization. Singapore stands as a prime example of this tantalizing desire to build a successful authoritarian market state.

Building the "Pragmatic" Market State

The birth and political evolution of Singapore exists in sharp contradiction to the accepted modernization narrative that successful marketization goes hand in hand with enhanced democratization. Despite decades of sustained economic growth, and the adoption of a parliamentary democratic system, the "city-state" nation has been dominated by the single-party rule of the People's Action Party (PAP). Under its leadership the country has rapidly marketized while strictly repressing free speech and other civil liberties. For this reason, Singapore generates "a debate, not about the survival of democracy, but rather about the 'transition to democracy' from 'soft authoritarianism'" (Means, 1996: 103). It speaks to the role of capitalist dynamics for bolstering durable authoritarian regimes (Rodan and Jayasuriya, 2009). More precisely, the persistence of the PAP's grip on power highlights the broader affective "grip" that authoritarian values currently have in relation to discourses of modernization.

Singapore, almost uniquely, marched involuntarily into statehood. Initially it was part of the Federation of Malaysia formed in 1963, but it was unanimously voted out of the federation in 1965 due to ideological differences with the Malaysian government and lingering fears associated with a race riot that occurred in Singapore in 1964. Over the next seven decades, the PAP led the country with a combination of soft, and at times hard, repression alongside the continuous marketization of the economy. This strategy was guided above all by their founder and long-standing Prime Minister Lee Kuan Yew. He focused his rule on rapid economic growth, support for business entrepreneurship, state-maintained social order, and strict limitations on internal democracy.

Since its inception, Singapore has been described in authoritarian terms. While there is a parliament, it is filled almost entirely by the PAP, who accepts almost exclusive responsibility for determining the country's short- and long-term direction. Early commentators depicted it, therefore, as a "dominant party state" (Bellows, 1970). However, as PAP rule extended beyond the 1970s and into the 1980s it was more and more understood as being an "administrative state" headed by a dominant party (Chan, 1975; Seah, 1999). Here, the government concentrated on modernizing the country through marketization by instilling corporate values of efficiency and productivity, with the primary aim of increasing economic growth. Liberal and more substantive forms of democratic deliberation and debate were deprioritized as ancillary and actually detrimental to these overriding economic ambitions. However, as inequality grew and the population progressively started demanding wider political and ideological choice, the regime evolved into a corporatist state (Jones and Brown, 1994) characterized by strategic forms of participation and inclusion so as to prevent a mass politics or real challenge to the country's neoliberal commitments.

Underlying this authoritarianism was an "ideology of pragmatism" (Beng-Huat, 1985). Originally, it was often associated with a type of "non-ideological" ideology (Chee and Evers, 1978) – a belief that the government was simply using its power to govern rationally and for universally agreed pathways toward modernization and mass prosperity. However, this rather neutral view was soon replaced by a more critical assessment of the PAP's intentions and rule. This appeal to "pragmatism" was explicitly and implicitly the handmaiden of policies favorably embracing global capitalism internationally and neoliberalism domestically. Thus:

> In short, Singapore's pragmatism is ideological because it hides – or at least makes more palatable – its association with neo-liberal globalisation, which in turn obscures the crisis tendencies and exploitative goals of global capitalism and the real political goals of the PAP government as it reassures Singaporeans of continued economic success. (Tan, 2012: 72)

These policies reflect a deeper politics of what has been explicitly referred to as "authoritarian capitalism" (Lingle, 1996b). The public sector, hence, is robust – concentrating on education and incentives for private self-sufficiency – but is by no means an example of traditional welfarism. Its official discourse, furthermore, at best deprioritizes and at worst directly eschews ideals of democracy and political competition, promoting instead a "market" government that is meritocratic and growth oriented (Rodan, 2004; Tan, 2008).

> PAP's one-party dominant state is the result of continuous ideological work that deploys the rhetoric of pragmatism to link the notion of Singapore's impressive success and future prospects to its ability to attract global capital. In turn, this relies on maintaining a stable political system dominated by an experienced, meritocratic and technocratic PAP government. (Tan, 2012: 67)

Tellingly, even the party's use of authoritarianism in practice was and remains intimately associated with market values. It seeks to repress opposition in the quite business-minded form of "calibrated coercion," acting tactically to deal with dissent with a minimum of political cost and maximum of political gain (George, 2007).

> Behind the stability of the press system, the Singapore government has made fundamental changes to its modes of control, with less frequent recourse to blunter instruments such as newspaper closures or arbitrary arrest ... Instead, less visible instruments are increasingly used, with the media's commercial foundations turned against themselves. (George, 2007: 127)

Moreover, citizens are commonly intimidated into silence not simply through the threat of imprisonment but by being financially bankrupted by the regime taking them to court on charges of slander (Tey, 2008).

All this points to the creation of a capitalist fantasy of building a "pragmatic" market state. In this spirit, the PAP, under the leadership of Lee Kuan Yew, linked its rule and popularity to its "non-ideological" guidance of the country's economic modernization. It was required to do so in order to attract foreign capital and internally ensure the continued efficient running of a market economy. Successful national development, significantly, demanded social order and political authoritarianism. Without these conditions, any chance the country had at keeping its modernizing going was put into jeopardy. According to the government, then, for marketization to work and advance the country it needed to be joined politically with a resilient and adaptable authoritarianism.

Protecting the Development of the Market State

A crucial component of this capitalist fantasy of authoritarian development was the need to constantly protect the market state. Perhaps more than anything else, the PAP's public raison d'être was to guarantee the nation's survival. As Lee Kuan Yew once declared, "Our Darwinian duty is to survive and prosper, as an independent nation, to the year 2050, at least, when most of you will still be around" (quoted in Hill and Lian, 2013: 37). This emphasis on mere survival soon transformed into one of protection and preservation. The state's importance was primarily connected to the need to safeguard the nation's particular brand of authoritarian development, and in doing so, preserve its continued modernization.

Throughout the PAP's reign, Yew and the prime ministers who followed him – first Goh Chok Tong and then Lee's eldest son Lee Hsien Loong – relied upon the construction of anti-state "enemies" imperiling the country's progress. This discourse was mobilized, for instance, at a mass level in the 1980s when emerging political opposition was disposed of as being a dangerous "Marxist conspiracy." In recent times, this has, as will be discussed more fully below, transformed into a call to protect the nation's "Asian values and democracy" (read authoritarianism and strategic illiberalism) to guarantee economic growth and prosperity. Significantly, this cultural appeal was based on an essentialist notion of Singaporean heritage and values as well as the party's historical success in guiding national development. It was associated with, drawing once more on an evolutionary metaphor, a "Darwinian process of mutation, competition and selection" (Yeo, 1990: 102) that would give the government the autonomy and flexibility it required to protect and perpetuate the country's economic development.

Specifically, it advocated its single-party rule and required limitations on democracy and dissent so that it could evolve to meet the challenges and opportunities of a dynamic and sometimes fraught global free market. Initially, the party, both discursively and practically, employed its authoritarianism to attract global capital, a policy that reassured investors of its stable and favorable investment environment (see Rodan, 1989; Tan, 1976). In particular, it advertised itself to its citizens and foreign business interests as a global city whose survival depended on international capital (Rajaratnam, 1972). Yet it was also exactly because of this "fragility" of being a nation in an uncertain global capitalist world that "the PAP government has been able to explain its political longevity and justify its extensive intrusions into aspects of economic, social and human life that would normally be regarded in more liberal political societies as private and off-limits to the state" (Tan, 2012: 70).

In the contemporary era, this hegemony has been legitimized, as mentioned previously, by drawing on discourses of "Asian capitalism" and "Asian democracy." The PAP exists primarily as a force for protecting the authoritarian values imperative for continued capitalist development. Democracy and liberalism are luxuries that a young modernizing country such as Singapore cannot afford. Consequently, "because of their function in de-legitimising potential sources of counter-capitalistic contradictions and counter-authoritarian dissent, 'Asian Values' enables the re-amalgamation, and even strengthens the mutual dependency, of authoritarianism and late-capitalism in Singapore" (Sim, 2001: 45). Modernization here is inexorably associated with economic neoliberalism and must be prioritized at all cost. It cannot be endangered by the prospect of inexperienced leaders or misinformed ideological debate.

The presence of the state therefore is inviolable, not so much to directly intervene within the economy but to defend the country's successful marketization against the threat of an ineffective "liberal model." Quoting Mutalib at length on this point:

> To the government, Singapore's rapid economic growth and political stability could not have been achieved if the country were to follow the Western liberal democratic path and its attendant notions of development. While gradually allowing for greater citizen participation in the formulation of policies in more recent times, the present leadership, mindful of opening up a Pandora's Box, is still cautiously wary of the growth of a more pluralistic political environment; hence, its preference for what can be described as an illiberal, (soft) authoritarian democratic culture. (Mutalib, 2000: 313)

Citizens are similarly expected to be "socially disciplined" to pragmatically solve problems and not negatively impact upon national development.

In this vein, the country's governance can be reasonably compared to that of the top-down organization of a corporation. Put differently, it is not simply that the PAP crafts its policies to cater to business interests domestically and globally. It is more that it models itself as if the country were in fact a large private enterprise. Writing in 1974, Louis Kraar explicitly likened the PAP's rule to a "country run like a corporation," observing that:

> Singapore has achieved this dazzling growth by stretching its meager means and using some extraordinary techniques of statecraft. The country is run very much like a corporation. Striving above all for efficiency, the government coldly weighs every move, from school curriculums to foreign relations, against cost-effectiveness. The key criterion, as one top-rank official puts it, is always: "What good can we get out of it?" (Kraar, 1974: 85)

Not surprisingly, other business-minded leaders, such as Thaksin in Thailand, have been directly influenced by this neoliberal view that "a country is my company" (Bowornwathana, 2004). First and foremost, both employee citizens and its executive leaders must rigorously and even ruthlessly prioritize the nation's continued profitability.

The persistent authoritarian refrain of survival and preservation deployed by the PAP thus represents the resiliency of neoliberal discourses of authoritarian modernization. The prospect of a repressive single-party rule remains attractive, or at least legitimate, as a means for ensuring and defending progress. In the age of globalization, this logic has been framed in terms of the need for a stable hand to guide the country through the treacherous but potentially profitable waters of an international free market. Consequently, to be modern in this context increasingly means to be dynamically authoritarian.

The Capitalist Fantasy of an Evolving Authoritarian Development

Singapore stands as a prime example of the contemporary "success" of combining authoritarianism and marketization. In particular, it severely puts to the test modernization beliefs that capitalism is an inevitable precursor to democratization. By contrast, it provides a paradigm for development that not only has failed to bring about greater democracy but also seems to actively eschew it as anti-modern. This reflects, moreover, an exportable authoritarian governing paradigm for other countries in the region and beyond (Zhang, 2012). Significantly, this capitalist fantasy is not terminal to a specific level of development. Instead, it is exactly the promise of constantly developing further that makes this repressive modernization so perniciously durable and potentially permanent in its affective appeal.

Specifically, the regime relies on a flexible yet stable vision of collectivist leadership and citizenship. Emphasized is the need to be socially and politically united around a government that can deal decisively with a fast-paced global economy. "We are not playing chess where the pieces remain static while we debate and deliberate at length," leading minister Teo Chee Hean pronounced in 1994, "We are playing football. Stop moving and the rest of the world will run rings around us ... let us not paralyse ourselves in perpetual conflict and debate" (Tan, 2012: 77). It is exactly for this reason that the government reserves the right to its "pragmatic" monopoly of power, as it stresses the country's continued vulnerability to global capitalism (Apcar et al., 2007).

This ongoing rationale for authoritarian rule, despite rather significant economic advances, was on full display when freshly appointed Prime Minister Lee Hsien-Loong (2009) declared that he was confident he could lead "a strong, clean and able Government to take us forward for the next twenty years. This will instill confidence in our long term future, among both investors and Singaporeans" (Tan, 2012: 80). Tellingly, the views and needs of foreign capital were as important as those of Singaporean citizens. It was expected that individuals join in the shared effort to keep creating the ideal conditions for outside investment. Any move toward greater welfarism or social instability was more than just unacceptable; it was directly counter to national progress (Lee, 2004). Citizens, thus, funded their social security through compulsory saving schemes as opposed to public pensions (Asher, 1995). The PAP, additionally, sought to internalize values of "performance based merit and working with, not against the government" among those it ruled (Hamilton-Hart, 2000).

Significantly, this authoritarian mentality, equally prevalent in the political elite and everyday citizens, was considered crucial to sustaining modernization due to the country's continued view of itself as a "developmental state" (Stubbs, 2009). This popular perception was highlighted in the PAP's slogan at the beginning of the twenty-first century: "From the Third World to First." The implicit threat in this celebratory rhetoric was that these gains were forever insecure and could be easily surrendered if the party's hegemony was ever challenged. The government was almost refreshingly frank in its justification of this authoritarianism to the country's precarious position in the global free market. As Lee Kuan Yew observed (quoted in Apcar et al., 2007):

> Supposing we had oil and gas, do you think I could get the people to do this? No. If I had oil and gas I'd have a different people, with different motivations and expectations. It's because we don't have oil and gas and they know that we don't have, and they know that this progress comes from their efforts. So please do it and do it well. We are ideology-free. What would make the place work, let's do it.

This work, importantly, is never finished. The state presented itself not as having a coherent vision but rather as being expertly attuned to the ever changing needs of global capitalism. Young student elites continued to see themselves as "responsible" for serving the country through continuing in an authoritarian neoliberal tradition (Sim, 2012). In place of the usual cynicism of many autocratic regimes, there appeared a sincere belief in their needed expertise for ensuring that the country continued to prosper in an uncertain international business climate. This included helping citizens embrace the proper attitude for collectively and individually profiting from this world market. The PAP made it a priority to promote ideals of the "entrepreneurial citizenship," especially through attracting "foreign talent" to energize the economy and influence "risk-averse" Singaporeans (Christensen, 2012). The recently implemented Character and Citizenship Education curriculum teaches students of all backgrounds from an early age values of social cohesion and cultural sustainability (read "Asian capitalism") as a way to instill in them the importance of being a responsible market citizen within their family, community, and world (Tan and Tan, 2014).

This attitude epitomizes the party's enduring capitalist fantasy of authoritarian development. It is one that is explicitly non-utopian and flexible, echoing the PAP's 1970s proclamation that it was instituting a market-driven "socialism that worked" (Nair, 1976). It remains "governed by an ad hoc contextual rationality that seeks to achieve specific gains at particular points in time and pays scant attention to systematicity and coherence as necessary rational criteria for action," contrasting it with "utopian rationality [that] emphasises the whole and at times sacrifices the contextual gains to preserve it, if necessary" (Chua, 1995: 58). It relies, in this respect, on a "crisis mentality," where the state justifies "pre-emptive interventions" and "possible course-changing as the positive result of its 'pragmatic' flexibility in policymaking and administration, rather than due to confusion or contradictions."

Vital to this affective discourse of "flexibility" and "pragmatism" is the need for the country to continually evolve to deal with a capricious global market. It follows, in this spirit, the regime's earlier use of Darwinian metaphors, updated for a new age of globalization. Up until the Asian crisis in the mid-1990s the regime was largely defined by a type of "disciplinary modernisation" in which:

> Singapore's high-speed post-independence economic development from the 1960s to the 1990s – an expression of a desire to be an insider within advanced capitalism – was wrought through a state-imposed "disciplinarity" that is here described as "disciplinary modernisation." The result was a protective-interventionist state that supported the free trade process. (Wee, 2001: 987)

Now the focus was on allowing the state to develop dynamically in line with changing domestic and international conditions, while never relinquishing its overall commitment to neoliberalism in principle or practice.

The ruling party, hence, no longer stands for a singular modernization narrative but rather modernization as a general principle. More precisely, while unwavering in its principles of marketization, the PAP presents itself as a pioneering force for finding every new cutting-edge way to take advantage of the global market. It resembles, in this sense, an "innovative" corporation that is always evolving, forever on the lookout for new ideas and possibilities that may profit its citizens and the country generally. Its campaign to foster "creative" citizens is a case in point as:

> The Pap now asserts that the passive citizens of Singapore Inc. are no longer desirable ... In place of state sanctioned passivity is now a new desire for messy creativity, for something less conformist that can spur Singaporeans' ability to maintain the city state's hub within global capitalism. The contradiction entailed is clearly significant: the interventionist state now hopes to tell its citizens how to be individually creative and non-conformist. (Wee, 2007: 98)

Significantly, these efforts are all done with the aim of increasing Singapore's global market share. The cultural industry is now transformed into a creative economy – contributing to the branding of Singapore as part of "New Asia" (Yue, 2006).

This is not to say the struggle and desire for democracy has been fully extinguished. Indeed, the 2011 elections, characterized by internet-driven debate and even dissent, represented real gains for the opposition party, but, nevertheless, remained confined within the ideological boundaries of an authoritarian modernization. Specifically, it continued to view leadership as a question of "who best to run the country" (Ortmann, 2011), making it more the transition from a dominant party state to "competitive authoritarianism." What remains key is that the legitimacy of any party that assumes leadership rests on its eternal ability for producing and reproducing modernization. Henri Ghesquiere (quoted in Mahbubani, 2009) observes how "the Singapore Government tinkers, almost obsessively, with its development strategy to cope with new challenges to its competitive position as soon as they emerge on the distant horizon. Yesterday's virtue can become tomorrow's obstacle."

Interestingly, this authoritarian fantasy has to an extent stood the traditional story of modernization on its head. Previously, it was thought that market societies would simply outgrow their authoritarian roots. Now it appears, as highlighted by the Singaporean example, that an authoritarian government is required to meet the emerging needs of its citizens as they enter into new phases of modernization. "The most recent phase of development has seen an emphasis in government policy, and in popular participation, on artistic and creative pursuits," according to Hill and Lian (2013: 10), "The concept of Singapore as a center of artistic excellence in Southeast Asia has been advanced, not only as a source of economic benefit, but also as a domain of aspiration for a new generation of citizens." Yet such transformations do not deviate from the country's core neoliberal values. In the wake of the 2011 elections, the PAP has undertaken a renewed campaign to create "future-oriented" citizens of globalization, instructing individuals in how to become a "Confident Person,"

"Self-directed Learner," "Active Contributor," and "Concerned Citizen" (Lee, 2013).

At the heart of this governance beats a capitalist fantasy of evolving authoritarian development. To this end, leaders stress that "Singapore's economy can be seen as a unique experiment to combine the best of available systems in a flexible, pragmatic, and unorthodox way – suited to its particular circumstances" (Mahbubani, 2005: 150). However, of even greater importance was how its continued single-party rule could help discover new states of development, leading to fresh heights of modernization. As Prime Minister Lee Hsien Loong suggested, in an unusual but revealingly utopian tone: "Up to now, Singapore has had the benefit of following and adapting best practices by others who are ahead of us … But as we move closer to the leading edge, we will have to break new ground ourselves, find fresh solutions, and feel our own way forward" (quoted in Peh and Goh, 2007). Thus, in the era of globalization it is the authoritarians who see themselves as the drivers of modernization, paving the way for national development so that the rest of the world can follow in their footsteps.

PRESERVING AN AUTHORITARIAN DEMOCRATIZATION: THE CASE OF MEXICO

A key feature of the prevailing modernization story is that democratization is an inevitable consequence of marketization. Yet, as this chapter has highlighted, the implications of neoliberalism are far from necessarily democratic, even institutionally, and are indeed often quite authoritarian. The case of Singapore is a prime example of such non-democratic modernization and the capitalist fantasy of authoritarian development it draws its strength from. However, this repressive character of neoliberalism, and the affective discourses sustaining it, is also prevalent in states that have officially, and to some degree in practice, more substantially conjoined their marketization to political values of democratization. Mexico's recent democratic reforms, inexorably linked ideologically with a neoliberal economic agenda, reveal this modern form of authoritarian democratization.

From Revolutionary Nationalism to the Promise of Democratization

There is an increasing acceptance that marketization and democratization are not inherent partners, as the above case of Singapore bears out. The examples of market despots and competitive authoritarians empirically put into question the triumphant belief that economic liberalization is the natural precursor to democratic liberalization. Yet relatively unchallenged is the durability of authoritarian capitalist governments, even when they do undergo ostensibly dramatic transformations toward liberal democracy. Such democratic repression obviously highlights the normative and practical limits of liberal democracy as a form of democratic governance. It also significantly reflects the underlying capitalist fantasies of authoritarian development driving such democratization.

The democratic transition of Mexico from a dominant-party state, ruled by the populist Institutional Revolutionary Party (Partido Revolucionario Institucional or PRI), exemplifies this trend of authoritarian democratization linked to present-day discourses of globalization.[1] The PRI dominated Mexican politics for almost the entirety of the twentieth century. Arising victorious from the country's civil war, which ended in 1920, it justified its rule on the back of a populist promise of economic justice and state-led modernization. For the next seven decades it used a mixture of hard and soft repression in order to maintain its monopoly on power. It stood as the primary force for guiding the country's economic development – taking a leading role in infrastructure building, natural resource governance, guiding domestic financial institutions, and managing employment relations. This authoritarian model for development – referred to as "stabilization development" – produced, at least initially, rather spectacular results, as the country saw growth rates of 6 percent annually from 1940 all the way to 1970 (Middlebrook, 2003; Philip, 1988).

This so-called "Mexican miracle" was preserved through the tightly controlled political hegemony of the PRI. Under the unifying power of the president, the party was able to dictate the country's direction as well as manipulate its limited popular democracy, judicial system, and military to its advantage (Araujo and Sirvent, 2005; Horcasitas, 1993). The PRI, moreover, used and strategically distributed Mexico's vast natural resources to control local government and offset national challenges to its power. It also relied upon more traditional authoritarian methods including assassination, illegal imprisonment, torture, and kidnapping alongside the tactical co-optation of resistance leaders (Hodges et al., 2002; Montemayor, 2009).

At the heart of the PRI's political hegemony was a modernization fantasy of revolutionary nationalism. According to its basic manifesto: "The role that historically corresponds to the Institutional Revolutionary Party is to secure and protect the continuity of the revolutionary nationalist current in the exercise of State's power through the cohesion and progress of the fundamental forces of the people" (PRI, 1979: 112–15).

Central to this affective ruling discourse was the ongoing promise of "national progress," through which the party was able to unite the economically stratified and culturally diverse nation (Córdova, 1979). This political cohesion was particularly associated with its claim to represent a project of "revolutionary nationalism" (Carmin and Meyer, 1998). It stated in its "Declaration of Principles" that "The Party assumes the revolutionary nationalism as the most consistent and conducive path to … get full access to the broad masses of people to enjoy the goods that our society produces" (PRI, 1979: 115). The utopian dimension of this discourse was captured in the PRI's vision of a new society where: "unemployment must be eradicated, all work must be fair and timely paid; the land must – without exception whatsoever – belong to those who work it, social security should be extended quantitatively and qualitatively … education and training, hygiene and welfare, must be fully and effectively guaranteed" (PRI, 1979: 178).

Politically, all those who opposed its rule were labeled as "enemies" of progress. Internationally, it positioned itself as the protector of Mexican development. In 1976, for instance, its leader publicly extolled that "we are not wealthy, we are not strong militarily and materially we are not great. However, we could be, because the resources of our territory are vast and because the possibilities of our people are endless." Its failure to do so would be catastrophic, resulting in the country's wholesale foreign exploitation. This sense of fear drove the president's authoritarian discourse: "[we must] carry out the development of [Mexican] man and natural resources, [we must] return investment into the country, [and] stop making other countries rich at the expense of ours" (PRI, 1979: 129).

Nevertheless, the popular appeal of "revolutionary nationalism" waned due to the economic crisis that hit the country at the end of the 1970s and throughout the 1980s. The causes of this long-term recession were several, including governmental corruption and inefficiency as well as a drop in international oil prices (Cansino, 2000). In order to address these issues, the PRI drastically departed from its previous "socialist" politics and economics in favor of neoliberal measures such as wage freezes, a reduced social safety net, decreased union power, and the privatization of certain state agencies in line with International Monetary Fund and World Bank structural adjustment plans (Romero, 2003).

The cracks in the PRI's power would only widen as the decade wore on. The former attractiveness of authoritarian modernization and its fantasy of "revolutionary nationalism" now appeared progressively hollow. In its place rose greater demands for democracy and a new narrative of national progress prioritizing democratization. Nevertheless, this desire for democracy would soon become incorporated within a repressive authoritarian discourse of neoliberal democracy.

Preserving Neoliberal Democracy

The profound challenge and gradual weakening of the PRI's legitimacy produced in its wake a new unifying political fantasy of democratization. The country's social ills were blamed principally on its failure to democratize and its continued reliance on authoritarian rule. Modernization, in this regard, came to be predominantly associated with political reform, the institution of competitive elections, and the ability to hold corrupt officials to account. These desires, while initially held and strategically utilized by parties across the ideological spectrum, soon became deployed in the name of implementing economic marketization at all costs.

This increasing replacement of "revolutionary nationalism" by desires for democracy was witnessed in the growing nationwide popularity of the left-wing National Democratic Front (FDN) candidate Cuauhtémoc Cárdenas (Leyva, 2007) as the 1988 elections approached. While many were drawn to his populist anti-neoliberal economic positions, even more embraced his demand to deliver real democracy to the country. Cárdenas explicitly associated socioeconomic justice with political democratization, presenting the latter as a necessary condition for the former. He declared: "We have gathered together to contribute to the formulation of viable alternatives to the national progress, [alternatives] capable to safeguard our independence and sovereignty … to promote the integral democratization of society and to impulse the equal development of the Mexicans" (Cárdenas and Ledo, 1987: 11). His democratic credentials were further bolstered by the public support for his candidacy of surviving members of the earlier 1968 student democracy protests that had been brutally suppressed by the PRI.

This affective narrative of democratization spread throughout the political classes. More precisely, it stood as a new hegemonic discourse for organizing public support and achieving ideological legitimacy. Indeed, the conservative National Action Party (PAN) echoed the FDN's call to dissolve the PRI and eliminate the "old system." It also extended to smaller radical parties, such as the Mexican Socialist Party (PSM), whose leader, Herberto Castillo, only days before the election, threw his support behind Cárdenas with the reasoning that "In this time of profound change, Mexico needs to advance towards its full democratization … The progressive forces must commit to uproot the authoritarian aspects of the Mexican State" (Castillo, 1988). The far-left Revolutionary Party of the Workers similarly denounced the presidential system entirely as despotic, advocating instead for "a new representation of national power organized from the bottom up" (Cárdenas and Ledo, 1987: 11).

The PRI meanwhile was undergoing an extreme political rebranding, now presenting itself and its neoliberal agenda as the only authentic force for achieving real democratic change. Whereas previously, democratization was at best a marginal and marginalized ideal in the party's broader aims of "stability development," it now took center stage, at least rhetorically. Throughout the 1988 campaign the PRI's candidate, Carlos Salinas de Gortari, made a point of including "democracy" alongside the country's other "four big challenges" of the "social," "economic," and "sovereignty" (Gortari, 1988). He, moreover, declared that it was now imperative that Mexico prioritize "practicing democratic methods and not authoritarianism [because] if politics does not modernize its everyday actions ... the great cultural and economic transformation of the country can become in anarchy or repression" (1988: 12).

Crucial to this strategy, as the above quote highlights, was the attempt by the PRI to condemn its opponents as "anti-democratic" and therefore a threat to progress. Importantly, this politics of demonization was one common to all the parties. During the campaign the FDN candidate championed how presently "modern fascism Mexico is rising up" (Alvarez, 1988). He repeatedly railed against the country's "democratic deficit" and the need to protect it from electoral fraud by the authoritarian PRI, noting "the government pretends to modify the electoral results in its favor and to close the roads for democratic participation" (Castro, 1988). These concerns seemed prophetic in the wake of the PRI's widely challenged official victory (Bruhn, 2010; Foweraker, 1989). In its immediate aftermath, all the major opposition parties joined with civil society leaders and intellectuals to form the "Commitment to Democracy" with the express purpose of safeguarding democratization. In their own words:

> [A public] mandate for the democratization of the country demands, as a starting point, the most strict respect of the effective suffrage and greater responsibility in the post-electoral qualifying dispute ... The Federal Electoral Commission and the Electoral Dispute Tribune constitute the only legitimate fundament to qualify the elections: finding another one can only lead to the dispurpose of claiming the annulment of the elections. (Azuela et al., 1988)

Not surprisingly, the PRI deployed an almost identical strategy of depicting its defeated rivals, especially the FDN, as "enemies" of democracy, which it was trying desperately to preserve. Hence, the PRI pronounced sanctimoniously after the election that "there is no justice without observing the law, just like there is no possible defense outside the resources that the law establishes" (PRI, 1988). This defamation campaign could be glimpsed even prior to the election results, evidenced in the Minister of the Interior, Manuel Bartlet's accusation of Cárdenas' criticisms as "anti-democratic." Their attacks on the ruling party revealed the FDN's "true political nature: authoritarianism and its obvious detachment from popular mandate" (Hiriart and Alvarez, 1988). Bolstered by the election, the party deployed its newfound commitment to democracy in order to strengthen its authoritarianism politically and neoliberal agenda economically. It quickly distinguished between its opposition, who were undemocratic "agitators," and the majority of Mexicans who in re-electing the PRI "demonstrate that it is through law that they want the changes and transformations in the country to be done maintaining the national sovereignty above all political and ideological differences" (Rodríguez and Tejada, 1988). Furthermore, they retrospectively legitimized their unpopular marketization policies as being democratically enacted. While campaigning, Salinas championed the economic liberalization measures of his predecessor, depicting him as "the leader that, democratically, has made possible the structural changes that Mexico needs" (Gortari, 1988: 7).

To this extent, democratization became inexorably bound up with market "reforms" in a broader official discourse of national modernization. Anti-market leftists, even those who primarily focused on the country's lack of democracy under the PRI, were portrayed as "populist Frankenstein." Simultaneously, the PRI's elite financial supporters, notably the influential entrepreneurial association Confederation of the Mexican Republic, openly warned that those who opposed marketization "undermined the progress of the country" by wearing a "democratic disguise that restricted economic, political and educative freedom" (Paredes, 1988). Their strategy could not be more transparent, in this respect the only road to democracy lay in marketization. For the sake of these political reforms, all those who dared to question this agenda must be repressed and eliminated.

The Capitalist Fantasy of Authoritarian Democratization

Ultimately, the PRI and its neoliberal values emerged victorious. The party would remain in power for another 12 years until finally being defeated by the right-wing PAN. However, their demise, while certainly ushering in a more institutionally democratic era, did not signal the end of either neoliberal democracy or the use of discourses of democratization for the purpose of closing off, forcefully if necessary, ideological and political contestation. In this spirit, PAN and those that followed would embrace the capitalist fantasy of authoritarian democratization created by the PRI.

The resiliency of this fantasy was witnessed throughout the 2000 campaign, specifically in the figure of PAN's charismatic candidate and soon-to-be president, Vicente Fox. Despite his deep commitment to marketization, he continually minimized these neoliberal beliefs in favor of affective themes of democracy (Klesner, 2004). In his post-election memoirs, tellingly entitled *Revolution of Hope*, Fox wrote that "I spoke straight to the people's hearts in a way every Mexican could understand, summing up the campaign as a crusade for democracy … the Mexican people wanted democracy. On the 2nd of July they got it" (Fox and Allyn, 2007: 183, 185, 191). This democratic "crusade" was waged at a time when social inequality was at record-breaking levels and showing no signs of diminishing (Mundi Index, 2011).

This affective modernization story of authoritarian democratization would become a persistent and defining feature of Mexican politics in the twenty-first century. The government was first and foremost responsible for protecting the country against anti-democratic threats. Any and all challenges to its authority were a danger to these political reforms and could lead the country into chaos or, even worse, fascism. These elements were on full display in the 2006 campaign. The PAN candidate Felipe Calderón Hinojosa campaigned heavily on the idea that electing his opponents – particularly his left-wing challenger from the Democratic Revolution Party (PRD) – would put the country at grave risk of returning to its authoritarian past. He intoned ominously during the campaign that: "Today ... we have a better country than we had in 2000. A country that lives a true democracy ... with economic stability and very solid social politics [Mexico] is now immerse[d] in a transformation process that should not be stopped but rather consolidated" (Partido Acción Nacional, Plataforma Electoral, 2006).

Despite these idealized appeals to democracy, the election results – as in 1988 – remained highly controversial, marked by charges of voting irregularities and fraud. In the face of civil challenges and street protests by the supporters of the PRD's Andrés Manuel López Obrador, who lost by fewer than 25,000 votes, Calderón called for national unity under the banner of national democracy, "even when there are differences stemmed from a very competed electoral process like the one we just experienced ... the Republic and the future of our democracy is one and indivisible" (Martínez and Aranda, 2006).

The next election in 2012 bore even greater witness to the neoliberal designs at the heart of this authoritarian call for democratization. The PRI once again gained power amidst promises of reduced civil violence and enhanced marketization. Its candidate, and newly elected president, Enrique Peña Nieto, pronounced, "I am convinced that the time has come to transform an essentially electoral democracy into a democracy of results" (Nieto, 2012: 1). In practice, these "results" included a sweep of neoliberal policies including the privatization of the Oil Mexican Company (PEMEX) and increased labor market flexibility. Notably, he blamed widespread student and social protests against his election – an election marred again by severe irregularities and accusations of manipulation – as being caused by "leftist" agitators and "anarchists" who opposed democracy.

This veneer of democratic reform often disguises the autocratic attempt by elites to implement neoliberalism nationally. The PRI was heavy handed and dictatorial throughout the 1990s in guiding the country toward marketization and an embrace of the global "free market" – witnessed in its negotiation of the North American Free Trade Agreement in the face of large social disagreement and even resistance (Kim, 2013). The election of Vincente Fox in 2000 did little to change this governing paradigm, as he continued the authoritarian implementation of neoliberalism begun by his PRI predecessors (Armijo and Faucher, 2002).

Crucial to this technocratic modernization is the belief by Mexican elites, many of whom were trained as free-market economists in the United States, in the need to "manage Mexico" (Babb and Babb, 2004). Teichman (2001) notes, similarly, that neoliberalism was implemented by a small clique of American-trained technocrats, characterized by an autocratic orientation who sought to implement marketization in a top-down way, free from popular discussion. Furthermore, they were extremely receptive and open to the opinions of foreign investors for guiding their country's policies, more so then their own fellow citizens. "The responsiveness to outside influences, which results mainly from an ongoing, wide-ranging policy dialogue, not from formal loan conditionality, aggravates the democratic deficit of technocratic decision-making: Foreign actors have significantly more influence than the presumed democratic sovereign, i.e., the voters" (Weyland, 2001).

Significantly, this authoritarian paradigm linked to discourses of democratization and neoliberalism has led concretely to increased social repression (see, for instance, Amnesty International, 2011). These abuses are directly connected to the country's opening relationship with the "global free market," which has produced greater organized crime (particularly connected to the drug trade) and enhanced government policing to deal with the rampant violence. Referring to twenty-first-century Mexican leaders as "globalization presidents," Olney (2012: 151) observes "globalization contributes both to the escalation of violence by increasing opportunities for criminals and disgruntled elites from Mexico's disposed revolutionary system ... and to a new political culture capable of supporting a stable, modern Mexican state."

The achievements of a stable liberal democracy harken back to the PRI's discourse of "stabilization development" used to justify its authoritarian program of state-led modernization. As the 2015 human rights report notes (Anon, 2015):

> [T]he government has made little progress in prosecuting widespread killings, enforced disappearances, and torture committed by soldiers and police in the course of efforts to combat organized crime, including during Peña Nieto's tenure. Other ongoing problems include restrictions to press freedoms, abuses against migrants, and limits on access to reproductive rights and health care.

Nevertheless, it continues to promote the need to work toward a "stable democracy" that can simultaneously fend off authoritarian populist protests, manage the country's escalating civil violence, and become a prosperous part of the global democratic community. These optimistic appeals stand in stark contrast to the country's declining economic situation, one where it has "[b]ecome a rentier nation living off of its cheap-labor and assembly-and-export, foreign-owned, manufacturing operations that have arisen largely as a result of the restructuring of US capital. But other rentier operations abound such as the de-capitalized national petroleum company, which is now targeted for privatization" (Cypher, 2013: 396).

Crucially, though, the failures of neoliberalism and persistence of state repression only serve to bolster a resilient capitalist fantasy of authoritarian democratization. The cure to all national ills is to strengthen its democracy. This affective narrative, in turn, bolsters the autocratic implementation of marketization; a process that is more responsive to foreign investors and capitalist institutions than it is to domestic democratic deliberation and popular opinion. Moreover, it positions the state once again as the primary protector of national progress, doing whatever is required to preserve the country's political and economic liberalization, an authoritarian necessity for achieving the country's dreams of democracy.

CONCLUSION

The dawning of the new millennium was meant to usher in a new century of modernization, characterized by the predicted flourishing of marketization and democratization across the world. The proliferation of capitalism internationally was championed as part of a broader narrative of liberalization, in which authoritarianism would gradually disintegrate as markets became more entrenched. Instead, the actual political effects of globalization have seen the reverse of these triumphant expectations. The new era is progressively marked, as the cases of Singapore and Mexico reveal, by the strengthening of autocratic and repressive market-oriented regimes. The happily-ever-after of capitalist development has transformed into a potentially cautionary tale of the persistence of authoritarianism in the global spread of capitalism.

Central to this authoritarian governing paradigm is a global capitalist fantasy of authoritarian development. Governments have re-established their right and, in fact, obligation to guide and protect the country's modernization against foreign and domestic threats. This strong arm of the state is especially needed in light of a fast-paced globalized market that brings with it both opportunities and challenges. More than simply protection, these emboldened regimes can optimistically lead the country to greater economic and political heights within an exciting, but dangerous, period of globalization. It must therefore be ready and willing to increase its authoritarian reach if it is to do so effectively. All actions, no matter how oppressive or intrusive, are potentially justified in the name of "modernization" and "democratization." Thus, just as the state in developing nations is retreating economically under the pressures of neoliberalism, it is expanding in quite worryingly non-democratic and despotic ways politically.

As will be shown, this paradoxical relation of capitalism and authoritarianism, and the affective fantasy sustaining it, is by no means confined to developing countries but can also be found in economically developed liberal democracies.

NOTE

1.   For a similar discussion of the linkages between democratization, neoliberalism, and authoritarianism in contemporary Mexico please see Montaño and Bloom (2014).

6. The tyranny of (neo)liberal democracy: a global capitalist fantasy of authoritarian freedom

On May 8, 2015 the United Kingdom (UK) woke up to a rather shocking political result. Against almost all professional expectations and predictions, the Tories had not only remained in power but had actually gained seats to form a majority government. They had done so on the back of a strong ideological commitment to neoliberal austerity policies. It would seem that this victory was another blow to "big government" in favor of free-market economics. Yet, rather surprisingly, one of the first measures this emboldened Conservative government proposed was the creation of new "tough anti-terror laws" meant to directly take on "poisonous Islamist extremist ideology" (Dominiczak and Prince, 2015). These measures echoed an earlier 2011 briefing by the London Metropolitan Police warning citizens to report such "threatening" groups as anarchists who advocate a "political philosophy which considers the state undesirable, unnecessary, and harmful, and instead promotes a stateless society, or anarchy" (Booth, 2011). Reflected in this seeming contradiction is one of the crucial paradoxes of the contemporary age – the more the state retreats economically, the more it seems to expand politically. It is this relationship between weakened economic sovereignty and strengthened political sovereignty that is at the heart of authoritarian capitalism, one which is witnessed not only in countries committed to "modernization" but also those that are ostensibly already fully "modernized."

While the end of the Cold War has produced with it certain democratic gains, these are often far from being substantively democratic or liberal. The proliferation of "defective democracies" is increasingly understood to be permanent rather than a temporary feature of the current global political landscape. "They tend to form stable links to their economic and societal environment and are often seen by considerable parts of the elites and the population as an adequate institutional solution to the specific problems of governing 'effectively,'" notes Merkel (2004: 33): "As long as this equilibrium between problems, context and power lasts, defective democracies will survive for protracted periods of time." Indeed, the problem of illiberalism has emerged as a defining issue of the twenty-first century, particularly when it appears that even in the face of challenges from state capitalism, the normative consensus – that it best represents idealized values of freedom and liberty – remains unshaken.

Perhaps most problematically, worries over illiberalism often appear narrowly confined to the non-Western world (Brownlee, 2009; Ekman, 2009). Tellingly, this is progressively associated with the pressures of corporate globalization internationally. The deepening of neoliberalism produces in its wake a reactionary politics combining traditional patriotism and expressions of jingoism, with quite predictable politically and socially repressive results. Referred to as "neothirdworldism" it notes that "in the post-cold war world order based on the hegemony of the USA weakens, rather than strengthens, the forces of democratic liberalism in Indonesian society – and reinforces the consolidation of an illiberal form of democracy" (Hadiz, 2004: 55). These interventions not only challenge optimistic modernization narratives but also highlight the imperialism central to current processes of economic and political globalization.

Yet these same illiberal trajectories, ones similarly justified in the name of preserving liberalism and democracy, are also witnessed in "developed" Western liberal democracies. Issues connected to globalization such as immigration have brought to the fore "illiberal liberal states," reflecting "a challenging new influx of illiberal practices among states that are supposed to bestow and adhere to the principles of liberalism and the rule of law" (Guild and Groenendijk, 2009: 1). This increasing illiberalism is, further, linked to the rising priority given to the need for security against terrorism following the attacks on September 11, 2001 in the United States (US) (Bigo and Tsoukala, 2008). As one scholar presciently asked, under this new security regime, are "security, risks and human rights" ultimately a "vanishing relationship"? (Tsoukala, 2008). These concerns are as valid in the UK, France, and the US as they are in Indonesia, Singapore, or Mexico.

Such formal and informal instances of illiberalism are, moreover, intimately and positively related to simultaneous policies of deepening marketization. The transition away from social democracies and the welfare state has led to fresh conceptions of "modernization," trumpeting the ability of post-industrial societies to provide individuals with greater forms of "human development" – associated with neoliberal values of individualism and choice – that are supposedly conducive to enhanced democratization (see Inglehart and Welzel, 2005). Nevertheless, in practice, it is more and more shown that greater economic capitalism serves to delegitimize even established democracies through its being controlled and supported by financial and political elites (Dutkiewicz et al., 2013). Additionally, they reinforce an "authoritarian syndrome" that manifests concretely in illiberal practices and rhetoric. It is not surprising, then, that Western Europe and the US have seen the growth of "right-wing populism," commonly championing a more coercive state to deal with domestic threats and internal foreign "others," as well as providing "law and order," directly connected to the prevalence of neoliberal culture (Berezin, 2009).

Underlying this present-day illiberalism is a deeper authoritarian logic, characteristic of and perhaps inherent to liberal democracy itself. A key tension of these regimes is that in the name of preserving and promoting "liberal freedom" they must rely upon the illiberal efforts of governments. To this end:

> (liberal) governments regularly find themselves compelled to formulate social policy with which to regulate some members' behaviour. Defending that liberal individualism has required government policy, a practice manifest in a range of government initiatives during the last century New Liberalism, Progressivism, the New Deal, the Great Society, the New Right, New Labor, Gingrich's Contract with America, and New Democrats. (King, 1999: 2–3)

This dependence on strong, not untypically illiberal, government interventions extends to neoliberalism. Marketization economically has been partnered politically with an "aggressive interventionism" that "is reflective of a distinctly 'Schmittian' liberalism, which aims to clarify the core values of liberal societies and use coercive state power to protect them from illiberal and putatively dangerous groups" (Triadafilopoulos, 2011: 861).

Represented is what can be called a tyranny of liberal democracy, one that has only grown in prominence and scope it seems with the advent of neoliberalism. It is tyrannical in distinguishable but ultimately complementary ways. First, in that it speaks to a coercive element often found within otherwise liberal democratic contexts. The existence of an inscriptive state for enforcing social norms in unequal and oppressive directions is so intertwined with this evolution and history of liberal democracy to make it appear fundamental. The second is that it defines and confines the limit of democratic participation, governance, and the expression of freedom to the boundaries (both figuratively, ideologically, and literally geographically) of liberal democracy. What it means to be "modern," "democratic," and "free" is delimited to liberalism conceptually and in practice. In the era of globalization and neoliberalism, this tyranny has only expanded, embracing the strategic and coercive deployment of the state to preserve marketization in the name of protecting and realizing a narrow but romanticized horizon of liberal democracy.

Imperative to this neoliberal project of illiberal liberalism is the promotion of a capitalist fantasy of authoritarian freedom. Here, the desire for agency in an otherwise overdetermined economic environment is transformed into a desire for a strong state actor who can safeguard the nation and its citizens' "freedom" against its internal and external enemies. The powerlessness felt in the face of a market economy that cannot be questioned nor regulated is translated into a renewed emphasis on the need for the state to ensure political security and social stability. This longing plays into authoritarian discourses and values of enhanced imperialism abroad and policing at home done in the name of spreading and protecting, respectively, "free market liberal democracy."

THE GLOBAL CRISIS OF ILLIBERAL DEMOCRACY

A predominant concern for current global politics is the prevalence of illiberal democracies. The proliferation of democracies internationally has not produced the liberal democratic "end of history" so confidently and optimistically expected. Rather, the world is now composed of a range of regimes that combine authoritarianism and illiberalism with certain democratic features such as elections. Put differently, whether or not a country is formally a democracy, they are increasingly marked by elite rule and internal repression. Tellingly, this authoritarian trend has strong linkages with the implementation and perpetuation of marketization internationally. Significantly, this neoliberal crisis of illiberal democracy is truly global, affecting developed and developing democratic (and non-democratic) states alike.

In order to account for this illiberalism, it is no longer assumed prima facie that the existence of democracy implies a concurrent liberalism, or even an evolution in that direction. Rather, there is the understanding that any democratic regime must be judged on this scale according to the power relations it affords, or encourages, as well as the governing practices that it permits and promotes. Accordingly, Larry Diamond (2002), rather famously, distinguishes between "electoral democracy" and "liberal democracy," the former denoting a regime that while democratically elected lacks a number of elements usually ascribed, at least ideally, to a liberal state – notably pluralism and an array of assured individual rights. Instead of theorizing a strict separation between these democratic typologies of rule, Diamond and those inspired by him have introduced the notion of "hybrid regimes." In this spirit, there is a further distinction made between "defective democracies" and "electoral authoritarianism," recognizing that otherwise liberal states can have dramatic democratic defects while functioning democracies can perpetuate quite stable forms of authoritarian government (Bogaards, 2009).

Just as significantly, historical understandings of "modernization" related to nations and democracy have undergone a substantial and necessary rethinking. Huntington (1991), very early into the post-Cold War period, theorized the existence of "reverse waves" of democracy, signifying the receding of democratization after initial periods of expansion (also see Kurzman, 1998). He contended, moreover, that a democratic victory leads in fact to the triumph of quite illiberal sociopolitical forces (Huntington, 1991). Recently, this "wave" history of liberal democracy has been put under serious question, as the presence of this illiberalism cannot be so easily charted or attributed, if at all, to regularized ebbs and flows (Doorenspleet, 2000). Regardless of its empirical validity or conceptual soundness, its appeal reflects the growing attempts to understand the crisis of democracy and fundamentally the challenges to the previously accepted modernization narrative of the global triumph of liberal democracy.

In an even more direct fashion, some commentators have argued that in this era of globalization, democracy and liberalism are not only not inherently allied but in fact often explicitly antagonistic. Specifically, the growth of democracy is a precursor for illiberal governance. Fareed Zakaria, the main proponent of this idea, thus contends:

> Democratically elected regimes, often ones that have been reelected or reaffirmed through referenda, are routinely ignoring constitutional limits on their power and depriving their citizens of basic rights and freedoms. From Peru to the Palestinian Authority, from Sierra Leone to Slovakia, from Pakistan to the Philippines, we see the rise of a disturbing phenomenon in international life – illiberal democracy. (Zakaria, 1997: 22)

This phenomenon has been observed empirically in a range of international contexts, including throughout Pacific Asia (Bell et al., 1995). To this effect, capitalist development, as discussed in Chapter 5, has strong affinities with a politics of illiberal democracy. "The developmental state seems indeed to be closely connected to illiberal practice (by design)," note Engberg and Ersson (1999: 19), "and this would suggest that the ideological pretensions of those who advocate illiberal democracy for the sake of economic growth and social achievements – perhaps have some argumentative leverage."

Key, in this regard, is the intimate connection of liberal authoritarianism ideologically and illiberalism in practice with contemporary processes of globalization. Similar to forms of "competitive authoritarianism," liberal authoritarianism appears to be on the rise. In particular, it is the acceptance of single-party regimes that, nonetheless, permit and even champion, despite their monopoly on power, a wide range of traditional liberal freedoms. This trend can be witnessed from as far afield as the Middle East (Dodge, 2002) to Botswana (Good, 1996). Notwithstanding these liberal pretensions, this reflects, in conjunction with illiberal democracies, the political authoritarianism and economic inequality central to strategies of neoliberal development. Consequently, "the deepening of market capitalism and global integration has, in many instances, appeared to consolidate authoritarian politics and predatory economic relationships. Even in the wake of the economic crisis and dramatic political change, these basic frameworks of power remain largely intact" (Hadiz and Robison, 2005: 220).

Such illiberalism and inequality extend beyond the sphere of political democracy. They also negatively affect the vibrancy, and in many cases the very existence, of democratic power sharing and decision making in the economic and social realm. Industrial democracy and unions have thus been strategically marginalized or co-opted by ruling parties, commonly in the service of financial elites, within hybrid regimes (Robertson, 2007). Globalization has also witnessed a reduction in industrial action and collective bargaining across the world (Piazza, 2005). Additionally, corporate globalization has resulted in a steep decline of civil democracy, once vibrant within established liberal democracies (Skocpol, 2013). Such market-led internationalization has, further, lessened the influence of unions within official democratic politics, which helps to explain, at least in part, the recent turn toward conservatism of a number of socially democratic political parties (Rudra, 2002).

This overall dampening of democracy and liberal ideals challenges the optimism of many who hoped that globalization would produce greater "participatory government institutions" (Avritzer, 2006) and "empowered participatory governments" (Fung et al., 2003), like those found in burgeoning participatory budgeting initiatives (Sintomer et al., 2008). These "new democratic spaces" would aim to expand the scope of democracy, making it more substantive than in liberal regimes while also renegotiating entrenched power relationships (Cornwall and Coelho, 2007). Instead, globalization has ushered in an enhanced ideological commitment to neoliberalism, and with it political authoritarianism and economic oligarchy. Reflecting specifically on the present-day Latin American context, but with clear international connotations, Boetsch (2005: 17) observes:

> In effect, neoliberalism – coupled with its strange brand of ballot box democracy – has managed to strangle the full array of political forces antagonistic to and resisting its project. Economic power has tended to concentrate in the hands of those social groups that share objectives of accelerated capital accumulation; benefiting themselves, their families, and their elite classes. Evidence of the undemocratic methods utilized by Latin American rulers of neoliberal democracies abound: the excessive use of presidential decrees in Menem's Argentina, the exclusion of popular leaders from consultative bodies in Salinas de Gortari's Mexico, or the application of strong arm tactics in Fujimori's Peru, could start a long list.

Along similar lines, MacEwan (2005) situates neoliberalism as the enemy of democracy, in particular "market power versus democratic power." Neoliberalism not only entrenches political illiberalism and economic elitism, in this regard, but also erodes the necessary culture and values for fostering an engaged democratic citizenship (Giroux, 2004). More recently, Duggan (2012) has referred to this hyper marketization as the "downsizing of democracy," while Wendy Brown (2015) warns of, as previously noted, its dangerous "undoing of the demos."

THE GLOBAL CAPITALIST FANTASY OF AUTHORITARIAN FREEDOM

While the global crisis of illiberal democracy is indeed alarming, underexplored is the affective appeal of this illiberalism linked to neoliberalism on the one hand and globalization on the other. Such authoritarianism, conjoined with the global spread of capitalism internationally and marketization nationally, is legitimized by an emotionally resonant political logic that extolls the necessity of a strong, often repressive, state. The structural need of a powerful government actor able to implement and sustain a neoliberal agenda is transformed into a broader political project championing the empowerment of liberal democratic regimes to safeguard values of political and economic freedom, associated with liberalism and markets, respectively. Reflected, in turn, is a new capitalist fantasy of authoritarian freedom.

Contrary to the triumphalism, until recently, of "modernization theorists," economic and political internationalism was not initially or primarily justified as a force for spreading liberal democracy. Rather, the first wave of capitalist internationalism was one marked by a telling pessimism of democracy for colonized populations. Even as vociferous a proponent of liberalism as John Stuart Mills doubted, for instance, whether democracy or liberal values could be extended universally (see Plattner, 1998: 176). Internally, liberal democratic societies relied upon formal and informal methods of coercion. As Mann (1996: 236) presciently observes, "Liberal 'civil society' contained a systematic tendency, lasting through the entire modern period, toward committing genocide ... and towards cruel coercion when merely employing labor. These two tendencies have an unmistakable tendency toward those of the SS state." Liberal regimes historically, then, in practice, have been legitimized and reproduced with reference to affective political discourses containing quite strong authoritarian characteristics. In the contemporary era, this combination of liberalism and illiberalism is witnessed in the prevalence and resilience of liberal autocracies globally. Indeed:

> It is now clear, both within and far beyond the Middle East, that liberalized autocracy has proven far more durable than once imagined. The trademark mixture of guided pluralism, controlled elections, and selective repression in Egypt, Jordan, Morocco, Algeria, and Kuwait is not just a "survival strategy" adopted by authoritarian regimes, but rather a type of political system whose institutions, rules, and logic defy any linear model of democratization. (Brumberg, 2002: 56)

Within established liberal democracies, Bloom (2015) notes the existence of a militaristic, and in the past literally genocidal, fantasy of a "liberal final solution" in which all social and political problems can be resolved, as well as idealized liberal values spread and realized, through the elimination of a malicious "enemy" – ranging historically from "native Americans" and communists to the current fixation on "terrorists."

This resonant politics of liberal authoritarianism gestures toward a deeper affective logic crucial to the general appeal of liberal democracy, specifically, the ability of a government to protect these cherished ideals from internal and external dangers threatening to destroy them. According to Freeden (1996: 268), "liberals have as a rule endorsed a strong state, precisely because they have entertained a passionate respect for the integrity of the individual and the need to protect that integrity from harmful intrusion." Significantly, this popular desire and structural need for a strong state concentrates, for obvious reasons, less in the economic sphere and more in the sociopolitical one with perhaps expected authoritarian results. Going even further, "liberal govern-ance actually creates the historical conditions of possibility for authoritarian governance as it distinguishes the legal and political order (of 'the state') and a 'liberal police' of what is exterior to it, classically conceived as 'civil society,'" creating, Dean (2002: 37) argues, "the injunction to govern through freedom into a set of binding obligations potentially or actually enforceable by coercive or sovereign instruments."

This reflects a broader capitalist fantasy of authoritarian freedom. It is not only that individuals long for a state to protect their freedoms. Nor that the desired need to "govern through freedom" provides the grounding for an authoritarian governing logic. There is also a profound market-based dynamic at work. Namely, the prominence of democratic values implies the ability for individual and collective self-determination, while economic liberalism entails the "natural" and "free" functioning of a market ideally external to human control. This tension has previously played out, especially during times of greater economic insecurity, into an enhanced acceptance of government inter-vention into the economy. However, its more typical manifestation, and one that is almost exclusively pursued in the evolution from liberalism to neoliber-alism, is the channeling of this desire of agency into the sociopolitical sphere. Concretely, this involves the emboldening of the state to protect the population against domestic and foreign threats, with the implicit or explicit intention of making the world and nation "safe" for liberal democracy politically and capitalism economically.

This fantasy has only become more attractive alongside globalization. While being extolled as the only path toward future prosperity, globalization is also presented as a worrying force, full of dangerous threats to national sovereignty and a secure world order. This fear attached to globalization, particularly after 9/11, has bred shared feelings of "global insecurity," contributing to a "globalization of domination." Bigo and Tsoukala (2008: 11) declare, to this effect, that:

> Even if we witness illiberal practices, and even if we attempted to use the argument of an exceptional moment correlated with the advent of transnational political violence of clandestine organizations in order to justify violations of basic human rights and the extension of surveillance is very strong, we are still in liberal regimes.

Importantly, it remains a "liberal regime" both in permitting for a wide range of existing freedoms but also in its continued reliance on a liberal democratic discourse of authoritarian governance. In this regard, at play is less a matter of a "unified strategy" or "Big Brother" and more a liberal authoritarian logic for protecting neoliberalism linked to a globalization discourse.

Connected to these challenges of globalization, voters expect governments to deal with problems of neoliberal globalization even as they have less resources to do so. In this respect:

> A crisis of governability has engulfed the world's most advanced democracies. It is no accident that the United States, Europe, and Japan are simultaneously experiencing political breakdown; globalization is producing a widening gap between what electorates are asking of their governments and what those governments are able to deliver. The mismatch between the growing demand for good governance and its shrinking supply is one of the gravest challenges facing the Western world today. (Kupchan, 2012: 62)

In response, the state has become the focal point for recapturing the agency perceived to be lost in the unstoppable rush toward globalization. Even more so, the previous ability under traditional liberalism to "govern" the market, and therefore exert control over it, is dramatically diminished in the era of neoliberalism.

Consequently, the state has become more assertive in its role for policing society, internationally and domestically, for the protection of liberal democracy and by association neoliberalism. Governments popularly legitimize their growing political and social interventions as simultaneously preserving liberal democracy and reasserting the ability of a democratic community to effectively "govern" itself for the public good. In foreign policy, this can be seen in the championing of a benign but nonetheless aggressive "democratic imperialism" (Kurtz, 2003; Spagnoli, 2004). Domestically, it is witnessed in the rise of liberal democratic security regimes, prioritizing enhanced government surveillance and a more militarized police force (Giroux, 2007; Wacquant, 2010). Emerging, hence, is an expanding capitalist fantasy of authoritarian freedom both at home and abroad.

THE NEW LIBERAL DEMOCRATIC IMPERIALISM: THE CAPITALIST FANTASY OF AUTHORITARIAN FREEDOM ABROAD

Western liberal democracies hold a hallowed place within the modernization narrative. They are the apogee of progress, the final stage of development toward which all less than fully "modern" countries must strive. Yet these success stories are shadowed by histories of colonial exploitation and imperial rule. Here, "liberal values" were often tools for justifying insidious economic and political practices abroad, a romanticized cover for the international expansion of authoritarianism, illiberalism, and hegemony. Crucial in this regard was the affective investment in a state empowered with the responsibility of simultaneously bolstering a superpower's global hegemony and spreading its superior moral "civilization." In the contemporary context, Western leaders have explicitly rejected the idea that their present policies have any relation to their imperial past. In the words of then President George W. Bush: "America has no empire to extend or utopia to establish, no territorial ambitions. We don't seek an empire. Our nation is committed to freedom for ourselves and for others" (quoted in Ignatieff, 2003). Yet behind this modern crusade lies a similar liberal dynamic for legitimizing the state in quite illiberal ways in the name of extending and protecting not just liberalism but neoliberalism.

Tracing out the Imperial History of Liberal Democratic Authoritarianism

Imperialism is commonly contrasted to democracy, not to mention liberalism. It denotes the submission of populations, cultures, and states to an encompassing and exploitive empire. Yet, even early examples of classical imperialism, such as in Athens, had "democratic roots" (Galpin, 1983; Orwin, 1986). Within relatively modern times, nineteenth-century European empires, with at least some rapidly developing democratic features domestically, were championed and partially driven by a "mission to civilize" the world (Conklin, 1997). This mission was linked largely to a race that was "transmuted into a more comprehensive notion of 'civilization'" (Anghie, 2000: 887). The resulting legacy of state-enforced slavery, apartheid, and continuing institutionalized racism reflects the potent mixture of liberal democracy and illiberalism central to the capitalist imperialism of the recent past.

Indeed, this governing logic of a "liberal authoritarian state" can be traced back to colonialism. Writing of the Caribbean, Ledgister (1998: 14) notes:

> The colonial state thus contained both liberal and authoritarian elements, and its ethos was simultaneously liberal and authoritarian. The civil servants, soldiers,

policemen and judges who administered the colonies both upheld civil liberties and provided certain basic services – education, healthcare, sanitation, poor relief – but were ever ready to discipline the masses if this was required in the interest of either colonial power, the local ruling class or both.

This combination of liberalism and illiberalism, democracy and repression, was also on display in metropoles. Whereas "conquest, exploitation and subjugation are old themes in world history," write Cooper and Stoler (1997: 1), "What was new in the Europe of the Enlightenment ... was that such processes were set off against increasingly powerful claims in eighteenth-century political discourse to universal principles for organizing a polity." Nevertheless, while such universalism brought with it a pronounced tension for ruling elites as to whom these values applied to, both in theory and practice, it also served as the foundation for legitimizing authoritarianism in the name of preserving these ideals. It situated the state as the primary force for safeguarding these cherished values, not only within its own borders but also the world over. If colonialism was inspired by private greed, it was certainly justified by an outward-looking state-enforced morality.

This empowering of governments was affective in two distinct but connected ways. It provided an appealingly ethical reasoning for the structural requirements of a strong state to sustain and expand capitalism internationally, intimately linked to the desire to spread liberalism universally. Yet, just as importantly, it maintained the indispensable need for sovereign agency without sacrificing the overall commitment to a "free market" economy, a condition that was especially imperative considering the democratic character of these societies domestically.

The Cold War carried over this liberal democratic authoritarianism even in the midst of the mass processes of decolonization following the Second World War. In place of direct rule was a new ideologically based imperial battle of wills between the liberal democratic US and the Communist Bloc led by the Soviet Union. Each tried to establish a sphere of hegemony for not only achieving their realist nationalist interests but also expanding the reach and dominance of their belief systems. In this way, "the Soviet Union intervened to spread Communist ideology (and/or counter US advances), while Americans did the same, ostensibly to spread democracy (and/or contain Communism)" (Von Hippel, 2000: 4). This framework for conducting international relations, in turn, reflected an affective capitalist political discourse of a robust state that at once defends liberalism and publicly represents the continued importance of democratically legitimized sovereignty that nonetheless simultaneously trumpeted the need for less government intervention economically.

Vital to this authoritarian project was the construction of an affective narrative of modernization. The upward and inevitable progression toward liberal democracy was an officially approved "ideology" (Latham, 2000), positioning Western governments, specifically the US, as an altruistic force in the global struggle for realizing liberal freedom. Here, liberal democracy was presented as the "highest stage" of modernization – a type of imperialism for spreading capitalist development (Gilman, 2003). Extolled in this romanticized story of capitalist development was the right and responsibility of governments to actively and forcefully implement marketization internationally. Max Milken, director of the MIT Center for International Studies, pronounced, therefore, that:

> A much extended program of American participation in economic development of the so-called underdeveloped states can and should be one of the most important elements in a program of expanding the dynamism and stability of the free world. The best counter to Communist appeals is a demonstration that these (development) problems are capable of solutions other than those the Communists propose. (Quoted in Gilman, 2003: 48)

In this regard, the very perpetuation of a modernization discourse arose in no small part out of an affective rationality of liberal democratic authoritarianism. It represented the marshaling of a democratically elected state to proliferate liberalism economically and politically. It echoed previous US justifications for expanding its territory across the North American continent, cloaking its militaristic (McCaffrey, 1994) and genocidal (Zimmerer, 2007) pursuit of this goal in the romantic discourse of "manifest destiny."

This belief in "manifest destiny" did not terminate in the nineteenth century but has continued into the contemporary era, legitimizing the country's military interventions in the 1990s (Coles, 2002) and after 9/11. Wickham (2002: 116) draws direct parallels, thus, between the "War on Terror" and the policies targeting Native Americans during the country's initial westward expansion.

The tragic events of 9/11 have unified most Americans against a new world of international terrorism. The psychological shock of America discovering its vulnerability began a period of intense national introspection, soul searching, and profound change to Americans' self-perceptions – both positive and negative. To many Americans, this period of reflection ignited a spirited revival of the nation's virtual state religion – one belief combining the sacred and secular into a Christian sense of mission with patriotism. A nineteenth-century variant of this state religion was America's divine "manifest destiny" to spread democracy and true civilization by territorial expansion and subjugation of native peoples.

Consequently, through discourses of modernization, the question of what is the role of democratic sovereignty in a market-based society is transformed into an affective discourse empowering the state to expand the market as part of its liberalizing mission to the world. Democracy – the ability to collectively shape social relations – becomes channeled into an overriding purpose of ensuring the survival and continued success of capitalism. This democratic obligation is, not surprisingly, fertile soil for producing illiberalism in practice with the aim of securing marketization and modernization worldwide.

The New Liberal Democratic Imperialism

The advent of neoliberalism brings into even starker relief the question of the liberal democratic state's function nationally and internationally. Domestically, if the country is already "modernized" and if the economy works best when "freed" from government interference, it is unclear where and to what ends democratic sovereignty should be directed. Beyond these national borders, the emergence of a global "free market" makes the need for a state-led liberal imperialism close to redundant – the spread of capitalism will arc naturally toward the universal realization of political democracy. Moreover, the failures of modernization to achieve these goals, in practice, produced new calls for the US to give up its "misguided mission" to democratize the world and focus "instead on spreading liberalism and preventing human rights abuses which will ensure better international security" (Farrell, 2000: 583).

Yet, as neoliberalism has steadily expanded across the globe, so too has the reach and power of liberal democratic governments. In the wake of the 2001 terrorist attacks, the US and its European allies, primarily the UK, proposed and initiated an ambitious foreign policy of "democratic imperialism." This strategy was exemplified in the controversial, and ultimately disastrous, American-led invasion of Iraq. "President George W. Bush's invasion of Iraq signaled the unambiguous return of 'democratic imperialism' in American foreign policy," Encarnación (2005: 47) observes, "entailing what is tantamount to the imposition of democracy upon a foreign country, this can be seen as the ultimate manifestation of America's traditional obsession with its role as a global moral crusader." Driving this "crusade" forward was the right and responsibility of Western governments to intervene as a humanitarian "force for good" (Davidson, 2012). This so-called "humanitarian imperialism" was "part of a strategy for defending the United States by establishing democratic regimes in the Middle East and throughout the world – peacefully, if possible, but by force if necessary" (Nardin, 2005: 21).

Neoliberalism, therefore, reasserted the obligation and power of democratic governments to spread their imperial will. Underpinning this reinvigorated sovereignty was a "liberal imperial perspective" (Bacevich, 2003; Cooper, 2002; Kurtz, 2003; Walker, 2002) that advocated for the state's "active assertive maintenance of order in the world, along liberal lines, to counter terrorism and WMDs [weapons of mass destruction], to end rogue states and help failed chaotic states, to intervene in humanitarian crises and prevent ethnic cleansing" (Green, 2005: 232). This triumphalist liberal agenda fed into a broader affective narrative associated with the anxieties of global terrorism, as:

> The terrorist assault on New York and Washington in September 2001 shattered the exceptionalist conceit that the United States was impervious to the carnage that had been a prominent feature of world history in the preceding century ... Americans were forced to recognize that the vulnerability of their society had increased even as their nation had emerged as the hegemon of the global order. (Adas, 2009: 387)

Importantly, this global expansion was meant to be decidedly different from past empires and forms of international interventions. It was explicitly distinguished from previous instances of imperialism, even by the US, that was done in the name of exploiting foreign markets and securing corporate interests. "America's empire is not like empires of times past, built on colonies, conquest and the white man's burden. We are no longer in the era of the United Fruit Company, when American corporations needed the Marines to secure their investments overseas," wrote Ignatieff in an influential 2003 *New York Times* article; rather, "The 21st century imperium is a new invention in the annals of political science, an empire lite, a global hegemony whose grace notes are free markets, human rights and democracy, enforced by the most awesome military power the world has ever known." *Wall Street Journal* editor Max Boot roundly echoed these sentiments that same year, declaring "A dose of US imperialism may be the best response to terrorism ... Afghanistan and other troubled lands cry out for the same sort of enlightened foreign administration as provided by self-confident Englishmen in jodhpurs and pith helmets" (quoted in Harvey, 2003: 4).

These statements may be read as merely particularly vociferous calls by an at best naïve and at worst complicit media in the immediate march to war. However, they also shed light on the popular legitimization of an enhanced and expansionist democratically elected imperialism linked to neoliberalism and the advancement of corporate globalization. Enacted was a similar framework of global relations as found in the Cold War, a militant and altruistic liberal America, safeguarding and preserving universal ideals of economic and political freedom against despots the world over. Such contemporized justifications for empire were crystalized in Boot's strident defense of US imperialism in *USA Today*. Rhetorically asking "American imperialism?" he declares "No need to run away from label":

> on the whole, US imperialism has been the greatest force for good in the world during the past century ... That doesn't mean looting Iraq of its natural resources; nothing could be more destructive of our goal of building a stable government in Baghdad. It means imposing the rule of law, property rights, free speech and other guarantees, at gunpoint if need be. This will require selecting a new ruler who is

committed to pluralism and then backing him or her to the hilt. Iran and other neighboring states won't hesitate to impose their despotic views on Iraq; we shouldn't hesitate to impose our democratic views. (Boot, 2003)

It is exactly this discourse of liberal imperialism that provides the grounds for the country to democratically sanction its own authoritarian practices globally. "Indeed, it is precisely American Liberalism that makes the United States so illiberal today," notes Desch (2008: 7). "Under certain circumstances, liberalism itself impels Americans to spread their values around the world and leads them to see the war on terrorism as a particularly deadly type of conflict that can be won only by employing illiberal tactics."

This legitimized recourse to "illiberalism" was done, if not fully in the name of at the very least in the service of, implementing and safeguarding neoliberalism abroad. Emerging was "a new phase of imperialism" that was "marked not only by increased conflict between center and periphery – rationalized in the West by veiled and not-so-veiled racism – but also by increased intercapitalist rivalry" (Foster and McChesney, 2003: 11). In this respect, globalization discourses of a peaceful "free market" transformed into struggles for political and economic supremacy between explicitly and implicitly competing authoritarian capitalist states (Harvey, 2007a). Within Western liberal democracies, it constituted "a project to restore class dominance to sectors that saw their fortunes threatened by the ascent of social democratic endeavors in the aftermath of the Second World War" (Harvey, 2007b: 22).

More though than simply a program of capitalist rule and domination, it reflected a specific neoliberal rationale for a resurgent and enhanced authoritarian state. While it minimized the role of democratic governments for shaping economic relations, it channeled this collective agency into utopian discourses of state-led empire. Consequently:

> The inner connection between the rise of these new imperial forms and the neoliberal counter-revolution engineered by capitalist class intent upon restoring and reconstructing its power is vitally important … And, in this project, the classical range of forces – military, political, cultural as well as economic – got freely deployed in highly destructive ways in the resurgent and enhanced role of the state. (Harvey, 2007b: 22)

In doing so, it provided liberal democratic governments with fresh authoritarian legitimacy to creatively and expansively manifest and preserve this new global neoliberal order.

Spreading the Capitalist Fantasy of Authoritarianism Freedom Abroad

This resurgent, and markedly authoritarian, liberal democratic optimism has had profound global consequences. The twenty-first century has been littered with not only the continued corporate exploitation of "emerging markets" but also costly Western-led military invasions, civilian casualties, and the strategic use of torture. Importantly, neoliberalism as an international project of economic transformation has brought with it an emboldened state actor, one who is charged with the "responsibility to protect" this world, whatever the cost. Such messianic political discourses represent more than mere affective justifications for capitalism, or the idealistic clothing of a national realpolitik. Instead, they illustrate the legitimization and organizing of contemporary politics around a capitalist fantasy of neoliberal authoritarianism.

Concretely, the US and its coalition of allies in Europe and internationally have waged a "War on Terror" characterized by direct military interventions, the use of drone warfare, and the legal deployment of "enhanced interrogation techniques." New evidence is continuously emerging regarding the sheer scale and brutality of these measures. The Iraq War caused hundreds of thousands of civilian deaths with potentially thousands more killed by drone attacks. Beyond these casualty figures have been shocking reports and images of prison abuse and torture, including waterboarding, rectal "feeding," and sleep deprivation.

For many, these actions symbolized a total denigration of the Western liberal democratic tradition. "There is this America today, profoundly corrupted by its twentieth century accumulation of power and wealth, untempered by thinking, responsibility and humility," wrote noted scholar Wendy Brown in the wake of the Abu Ghraib prison abuse scandal, "where 'democracy' stands for little more than decadent indulgences, ignorant supremacism and imperial designs" (Brown, 2004). Speaking to similar sentiments of outrage, the prominent philosopher and social critic Slavoz Žižek railed against the "moral neutrality" which films like *Zero Dark Thirty* provided to the American reliance on torture:

> Torture saves lives? Maybe, but for sure it loses souls – and its most obscene justification is to claim that a true hero is ready to forsake his or her soul to save the lives of his or her countrymen. The normalisation of torture in *Zero Dark Thirty* is a sign of the moral vacuum we are gradually approaching. (Žižek, 2013)

By contrast, those perpetuating these offenses portrayed their aims in almost messianic terms. In defense of the American Iraq invasion, then President George W. Bush revealed, "God told me to liberate Iraq." The struggle against terrorism was framed, fundamentally, as war not just between enemies but entire ways of life. According to Bush, "This struggle has been called a clash of civilizations. In truth, it is a struggle for civilization." More precisely, it was all in the service of realizing a liberally inspired utopian vision, where the "common danger" of terrorism was "erasing old rivals" and, "in every region," Bush gushed, "free markets and free trade and free societies are proving their power to lift lives" (Bush, 2002).

It is perhaps tempting to explain this democratically sanctioned global repression as merely the latest propaganda for the global expansion of capitalism or the real politics of the US, or more likely both together. Indeed, this has been an early and ongoing critique of this updated form of "liberal imperialism." To this effect:

> [R]ather than a moral shift away from the rights of sovereignty, the dominance of the liberal peace thesis, in fact, reflects the new balance of power in the international sphere. Justifications for new interventionist norms as a framework for liberal peace are as dependent on the needs of Realpolitik as was the earlier doctrine of sovereign equality and non-intervention. (Chandler, 2004: 59)

While such critiques are warranted, they are by no means exhaustive. Notably, the concrete prospects of security, the "realist" calculations for how to best achieve the safety of the nation, are arguably best ensured not through continual top-down superpower interventions but rather the global encouragement of bottom-up democracies. "Thus the emergence of diverse democracies strongly influenced by the interests of ordinary citizens – nondomineering regimes domestically," hypothesizes Gilbert (1992: 12), "would contribute to the existence of nonaggressive norms and regimes internationally." Yet, they also fail to capture the affective appeal of these liberal democratic sovereign discourses of international intervention and imperialism.

Significantly, the attractiveness of this empowered and expansive state was linked to the failures of previous liberal democratic notions of modernization. Rather than give birth to an international order of flourishing democracies and prosperous democracies, as predicted at the end of the Cold War, the new millennium witnessed the rise of terrorism and failed states. Into this political vacuum, neoliberalism emerged as a new modernization fantasy, replete with a global vision of historical progress. As Latham (2011: 158) notes:

> With modernization discredited and no single overriding narrative of progress to replace it, neoliberals took the field with their own promises of accelerated, benevolent change … Neoliberalism, in other words, prevailed precisely because it revived a vision of the global mission of the United States and made the same sort of transformative claims that modernization had.

These desires tapped in, further, to growing anxieties linked to an ever danger-ous world, filled with the permanent specter of terroristic threats. At stake then was the arrival of a new affective political discourse, combining the certainty of market-driven economic development and the passionate belief in the continuing need for a strong state to protect it. This dual embrace of marketi-zation and sovereignty was reflected in the enhanced rhetoric of unilateralism deployed by the Bush Administration, a relative departure from the multilater-alism of the previous decade (Leffler, 2003). Such discourses of liberal demo-cratic authoritarianism feed into a mentality of unilateralism, which reflects the desire for agency (specifically state agency) in an existentially insecure world.

Illustrated is the precise political dynamic associated with neoliberalism that bolsters affective rationalities of authoritarianism. It is one premised on the capacity of a national government to construct and safeguard the "correct" path toward global development, not only for themselves but also for others. It is a longing to "feel in control" of "natural" economic forces, to assert a sense of human agency into an already proscribed "modernization" history. Such political longings, and their interventionist results, were integral to the very beginnings of neoliberalism. It was part of a "Wilsonian mission" in which US intervention was needed to create a peaceful neoliberal order (Smith, 1994). Since 2001, these impulses have only been enhanced and strengthened. To quote Smith (2012: 385–6) at length on the topic:

> Under the terms of the "responsibility to protect," the progressive imperialism became a form of just war and the American military that George W. Bush announced was "beyond challenge" was tasked with ushering in a new dawn of freedom worldwide. For in a uni-polar world, a global mission was conceived, as in neo-liberal and neo-conservative hands neo-Wilsonian evolved into a hard ide-ology, the equivalent in conceptual terms to Marxism-Leninism, with a capacity to give leaders and people a sense of identity and worldwide purpose to a degree that liberalism had never before possessed.

At stake was the rise of a resonant and dangerous global capitalist fantasy of authoritarian freedom abroad, and as will be shown, also at home.

THE NEW LIBERAL DEMOCRATIC POLICE STATE: THE CAPITALIST FANTASY OF AUTHORITARIAN FREEDOM AT HOME

The economic expansion of neoliberalism internationally has been accompa-nied by an emboldened and quite authoritarian imperial state politically. This authoritarian governance has also spread inward. There is, moreover, a deep interconnection between this outward- and inward-looking authoritarianism. As Gilbert (1992: 12) observes, the "interconnection between power-rivalry, the ideologies of anti-radicalism and 'racism' that make enemies of most international and domestic rivals, and the constriction of democratic options at home." Indeed, the central features of this affective political discourse – the desire for agency in the face of economic marketization and protecting liberal democracy from existing and future threats – holds true, if not even more so in the domestic sphere.

The History of Liberal Democratic Authoritarianism

The function of the state in liberal democracies is at once a structurally necessary and politically ambiguous one. On the one hand, it has a structural importance for supporting capitalism and capitalists as well as enforcing liberal rights. On the other, a supposedly distinctive feature of these market-based societies is the limited role of governments in the economy and the personal life of its citizens. Nevertheless, as discussed in Chapter 2, there is a long history of authoritarianism, both in the public and private spheres, within actually existing liberal democracies.

Capitalism traditionally, at least rhetorically, is commonly put at odds with state power in favor of a "free market." Murray (1971: 88–91), however, lists six general functions of the capitalist state for capitalism: (1) guaranteeing of property rights; (2) economic liberalization; (3) economic orchestration; (4) input provision; (5) intervention for social consensus; and (6) management of the "external relations of a capitalist system." Moreover, market building is inexorably connected to state building, not only structurally but also sociologically (Fligstein, 2001).

The state, thus, has always had a part in intervening to maintain the power of capitalists as well as the overall wellbeing of the market system (Taylor, 1972; Wolfe, 1977). In the context of liberal democracies, the question was how to balance the requirement of the state for the survival of capitalism with the overriding normative ideologies of limiting such intervention whenever possible. "Perhaps the chief task of economists at this hour is to distinguish afresh the Agenda of government from the Non-Agenda," Keynes famously remarked, "and the companion task of politics is to devise forms of government within a democracy which shall be capable of accomplishing the Agenda" (Keynes, 1926). In practice, this commonly meant an, at times, almost "invisible" empowering of the state. The US in the nineteenth century, for instance, had:

> [a] government that was often most powerful in shaping public policy when it was hidden in plain sight. Such was the case when the government created and nourished a corporate-driven market, stimulated expansion by subsidizing exploration and removing the Indians and influenced trade patterns through communication and transport policies. (Balogh, 2009: 4)

One area domestically where the role of the state was not so "hidden in plain sight" but actively celebrated was as a policing force for ensuring social stability. This policing function can be traced, in part, back historically to the empowering of the state by the bourgeoisie in the early nineteenth century to deal with the rise of unionism at the dawn of the industrial revolution. Capitalists realized early on that in order to stop this trend they would have to combine legal restrictions with local control and governance (Foster, 2003). This historical precedent transformed into a broader government "responsibility" to "police" in order to "give security against the perpetuation of dishonesty, extortion and violence," a responsibility asserted even by Adam Smith (Viner, 1927: 223–4). This perceived obligation would play out across diverse liberal democratic contexts, which despite differences were all similarly marked by "the expansion of bureaucratic states as power structures maintaining police and military control over potentially rebellious populations and reproducing the conditions of capitalist accumulation" (Alford and Friedland, 1985: xiii).

Present, then, was the legitimate right of the state to police society. This right could be, depending on the society and historical moment, quite limited or expansive in scope. Tellingly, regardless of the extent of its reach, its purpose was to create the structural conditions required for fostering a flourishing private sector. Its duties in this capacity could range from the "enforcement of peace and of 'justice' in the restricted sense of 'commutative justice,' to defense against foreign enemies, and to public works regarded as essential and as impossible or highly improbable of establishment by private enterprise or, for special reasons, unsuitable to be left to private operation" (Viner, 1960: 45).

Normatively, governments were also formally and informally expected to police "unjust" behavior that was deemed detrimental to the market and its citizens. More to the point, "norms of support for a policing agency follow logically from disapproval of the moral equivalent of trespassing and theft" (Swenson, 2002: 29). For instance, in Sweden, practices such as employee "poaching" and low wages were not only illegal but also traditionally socially disparaged as "disloyal recruitment" and "black market wages." As such, the "full exercise of freedom in an unregulated market was not a capitalist virtue" and demanded government intervention (2002: 29–30).

Contained in this mandate are the components of a capitalist fantasy of authoritarian freedom. The a priori desire to limit the government's intervention into the economy, except when necessary, produced in its wake both substantive questions as to what was the proper role of government as well as an affective longing for collective agency within these marketizing contexts. While the structural problems of capitalism, manifested in symptoms like poverty, inequality, and racism, seemed almost impossible to solve – particularly so through the overbearing hand of the state – what could be controlled were "troubling" individuals and populations. Bittner (1967) speaks, in this regard, of the American policing of "skid row" as a type of "keeping the peace" rather than "law enforcement." In the past, this repressive and exclusionary mentality has been directed at an array of marginalized communities, from African-Americans to immigrants to the poor.

This type of authoritarian policing has been heightened as liberal democracies have experienced increased economic marketization at the end of the twentieth and beginning of the twenty-first century. On the surface, it would appear that certain state-sponsored forms of social policing in the service of maintaining privilege have been diminished. Bobo et al. (1997: 17) refer to "laissez faire racism" where "Rather than rely on state-enforced inequality as during the Jim Crow era, however, modern racial inequality relies on the market and informal racial bias to recreate, and in some cases, sharply worsen racial inequality." Nevertheless, the state has retained its crucial role for intervening to "safeguard" this unequal liberal democratic order. "Laissez-faire racism" has been joined by growing police brutality, inordinately affecting African-American citizens but also extending to the population generally.

The democratic dimension of this repression is central to the modern perpetuation of this rising authoritarian capitalism within liberal democracies. The general powerlessness to literally regulate the economy and existentially shape economic relations has become channeled into a democratic mandate for politicians and law enforcement to use their power and agency to preserve "law and order" (see Beckett, 2000; Stenson, 2001). The "declining support for social welfare," in this respect, "is part of a punitive policy development in which the state has a substantial and active role" (Beckett and Western, 2001: 43). Significantly, the controlling of certain "problematic" demographics is symbolic of a greater desire by democratic communities to reassert a sense of control in an era where such sovereignty seems to be rapidly deteriorating. That state is then popularly charged with repressing those that trespass against liberal democratic and market values. The contemporary democratic impulse for collective rule has become concentrated on enhanced demands for, and practices of, social policing targeting specifically all those that behave economically and politically "irresponsibly."

The New (Neo)Liberal Democratic Policing State

Liberal democracies are not conventionally thought of in terms of being police states. While the need for some forms of government intervention and social regulation is understood to be necessary, these practices must always be balanced by an ethos of "self-restraint" on the part of the state (Schedler et al., 1999). This is perceived to be perhaps especially true in the age of neoliberalism, where all forms of government activity are thought to be in retreat.

However, this onrush of marketization is actually connected to a widening and diversifying liberal democratic set of policing regimes. Specifically, "In the name of public and private security, life has been accorded a 'social dimension,'" observes Rose (1996: 144), "through a hybrid array of devices for the management of insecurity." While such social management extends deeply into the "private sphere" – ranging from the enhanced power of managers to demands for "self-discipline" – it has also granted fresh capabilities and justifications for state power. Hence, the established policing function of the state under traditional liberal democracy has transformed progressively into a neoliberal democratic policing state.

Contrary to popular assumptions, early neoliberals championed the continued and in some cases expanded role of the state for preserving capitalist values both ideologically as well as in practice. As Jackson chronicles: "Neo-liberals of the 1930s and 1940s therefore believed that the legitimation of the market, and the individual liberty best secured by the market, had to be accomplished via an expansion of state capacity and a clear admission that earlier market liberals had been wrong to advocate laissez-faire" (Jackson, 2010: 129).

In the present age, its supporters vocally advocate for less government in favor of freer markets. The "march of the neo-liberals" is "grounded in the 'free, possessive individual' with the state cast as tyrannical and oppressive. The welfare state, in particular, is the arch enemy of freedom ... The state must never govern society, dictate to free individuals how to dispose of their private property, regulate a free-market economy or interfere with the God-given right to make profits and amass personal wealth" (Hall, 2011). Yet this anti-statism is belied by the fact that under neoliberalism the public sector and its bureaucracy have been increased, often dramatically so. Indeed, "across the world the state is, after several decades of accelerated globalization, in most cases larger and more entrenched in social relations than ever" (Scholte, 1997: 441).

This seemingly contradictory expansion of the state associated with marketization becomes clearer when seen in terms of the strengthening of the government as a social policing institution. Tellingly, even as early as the 1980s, the "neo-conservative revolution" was witnessing dangerous levels of policing for ostensibly liberal democratic states. "Police involve themselves in too many areas of public life and are capable of upsetting the delicate constitutional balance between individual and state that must exist in a liberal society," reported Uglow (1988) at the time; "Modern policing reflects the increasing authoritarianism of liberal society." For some, these emerging forms of "state-making" were akin to "organized crime," a type of mafia-like protection "racket in which a local strong man forces merchants to pay tribute in order to avoid damage – damage the strong man himself threatens to deliver" (Tilly, 1985: 170). Thus, whereas neoliberalism "is in the first instance a theory of political economic practices" fixated on spreading individual freedom through the freeing of the market, the state, nevertheless, must "create and preserve an institutional framework appropriate to such practices" including "police and legal structures and functions required to secure private property rights and to guarantee, by force if need be, the proper functioning of markets" (Harvey, 2005: 2).

Consequently, neoliberalism was initially associated, under Thatcher in the UK and Reagan in the US, with a politics of "authoritarian populism" (Gamble, 1979: 6). Hall (1978) proposed that this authoritarian populism results from the ways Thatcher was able to tap into large-scale discontent with the economic order and mobilize mass support through a populist appeal to free-market fundamentalism, social conservatism, and a strong coercive state able to "police the crisis." Importantly, this was a form of "consensual authoritarianism" in that it simultaneously evolved from the coercive role of the police in liberal societies and built mass support for these repressive "crime and order" strategies (Norrie and Adelman, 1988).

Notably, these populist appeals point to a broader affective political discourse of authoritarianism central to the advancement of marketization agendas within established liberal democracies. They represent a desire to recapture social agency through a reinvigorated coercive state, revolving around the policing of foreign and domestic "enemies" within a sociopolitical backdrop of permanent crisis. While perhaps exaggerated, this shift is indicative of a broader move toward authoritarianism within these societies. Speaking to the twenty-first-century US context, Giroux (2007: 98) contends that "the United States is not simply governed by a center-right party supported by the majority of the populace, it is a country that is moving rapidly towards a form of authoritarianism that undermines any claim to being a liberal democracy," characterized by "the attack on immigrants and people of color, the assault on civil liberties, and the growing concentration of wealth in the hands of the rich and elite corporations."

This affective authoritarian governance significantly emerges from, and is a response to, the structural problems created by neoliberalism. Concretely, greater policing is needed to deal with the fallout from the diminishing welfare benefits once provided by a now retreating state. It is also required to help implement, forcefully if need be, these economic changes. Law and order policing should "be properly understood as one component of a broader monetarist and neoliberal state strategy geared towards inhibiting working peoples' opportunities to avoid the worst forms of wage labor and, concomitantly, diminishing their expectations with respect to wages and job security." As such "neoliberal restructuring has not resulted in less state, as is fashionable to argue in some circles today, but in a different, often more coercive, role for the state" (Gordon, 2005: 53–4).

Yet it is also borne out of the profound social and political dislocations caused by neoliberal transformations. The "creative destruction" at the heart of neoliberalism serves as a primary means for the legitimization of the state as a repressive force for policing this crisis rhetorically and in practice. More precisely, enhanced policing is linked to the social construction of a profound cultural and political insecurity. The existential fears over the ability of traditional liberalism and social democracy to provide for collective economic security and prosperity are currently translated into a strategic promotion of a "crisis" logic for simultaneously spreading coercive state power and economic marketization. Brenner and Theodore (2002: 349) maintain: "Throughout the advanced capitalist world ... cities have become strategically crucial geographical arenas in which a variety of neoliberal initiatives – along with closely intertwined strategies of crisis displacement and crisis management – have been articulated."

More broadly, this reveals a contemporary liberal democratic politics linked to "neoliberal penality." Critically, it points to the shift from "mass" to "hyper" incarceration, signifying the "rolling back of the stingy social state and rolling out of the gargantuan penal state that have remade the country's stratification, cities and civic culture" (Wacquant, 2010: 74). This "neoliberal" penality is also evidenced in the UK, where the prison population has more than doubled between 1993 and 2012, increasing from 41,800 to over 86,000 (see Ministry of Justice, 2013; also Berman and Dar, 2013). Present is "the distinctive paradox of neoliberal penality," whereby "the state stridently asserts its responsibility, potency and efficiency in the narrow register of crime management at the very moment when it proclaims and organizes its own impotence on the economic front, thereby revitalizing the twin historical cum myths of the efficient police and the free market" (Wacquant, 2009: xviii).

More than just being penal in character, present is an authoritarian policing logic at the core of present-day (neo)liberal democracies. This paradox is manifested in the expectation of governments to deal with an ever proliferating set of "enemies." The increased militarization of the police (beginning in the 1990s), for instance, reflects "the aggressive turn many law enforcement agencies are assuming behind the rhetoric of community and problem-oriented policing reforms" (Kraska and Kappeler, 1997: 1). It is, moreover, witnessed in the ongoing "War on Drugs" that has combined with the private prison-building industry and the effects of economic globalization to explode incarceration rates within advanced liberal democracies (Reynolds, 2008). To this end, this domestic "war" constitutes a "global lock down" that affects marginalized populations across the world, disappearing the national boundaries of governments to police vulnerable "irresponsible" citizens (Sudbury, 2014). This authoritarian policing logic produces systematic police brutality (Cooper,

2015) that is "much more diffuse, insidious and variegated" than often scholarly or popularly assumed (Lynch, 2012: 175).

The Capitalist Fantasy of Authoritarian Freedom at Home

While not completely unprecedented, neoliberalism has introduced a rather novel paradigm for legitimizing and maintaining a liberal democratic policing state. Harvey (2005: 202–3) characterizes neoliberalism as the "brutal withdrawal of the state from all social obligation (except policing and surveillance)." Such a mentality, if not always a reality, provides the grounding for an affective authoritarian political discourse, increasingly defining liberal democratic governance. It is one where democratic power is chiefly, almost exclusively, fixated on the disciplining and often coercive "managing" of social relations. Crucial to such authoritarian justifications is an emerging capitalist fantasy of neoliberal authoritarianism.

Revealed, in turn, is a globalized model for deploying illiberal tactics for "preserving" liberal democracy and the free market. Critical, in this respect, is delimiting democracy to its traditional liberal boundaries, especially when it endangers the prevailing hegemony of financial capitalism and its elites. This policing for the sake of preserving liberal democracy was displayed in the use of "strategic incapacitation tactics" against Occupy Wall Street which focused on issues of social control and coercive preventative measures in the name of risk management.

The employment of state power to "incapacitate" this expansion of democracy beyond the limited confines of liberal elections and rights represents existing "conflicts over the use of space both public and private, contentious efforts to control the production and dissemination of information, and unprecedented levels of surveillance" (Gillham et al., 2013). It is similarly apparent in surveillance legislation, such as the 2015 French bill that:

> [a]uthorises the government to engage in preventive surveillance of private communications and public spaces for a broad range of motives – from terrorism to economic espionage and the monitoring of social movements – without proper ex ante control. It also orchestrates the legal whitewashing of mass surveillance, and legalizes tools and policies that directly echo those of other surveillance superpowers, like the US, the UK or Germany. (Treuger, 2015)

Less explored is the "ideological" appeal of this repression associated with neoliberalism. To this end, the failures of social democracy and Keynesianism produced the need for new "liberating" discourses. "Neoliberalism owes its strength to its ideological appeal," argues Clarke (2004: 60), "The point for neoliberalism is not to make a model that is more adequate to the real world, but to make the real world more adequate to its model." This has been met with affective authoritarian discourses of policing, centered on a strong state or person for "providing order" to what appears to be a crime-ridden, poor, and chaotic social situation. This discourse is not only linked to globalization but is also an increasingly global paradigm for affectively justifying a more despotic state presence in public discourse. Exemplifying this progressively universal trend was the adoption of former New York City Mayor Rudolph Giuliani's "innovative" policing methods in Mexico City.

> Giuliani's policies in Mexico City constituted a performance: policing in drag, a dressing up of policies cloaked in the language of control, and alternatively marketed with Giuliani's masculinity and reputation as a "tough guy." This performance is part of the "making up" of neoliberal policy to mask as effective, comforting, logical, and inevitable a set of policy prescriptions that has led to more insecurity, not less. (Mountz and Curran, 2009: 133)

The key here is not the achievement of security but the constant attempt to achieve security, and therefore paradoxically the need to continuously maintain insecurity. Crisis grants to governments new capacities attached to new fantasies for preserving capitalism. For instance, the Great Depression legitimated the state to regulate and intervene in the private economy in quite novel ways (Skocpol and Finegold, 1982). In the present era, the "crisis" of liberal and social democracies is now a continuous process of governments managing crises – similar to a corporation that must constantly discipline workers and police internal problems for the sake of maintaining order and profit. This is especially true in relation to a competitive global "marketplace." For this reason, "politics everywhere are now more market driven. It is not 'just' that governments cannot manage their national economies; to survive in office they must increasingly 'manage' national politics in such a way as to adapt them to the pressures of transnational forces" (Leys, 2003: 2).

Politically at stake is the turning inward domestically of the international policing mentality that legitimizes modern neoliberal authoritarianism. Just as following 9/11 the US and other great powers were supposedly justified in policing the world to "manage crisis" (Rana and Rosas, 2006), so too are they expected to regulate the country to safeguard its cherished liberal values. Emerging is an affective liberal authoritarian discourse connected to an increasingly conservative politics. It is one that simultaneously embraces the decreasing of state power in the "private" economy and its increase for preserving patriotic ideals as well as law and order. The US Tea Party represents, in this respect, a potent mix of hope and fear combining a neoliberal disdain for big government economically with a desire to restore "national values" (Skocpol and Williamson, 2012). This present-day "reactionary politics" (Parker and Barretto, 2014) strongly echoes the authoritarian populism accompanying neoliberalism in the 1980s. Tea Party spokesman Rob Kuzmanich declared "Conservatives are trying to conserve America's liberating values ... the Tea Party unites around three values: limited government and the rule of law, free market capitalism and personal responsibility" (quoted in Parker and Barretto, 2014: 1). Tellingly, while at least ideologically opposed to government overreach economically at home, they share a commitment to unilateralism and enhanced national sovereignty in the world (Mead, 2011).

Present is a broader attempt to deploy this affective authoritarian discourse for expanding marketization domestically. "The current attack on employee unions and public school teachers should be example enough of the anti-democratic bias of free market fundamentalism," according to Shapiro and Tomain (2014: 72). "Not to put too fine a point on the matter, the future regulatory state requires public policies to recapture the lost generation of economic and political gains." What cannot be ignored, however, is that neoliberalism is fundamentally regulatory, and significantly state based in its expected regulation. It requires governments to "police" the population to ensure its stability and survival.

Reflected, thus, not only in these right-wing politics but also generally, is a capitalist fantasy of neoliberal authoritarianism. Witnessed, in this respect, is the "rise of the competition state" in which "both state and market actors are attempting to reinvent the state as a quasi-'enterprise association' in a wider world context ... this process does not lead to a simple decline of the state but may be seen to necessitate the actual expansion of de facto state intervention and regulation in the name of competitiveness and marketization" (Cerny, 1997: 251). The state is considered necessary to ensure that the nation remains competitive through policing existing and potential threats. This policing focuses on the political (e.g. those sources that are "non-liberal") and social (e.g. those whose behavior is making us less competitive, such as welfare cheats and drug users, immigrants, and terrorists). Underpinning this need is an affective liberal democratic politics of authoritarianism – whereby policing becomes the primary means for populations to assert collective agency in shaping social relations and preserving its cherished, and largely unquestioned, ideals of "freedom."

CONCLUSION

Authoritarian capitalism is not limited to "developing countries" or newly economically and politically "modern" ones. It is also found within established liberal democracies. Significantly, such authoritarianism is not counter to liberal democratic values but rather expands upon them in quite coercive ways. More precisely, it channels desires for democratic sovereignty and power as well as liberal notions of the state as a "protector" of rights, into a political fantasy in which governments must be illiberally empowered to safeguard freedom understood as the simultaneous presence of liberalism, democracy, and the market. The need to shape, and discipline, individuals to become "responsible" neoliberal subjects is transformed into the duty of the state to control the population for the same ends.

Revealed is an increasingly global form of affective governance for legitimizing enhanced state repression and economic marketization. Thus far, this analysis has largely focused on the internal policies of national governments in regards to its citizens. Yet the globality of this authoritarianism is additionally present in the reconfiguring of how the state relates to the international order. The growing influence of transnational capitalist institutions and actors has produced a complementary type of national governance, empowering governments to enforce its "correct" economic policies nationally while also ensuring that countries remain financially "responsible" states. Chapter 7 will examine in greater depth the global evolution from liberal democracy to authoritarian capitalist sovereignty – one in which powerful international financial institutions coercively "discipline" nations that fail to be financially "self-disciplined" based on global capitalist standards of "good governance."

7. A responsible global hegemony: the capitalist fantasy of authoritarian "good governance"

On January 25, 2015 the leftist coalition turned political party, Syriza, was elected to power on an explicit platform of "anti-austerity." They ran on the need to challenge its European and international creditors – collectively referred to as the "Troika" – in regards to its looming debt repayment. As one Athenian citizen observed: "They were voted in to say no. No to the same old, same old. Because the people have been desperate, they have felt humiliated and impoverished" (Hurst, 2015). While commentators focused on their potential to offer a "new economic agenda" challenging the reigning domination of neoliberal austerity, it also hinted at an emerging and dangerous political reality. Namely, it gestured toward the ability of international and regional actors to impose neoliberalism on national states, forcing them to accept economic austerity and a politics that would enforce it. The democratic resistance of the Greek people to these increasingly coercive capitalist regulations put into sharp relief the increasingly authoritarian character of this international market order, one in which democracy is often the enemy of "good governance" and thus needs to be continuously disciplined.

These negotiations starkly reveal the profound foreign influence on contemporary democracy. External actors can often have as strong if not stronger political effect on countries than economic (Bratton, 1989). Empirical studies show that external incentives and conditionalities strongly impact democratization, and as such, democracy is not, as commonly assumed, a "domestic affair par excellence" (see Ethier, 2003). Positively, many modernists believed that in the new millennium democracy would soon become a "global entitlement ... that increasingly will be promoted and protected by collective international processes" (Franck, 1992: 47).

Despite such optimism, the positive international impact on democracy promotion has been ambiguous at best and negative at worst. There is little evidence, for instance, that foreign aid positively effects democratization (Knack, 2004). Moreover, such efforts are found to be most successful when there is a strong incentive for countries to accept and become part of an unequal neocolonial order, such as the prospect of entering into the European

Union (EU) (Schimmelfennig and Scholtz, 2008). There is also often a failure to empirically analyze the actual as opposed to assumed political impact of international organizations like non-governmental organizations (NGOs) on democratization, leading scholars and policy-makers to adopt "inadequate, explicitly normative interpretations" (Clarke, 1998: 40).

Critically, it should not be overlooked how foreign influences can explicitly work against democracy. In the immediate post-Cold War era, despite fresh claims of the "end of history" with the triumph of liberal democracy globally, realpolitik on the part of dominant powers often trumped democratic concerns. Under President Clinton through the 1990s, Middle Eastern democracy promotion was, for instance, marginalized due to fears that it would bring to power anti-American regimes (Hawthorne, 2001), while Europeans were worried about the threat of political instability on their borders (Xenakis, 2000).

This trend has continued into the twenty-first century, especially linked to the proliferation of neoliberalism internationally. Scholars note that this hyper-capitalist paradigm actively limits the ability of NGOs and other external actors from fulfilling their democratic role (Edwards and Hulme, 1996; Farrington and Bebbington, 1993; Fisher, 1997; Roberts et al., 2005; Zaidi, 1999). Institutionally, it allows former political elites to move into international organizations, notably "democracy-promoting" NGOs. Such transfers, in practice, limit the scope and ability of populations to either ideologically challenge neoliberalism or create the foundations of a mass-based democracy (Farrington and Bebbington, 1993). Further, authoritarian governments use the "threat" of these democratizing "foreign" organizations to legitimize their power and enhance repression domestically (Carapico, 2002).

More broadly, "neoliberal globalization" can be understood as "a new [United States] based form of imperial globality, an economic-military-ideological order that subordinates regions, peoples and economies world-wide" (Escobar, 2004: 207). Rather than democratization or the nurturing of greater popular participation, international institutions committed to a neoliberal agenda promote a "one-size-fits-all" market-based technical solution to national development. Consequently, "Any agenda for social and political change is lost in this technocratic discourse that essentially argues that NGOs be utilized to legitimize World Bank-sponsored attempts to foster widespread acceptance of the neoliberal ... state" (Mercer, 2002: 18). Concretely, this entails the decrease and elimination of needed social services, in the process weakening the legitimacy of the state (Fowler, 1991; Marcussen, 1996; White, 1999). For this reason, global organizations and their partners are commonly referred to as a "parallel state" (Clarke, 1998) and countries as a "franchise state" (Wood, 1997) within this expanding neoliberal order.

Nevertheless, it would be a mistake to assume that the state has been irrevocably neutered or even completely disempowered. If globalization poses a threat, it is to democracy not to the power of the state (Scholte, 1997). The growing private sector (and privatization of politics) still requires a strong state to protect its profitable interests and uphold social order. Yet this role transcends that of a mere sovereign "night watchman." Instead, it grants the state and its affiliated political agents a renewed right and capability to do what is necessary to implement and preserve these capitalist "reforms." Thus, the proliferation of civil society is needed to limit the state economically but also strengthen it as a legitimate authority (Diamond, 1994). Concretely, "NGOs have become harnessed by the state and [have] been used as a tool to implement the neoliberal model" (Gideon, 1998: 304).

Reflected is a global capitalist fantasy of national and transnational sovereignty, one that centers on the empowering of national governments and, if necessary, international bodies to encourage, protect, and deepen neoliberalism. Present is a political project for spreading capitalism globally, one nation at a time. The triumphant rhetoric of democracy promotion is transformed into a discourse for neoliberal justification. Martell (2007: 173) notes, "Third wavers propose globalist cosmopolitan democracy ... when the substance of their arguments do more in practice to bolster the sceptical view of politics based around inequality and conflict, nation-states and regional blocs, and alliances of common interest or ideology, rather than cosmopolitan global structures." This global "common interest or ideology" is manifested in the increasingly coercive demand for national governments to adopt practices of "good governance" compatible with neoliberal beliefs and expectations.

Significantly, a vital element of this fantasy is the strengthening of the authoritarian power of the state as well as international organizations. It is progressively the "responsibility" of governments to be "responsible" or face threatening international consequences for their "irresponsibility." This means that the states must be equipped and given the political ability to enforce this neoliberal paradigm, even in the face of popular dissatisfaction. It also means that the World Bank and International Monetary Fund (IMF) must be allowed to directly involve themselves in the political affairs of countries as well as punish those that deviate from this "correct" path.

This chapter sheds light on the authoritarianism crucial to the contemporary international spread and maintenance of capitalism, specifically its modern neoliberal variety. Rather than a weakened state or merely transnational forms of sovereignty, it illuminates its continued reliance on an emboldened governmental force for its protection. The promise of "good governance" exists as an affective discourse for increasing the scope of national governments to broaden the limits of its coercive power in order to "secure" marketization domestically against popular threats. In this respect, corporate globalization has produced "self-disciplining" neoliberal states. It has additionally dramatically expanded the authority and subsequent authoritarianism of international actors to influence and directly determine a country's politics to reflect these neoliberal values. Present, as will be shown, is a multilevel global authoritarian fantasy of capitalist good governance.

TOWARD A "RESPONSIBLE" INTERNATIONAL HEGEMONY

Globalization presents a profound contradiction for international relations. On the one hand, the current ethos is one of universal democracy – the construction of a global society composed of cooperating and peacefully competing democracies. Implicit for this perspective is the inherent right of all countries to self-determination. On the other hand, international organizations have placed on nations quite strong conditionalities, directly and indirectly dictating their economic policies and increasingly political arrangements. Reflected is the expansion and cementing of a "responsible" international hegemony, the governing of countries to adopt and maintain neoliberalism economically and politically.

Crucial to this shift has been the supposed transition from governments to governance. The ascendancy of capitalism in the 1990s was met with prevalent fears that established forms of sovereign government were no longer capable of managing the complexities of the modern economy. As Kooiman (1994) observed at the time, "the growing complexity, dynamics and diversity of our societies as caused by social, technological and scientific developments put governing systems under such new challenges that new conceptions of governance are needed." This shift toward governance rather than governments was directly associated with globalization. It was thought that:

> states are no longer the only actor who initiate and dominate the cascades which radiate out from the epicenter … [thus] a theory needs to be developed that treats globalized space as the locale of the epi, as a vast arena composed of actors and processes that are not limited by territorial boundaries of sovereign rights, as a bifurcated system composed of both state-centric and multi-centric worlds. (Rosenau, 2000: 188)

Ironically, though, this trumpeting of the need for governance was associated in practice with the reaffirmation of both the nation and the state. The almost exclusive association of democratization with liberal democracy confined such changes to national boundaries. As Ahrne et al. (2005: 3) maintain, "Since political parties as organizations … are strongly related to the nation state for gaining power, there are few incentives in the short run for political parties to work outside the nation state." This on-the-ground reality belied the hope of some to build upon this embrace of transnational governance to similarly "reconstruct contemporary democracy" (Scholte, 2008). In fact, the engagement in regional forms of governance by states is commonly done for the purpose of "sovereign boosting" by national governments seeking to popularly legitimate their power domestically (Söderbaum, 2004).

Further, such democracy promotion is undermined by the overriding aim of needing to ideologically and practically reinforce neoliberalism within these countries. The fostering of a strong and independent civil society has perpetuated and deepened marketization, marginalizing popular and participatory movements. Here, the replacing of state function by NGOs, for example:

> undermines the institutional capacity of Latin American countries to define and defend alternatives to the development agenda articulated by international financial institutions and development agencies. This mutes voices of opposition and fundamentally weakens democratic political processes. It is ironic that NGOs, which generally see themselves and are often seen by others as agents of democracy, have been instrumental in undermining the institutional bases of political participation in this way. (Arellano-López and Petras, 1994: 567)

At the international level, activists committed to the global spread of democracy commonly feel as if they are "double agents" having to simultaneously serve the cause of nurturing genuine political change and the interests of their superpower backers (Guilhot, 2005).

Crucial in this respect is the prioritization of stability above all other normative political considerations. Despite rhetoric to the contrary, "donors' goals of democracy promotion is balanced against – or outweighed by – their desire for political stability in a country or a region" (Brouwer, 2000: 22). These realist considerations represent the fundamental desire of elite national and international actors to retain their influence and advantage. Accordingly, "Western democracies do not unequivocally engage in democracy promotion. Similar to nondemocratic regimes, they have a tendency to prioritize stability and security over democratic change." Moreover, "non-democratic regimes do not necessarily engage in autocracy promotion. Rather, they seek to undermine Western efforts at democracy promotion if they see their political and economic interests or their political survival at stake" (Börzel, 2015: 520).

This emphasis on stability is meant ultimately to ensure the success of neoliberalism. Specifically, "civil society serves as an arena where different groups manifest and use political and economic power to perpetuate or balance out pre-existing power dynamics within an/or between the economy and the state" (El-Mahdi, 2011: 26). Likewise, the state is empowered to regulate the civil sphere to minimize threats to this system. As Jha (2004: 531) observes, "globalization is basically the extension of capitalism by other means." It involves a continually evolving reshaping of civil society and the state for imposing economic marketization.

This simultaneous and compatible emphasis on stability and marketization combines to encourage political authoritarianism. Importantly, "the 'rhetoric' of globalisation is paralleled by and facilitates the emergence of more authoritarian or at least autocratic forms of governance" (Swyngedouw, 2000: 63). A strong sovereign actor is required to maintain order, especially as globalization seems to be undermining traditional political and social safety nets. Thus, the "end of history" has been witness to the rise in some places of new strongmen able to deliver social stability, regardless of the cost. Duffield (1998: 65) observes:

> Warlords, for example, have forged new and viable links with international organizations and global markets ... At the same time, many post-adjustment rulers, in terms of state debureaucratisation and the embrace of the free market have adopted warlord-type strategies. The changing architecture of the nation-state has also weakened the rule of law and blurred traditional responsibilities. This has created a demand for private protection at all levels within the emerging system.

Such insights challenge established understandings of globalization and governance as a fundamental process of weakening state power. Echoing this perspective, Scholte (2005: iii) argues: "In terms of governance, the key trend promoting neoliberal policies has been a shift from statist to decentered regulation. With respect to production, the pre-eminence of neoliberalism has resulted from certain turns in contemporary capitalist development." Nevertheless, the state has by no means disappeared or even been substantially disempowered. Rather, its role has been redirected away from economic regulation and toward social and political regulation. Bowles (2005) notes that "neo-liberal globalization" is less a singular definition and more a set of perspectives for reconfiguring the relation of the state and market. In this respect, corporate globalization has produced a "reconstructed state" that must serve global as well as national constituencies (Scholte, 2005: 193).

The central function of this "reconstructed state" is to ensure a country upholds its global economic "responsibilities." More precisely, that regardless of any other desires it or its population may have, that they maintain their commitment to marketization. Sarfaty (2012) speaks of competing post-Cold War logics between efficient markets and "social contract liberalism." The World Bank, for instance, usually does not take human rights into consideration when lending and implementing policies, yet those within the World Bank who do care about these issues must justify them in the language of neoliberalism (Weiss, 2000). Analogously, to retain its international legitimacy, governments must make their policies and aims compatible with priorities of deepening economic marketization.

THE GLOBAL CAPITALIST FANTASY OF AUTHORITARIAN "GOOD GOVERNANCE"

Vital to this process is the empowering of the state as an authoritarian actor for the sake of "good governance." This conforms to the more fundamental authoritarian dynamic of capitalism discussed throughout this work, that the increase of marketization produces, formally and informally, the need for a stronger state for its safeguarding and reproduction. Moreover, it is underpinned by a similar fantasy of capitalist development. The promotion of "good governance" stands as an affective discourse for justifying not only neoliberalism but also the enhancement of a coercive national and transnational sovereign power to implement and protect this status quo.

Importantly, governance is now predominantly associated with the governing of and for capitalist interests. Whereas it was previously linked to internationally accepted ideas of decolonization, localization, and human rights (Weiss, 2000), it has presently come to be inexorably linked to neoliberalism. More than just a set of guiding principles, good governance is currently a hegemonic idea. It exemplifies how "powerful states (notably the USA), powerful organizations (such as the IMF) and even, perhaps, powerful disciplines (economics) exercise their power largely by 'framing': which serves to limit the power of potentially radical ideas to achieve change" (Bøås and McNeill, 2004: 1).

This direct expansion into politics is a significant departure from the past. Previously, foreign aid was not contingent on political conditionalities. Rather, it was linked to the geopolitical considerations of the superpower donor or focused on the completion of specific development projects. "Cold War era aid programs rarely ventured beyond economic and social development projects into explicitly political affairs ... so good governance was a new sector for traditional aid donors," writes Carapico (2002: 381). It represented the extension of the scope of international organizations and foreign powers on those they were subsidizing. This enhancement of their sovereign power was cloaked in the language of rather universally accepted political and welfare goals. Indeed "most development assistance agencies adopted democracy promotion, rule of law, and civil society projects in the 1990s, alongside loans and grants in traditional aid sectors like agriculture, communications, and health" (2002: 381).

Despite its touted development objectives, this discourse of "good governance" perpetuated a troubling and potentially dangerous image of these developing countries. It portrayed them as chaotic and weak, therefore implicitly requiring the guidance and possible intervention of stronger external actors. As Mercer (2002: 11) contends:

> in highlighting the "incivilities" within NGOs and civil society (such as ethnic and regional tension, undemocratic practice and weak capacity), much of this critical NGO literature runs the risk of reinforcing the widespread perception that civil societies in poor countries are indeed "fragmented," "weak" and "unorganized." The assumption is that civil society (in its familiar western guise) has somehow gone wrong in the developing world; that these societies are incapable of becoming "civil."

On the basis of these assumptions, the World Bank and other international financial institutions (IFIs) reserved the right to dictate the national politics of donor countries. Economically, this entailed allowing "market forces and competitive pressures" to guide "resources into activities that were consistent with comparative advantage and, in the case of labor intensive exports, laid the foundation for learning international best practice and subsequent industrial upgrading" (World Bank, 1993: 325). The adoption of these neoliberal strategies would ensure long-term national development and a stable international financial order.

Such development discourses, thus, reflected prevailing ideas of what constitutes good governance. These narratives "embody particular theories about rationality, institutional embeddedness, and agency, as well as a historical story" (Bevir 2003: 200). Two dominant governance narratives were "neoliberal" and institutionalist "governance as networks" (see Bevir, 2003), as well as an "Anglo-governance school" (Marinetto, 2003) According to Richards and Smith (2002), the "story of governance" has three parts: (1) "government," where governments took the lead in implementing policy following the Second World War; (2) "governance," where multiple actors took the initiative in implementing policies; and (3) "joined-up government," where governments sought to re-establish a more central role for government. Tellingly, this reinforcing of the state's role helped to entrench a redefinition of politics as primarily focused on proper economic management (Doornbos, 2003; McGregor, 1993).

Present, in turn, was a new modernization narrative based on the partnership between international organizations, non-governmental actors, and the state for correctly implementing neoliberal reform. In the 1990s, NGOs were increasingly touted as important actors for ushering in democratization (Dicklitch, 1998; Farrington and Bebbington, 1993; Ndegwa, 1996). Notably, such democracy promotion was confined to that of liberal democracy, as it was understood that there were "no other games in town" (Baker, 1999). This was soon transformed, however, into a stronger focus on reforming the state so that structural adjustment policies could effectively improve the economy and popular welfare. This represented a shift in international development discourses from "getting prices right" to "getting institutions right" (Choudhary, 2007). As declared by United Nations Secretary-General Kofi Annan, "good governance is perhaps the single most important factor in eradicating poverty and promoting development" (Annan, 1998).

Emerging was a capitalist fantasy of good governance, in which "getting institutions right" served as an affective promise for resolving all of the country's social, economic, and political problems. The World Bank's limited view of governance was merely "the manner in which power is exercised in the management of a country's economic and social resources for development" (World Bank, 1992: 1). Yet this rather narrow perspective was coupled with a quite heightened rhetoric about the need for change and reform. In 1989, the World Bank declared that "a crisis of governance" underlay "the litany of Africa's development problems" (World Bank, 1989: 60–1). Nanda (2006: 269) observed that "'good governance' ... has assumed the status of a mantra for donor agencies as well as donor countries." Indeed:

> From the early 1990s onwards, the call for less state has gradually been substituted by a call for a better state. This new approach should not be confused with a plea for a return to the strong (Keynesian or socialist) state. Rather it implies better and transparent governance of what is left of the state after neoliberal restructuring has been implemented. (Demmers et al., 2004: 2)

Here the traditional modernization narrative was turned on its head, as such good governance would provide the required market economy for gradually achieving liberal democracy (Leftwich, 1993: 605).

Nevertheless, this global capitalist fantasy of good governance legitimized authoritarianism. In particular, "this new governance paradigm represents a market/private sector model of development which signifies the current era of globalization" (Choudhary, 2007: 3). Yet, while this definitely constituted the move away from centralized national economic planning, it was not a shift away from centralized policing or social regulation. To this end, governance as a discourse promotes a "managerial" notion of democracy in which democratic aspects are a concession to the broader correct management of society (Jayal, 2007). Other values must therefore conform to this overriding drive for structural reform, empowering governments to do what it deems necessary for putting in place and preserving this neoliberal agenda. As the then World Bank President Barber Conable put it, "[i]f we are to achieve development, we must aim for growth that cannot be easily reversed through the political process of imperfect governance" (quoted in Doornbos, 2003).

This affective discourse of authoritarian good governance disciplined populations in the name of achieving development through enhanced marketization. For instance:

> through the good governance agenda, human rights advocacy, far from adopting an outsider or independent critique to the neo-liberal economic policies of the World Bank or International Monetary Fund (IMF) ... [instead] adopted an approach based on finding complementarity and compatibility between human rights advocacy and the economic and financial policies of the World Bank and IMF. (Gathii, 1999: 107–8)

More broadly, it signified a potent combination of political authoritarianism and self-disciplining, the mixture of coercive governance from "above and the governance of self" that "compels state and policy structures in individual countries to conform to the norms set by global institutions" (Doornbos, 2003: 6).

In this context, "governance" therefore designates "the application of power and authority in a way that commits relevant political actors to managerial decisions" (McGregor 1993: 182), a process entirely consistent with the World Bank's agenda. In effect, this amounts to the seemingly paradoxical outcome of depoliticizing the exercise of political power – a point made by a number of scholars in the literature on economic development (e.g. see De Alcantara, 1998; Doornbos, 2003; Jessop, 1998; Jose, 2007; Kiely, 1998). The effect of this, note Demmers et al. (2004: 10), "is the seemingly paradoxical coincidence of this type of democratisation with nothing less than a depolitisation of democracy ... the state, and politics itself has disarmed, paralysed or even brain-washed most of capitalism's previous critics and reformers, such as socialists, social-democrats, nationalists and communists."

Vital to this authoritarian development was the affective promise of good governance. It provided international organizations with not only greater scope in guiding a country's politics, it also served as the foundation for the coercive regulation of these reforms by transnational and national actors. Consequently, the fantasy of good governance re-established sovereign power, though in a somewhat new neoliberal direction. It limited the state's influence within the economic sphere while simultaneously empowering it, and if necessary its international partners, to politically police the implementation and maintenance of these marketization policies. Under the banner of promoting good governance, what is emerging are authoritarian "self-disciplining states" as well as the authoritarian right of international organizations to discipline states that refuse to act "responsibly."

THE SELF-DISCIPLINED CAPITALIST STATE: THE NATIONALIST CAPITALIST FANTASY OF AUTHORITARIAN "GOOD GOVERNANCE"

The proliferation of corporate globalization has commonly led many to assume the overall weakening of national sovereignty. The state is sidelined in its power in favor of transnational actors and international financiers. Yet, in practice, governments remain responsible for their country's economic wellbeing. More precisely, they have the "responsibility" to make sure that the nation maintains its commitment to neoliberal reforms, if necessary through quite coercive measures. Arising is the politically authoritarian "self-disciplined" modern capitalist state.

A History of the Responsible Market State

There is a long precedent of international capitalist actors justifying political authoritarianism nationally in the name of sustaining a "responsible" economic agenda. Indeed, a vital issue that confronted the IMF and World Bank in the post-war era, at least from the mid-1970s onward, was how to deal with popular resistance to its proposed capitalist reforms. While modernization narratives painted a theoretical picture of capitalism being the exclusive pathway to democracy, in practice marketization often had profoundly authoritarian consequences. The expectation of governments to effectively deal with domestic threats to capitalist changes served as a precedent for the present self-disciplining neoliberal state.

The 1980s ushered in resurgent demands by donor countries and international financial organizations for developing countries to adopt widespread market reforms. Central to these strategies was increased privatization, a more competitive labor market, and a sharp reduction in public spending on social welfare. The freeing up of "market forces" was aimed, rhetorically at least, at encouraging economic growth. More than suggestions, these reforms were conditions for countries to receive IMF loans and, as such, remain financially solvent. By the latter part of the decade though these loan conditions were increasingly subject to the "distribution critique" as across the developing world these changes resulted in a substantially lesser share of labor income and rapidly increasing inequality (Pastor, 1987).

Not surprisingly, these measures catalyzed quite strong public dissent.

The erosion of social safety nets alongside a lessening stake in the economy created widespread dissatisfaction with these reforms and the governments who supported them. Politically, this meant that states had to progressively turn to authoritarian measures to protect these capitalist policies from democratic challenges. Within the Latin American context, for instance, it was observed that:

> governmental elites, if they are to remain in power, must also answer to (or repress) their own populations. And the price to be paid for external help with "liquidity problems" has typically involved politically dangerous stabilization measures (devaluations, wage and credit restrictions, and fiscal deficit reductions) – measures that often arouse the strong opposition of major social forces. (Kaufman, 1985: 473)

Pastor (1989) notes, in this respect, that governments had to navigate between the external pressure of neoliberal reforms to deal with debt and the internal pressure with populations upset at these reforms and the international actors who imposed them. This tension gave birth to a broader global discourse on the need for "political stability," an idea that justified either outright authoritarianism or democratic illiberalism within developing countries being forced to accept these structural readjustment policies (see Foxley, 1983; Frenkel and O'Donnell, 1979; Sheahan, 1980). Transnational capitalist organizations (both in their structure and influence) similarly created conditions for authoritarian politics in Africa (Bangura, 1991).

This was true even in countries that had recently experienced democratic transformations. "Southern cone countries such as Argentina and hopefully Uruguay and Brazil, are now returning to civil democracy after years of military rule … But they are faced with enormous debt problems, which seriously endanger the process of democratic transition," wrote former president of the Latin American Studies Association, Helen Safa (1985). She continued that "the policies of the International Monetary Fund are hindering the democratic process in these countries, not only by forcing the new civilian governments to institute harsh unpopular measures regarding wages, inflation, and investment policies, but by seriously weakening the strength of labor unions."

Underpinning this emerging reality of capitalist authoritarianism was the idea that without these coercive state measures countries would face not only economic ruin but also political anarchy. The successful implementation of these reforms was thus directly linked to the ability to portray the situation as one of "crisis" requiring immediate and drastic change (Remmer, 1986). As one scholar emphasized, "the only alternative to planned and guided adjustment is chaotic adjustment, entailing higher costs in terms of controls, scarcities, inflation, unemployment, and atrophied output and growth" (Nelson, 1984: 81).

This early legitimization of an empowered state tasked with policing the successful maintenance of marketization set the foundations for present forms of national self-disciplining. Tellingly, the economic justification for this authoritarianism is based on quite limited historical evidence. Andrews (2008:

380) notes that prevailing models of government effectiveness are "like telling developing countries that the way to develop is to become developed" and that the "'one-way-best model' of governance ignores institutional variation across well-governed states" (also see Pritchett and Woolcock, 2004). Instead, it is based on a new capitalist fantasy of development that combines "responsible" policies of economic marketization with political authoritarianism.

The Rise of the Self-Disciplining Capitalist State

The present era has witnessed the evolution of a state that while reducing its responsibility for economic regulation has promoted its increased obligation for managing the political and social sphere. The overriding emphasis is one of maintaining capitalist discipline, not giving into the lures of corruption or the populist but ill-conceived desires of many of its citizens. Governments, in this respect, have taken on an almost paternalistic role, forcing their populations to be "responsible" and "self-disciplined" as if the acceptance of neoliberal reforms was a matter of personal and national maturity. To ensure this "mature" perspective states must be willing to act decisively and at times coercively to stamp out the threat of "irresponsibility."

Economically, there is a renewed sense that developing countries should become self-sufficient. The reliance on loans or donor aid is seen as simply a transitionary stage to a point where they can compete independently without assistance in the global marketplace. This idea is captured in the call for such countries to evolve from a "rentier" to a development state (see, for example, Verkoren and Kamphuis, 2013). Ignored are the power dynamics that prevent developing countries from attaining such autonomy. Yet it also represents an affective narrative of neoliberal modernization, where all that is needed to economically develop successfully is to faithfully adhere to the capitalist reforms proscribed by international organizations.

Crucial to this discourse is the broader notion that financial solvency is directly linked to countries taking "personal responsibility" for their economic health. It involves being willing to make "hard sacrifices" in the form of spending cuts to decrease national debts. This sentiment was especially relevant in the wake of the 2008 financial crisis. Here the crisis was framed as a moment to, if not completely transform the financial system, to at the very least reform it. It soon, however, turned into an opportunity for strengthening these financial ideologies, as the crisis:

> has been ideologically reworked, at least in the UK, from an economic problem (how to "rescue" the banks and restore market stability) to a political problem (how to allocate blame and responsibility for the crisis): a reworking that has focused on

the unwieldy and expensive welfare state and public sector, rather than high risk strategies of banks, as the root cause of the crisis. (Clarke and Newman, 2012: 2)

Central to this shift was the exporting of austerity globally as the "appropriate" response to deal with this near economic meltdown. In this spirit, Britain was "repositioning itself as a model of probity and good fiscal housekeeping" to the world (Clarke and Newman, 2012: 2).

Reflected was a prevailing ethos in which countries must actively create the policies and institutions necessary for meeting these now moral demands of austerity and structural readjustment. Even before the crisis, in 2005 the G7, with the support of leading international organizations, emphasized the concept of "national ownership" associated with the increasingly coercive expectations of "good governance." Such demands for countries to be responsible have reconfigured state power. As early as the 1990s it was apparent that "On balance, stabilization and structural adjustment programs ... facilitate a major continuation of some forms of intervention (influence and mediation), redirect others (regulation, mediation, and distribution), and reduce those associated with state production and planning" (Biersteker, 1990: 477). In the twenty-first century, as marketization became as much a moral principle as an economic priority, governments were increasingly ethically legitimized as an authoritarian force for capitalist self-disciplining.

Ironically, but perhaps not unpredictably, discourses of democracy promotion and liberalism were used to justify market-based authoritarianism. Civil society, once the touted harbinger of democratization, was transformed into a social sphere whose principal aim was to remain "apolitical" in its commitment to implementing and preserving marketization (Hawthorne, 2004). Yet it was also politicized in the name of forcing unwilling governments to adopt neoliberal reforms, ostensibly for "the good of the country." These predominantly middle-class "reform movements" were directed against widely supported elected populist governments, challenging democracy when it threatened "good governance" (Thompson, 2004).

Further, the depiction of developing countries as lacking certain telltale modernization traits such as a "democratic culture" or "entrepreneurial spirit" were continually given as reasons "to extend the control of states and international financial institutions over their ostensible beneficiaries, while concealing their own essentially political character" (Abrahamsen, 2000). Tellingly, the rise of a "self-disciplining" state extended to all social and political spheres. A chief "promise of good governance" was the possibility of a decentralized power structure more responsive to local populations (Grindle, 2007). Yet this power was largely contingent on local governments being "responsible," as even a proponent like Grindle admits. Additionally, this disciplining capitalist morality came to include in many contexts the respect for, or at least acceptance of, the authoritarian state. As Dalmasso (2012: 222) observes in the Arab context, "human rights campaigners had to depoliticize their demands, and sometimes their structures" so as not to directly challenge non-democratic "good governance" regimes "in order to obtain their desired reforms."

Evolving was a clear differentiation globally between states that governed themselves "properly" and those that did not. In the immediate post-Cold War era the international order was characterized by "an increasingly sharp division between 'core' states who share in the values and benefits of a global world economy and polity, and 'marginalized' states, some of which are already branded 'failed' states" (Hout, 1996: 168). During this time, the World Bank portrayed "good governance" and therefore politics as a whole simply as "purely technical questions of policymaking, such as 'getting the basics right'" (Kiely, 1998: 81).

At the heart of this "good governance" was thus the effort to produce "self-disciplining" neoliberal states. It represented "new forms of transnational control accompanying the rise of global capitalism ... to replace coercive means of social control with consensual ones in the South within a highly stratified international system" (Robinson, 1996: 616). Significantly, whether or not a country was democratic ultimately mattered very little. What was chiefly important was the degree to which they embraced marketization. As Schmitz (1995: 69) argues: "The key thing to ask of developing countries was not whether they were democracies or autocracies ... but whether they had the governing will and wherewithal to create the 'appropriate policy framework' required to achieve efficient markets and the successful implementation of donor and creditor-mandated economic liberalization programs." This over-riding emphasis on states to be "self-disciplined" would become, even more troublingly, ever more authoritarian.

The Self-Disciplining Capitalist Fantasy of Authoritarian Good Governance

The once celebratory narrative of capitalist democracy has been gradually replaced and progressively undermined by new priorities of "good govern-ance." The expectation that governments have a moral not just economic duty to be financially "responsible" grants states new legitimacy to use their sovereign power to protect these reforms. Governance in the present context is a pretext for the government's enhanced regulation of the civil and political spheres to preserve marketization. It is "good" if neoliberalism flourishes and "bad" if it does not. The "good" in "good governance" also has a strong affec-tive dimension – symbolizing the fantasy that if countries follow neoliberal development principles and organize their politics effectively to this end, they will soon achieve both economic growth and shared prosperity. Yet it relies on an authoritarian cycle of "self-disciplining," whereby states are granted ever more power to police "irresponsible" domestic threats blamed for undermining "good governance" and thus stalling national progress.

Western governments and IFIs draw on this affective promise of marketization linked to "good governance" for extending their influence and strengthening neoliberalism ideologically. They subsume all efforts for sociopolitical change into an approved narrative of capitalist development. Demands for more employment, greater economic welfare or increased democracy are translated into a call for "better institutions" so that free-market policies can work more successfully. This is true even in contexts where such policies are being explicitly resisted. European support for the Arab Spring was in fact an attempt to promote neoliberalism "in order to foster a mode of subjectivity that is conducive to the EU's own norms and interests" (Tagma et al., 2013: 357). More to the point, it signifies Europe's efforts to subjectively govern these movements, exemplifying a contemporary "form of politics and economics that seeks to subject the agency on the 'Arab street' to EU standards" (2013: 357).

Such governance demonstrates a contemporary type of colonial neoliberalism. Foreign powers defend and bolster authoritarian regimes across the world as a primary method to ensure stability. Countries with direct political and economic strategic importance to Western countries are most able to retain non-democratic rule (see Brownlee, 2005; Carothers, 2003; Dalacoura, 2005; Diamond, 2010; Dunning, 2004; Levitsky and Way, 2002; Schedler, 2002). This support for authoritarianism denotes an increasingly global model for ensuring the successful spread of neoliberalism. Consequently: "The failure of Western democracy promotion is rooted in the contradiction between the dominance of global finance capital and the norm of democratic equality; in the periphery, neo-liberalism is most compatible with hybrid regimes and, at best, 'low intensity democracy'" (Hinnebusch, 2015: 335).

These realist considerations are bolstered by an affective politics of crisis and reform, one where the state takes center stage as driver of "good governance" change. Autocracy and illiberalism is deemed a "necessary evil" to furthering economic development. The fantasy of "good governance" as the silver bullet to mass progress provides the basis for "strong" states to reassert their right to rule and effectively deal with threats to their power. They do so often with the full backing of the international community. "In a context of economic crisis and political liberalization, external support from foreign powers can strengthen the capacity of regime incumbents to maintain tight control over democratic reform processes," observe Yom and Al-Momani (2008: 39), "foreclosing the possibilities of opposition victories in their struggles to capture larger slices of state power and hence ensuring continuity in the autocratic system."

Politics, in turn, is transformed chiefly into a type of authoritarian capitalist "self-disciplining." Autocratic governments, like Tunisia before the
Arab Spring, used statistical and data collection procedures to "develop the
fiction of the regime as a model student" of market capitalism (Hibou et
al., 2011: 12). This manipulation of official statistics by rulers reinforced
the capitalist fantasy of authoritarian good governance both internationally
and domestically. Specifically, these non-democratic governments trumpeted
their "economic discipline" to outside actors while repressing internal dissent
arising from the less ideal reality of these reforms. Returning again to the case
of Tunisia:

> While the fundamentals of the economy might indeed have been good enough
> for global markets and international investors and trading partners, the economic
> miracle of Tunisia had a very dark side where under-employment, unemployment,
> difficult access to the labor market, income inequalities and wide regional gaps were
> the main features. (Cavatorta and Haugbølle, 2012: 184)

The new global order of "good governance" thus creates the conditions for
a pragmatic authoritarian state. Writing of the effectiveness of EU democracy
promotion in the Middle East following the Arab Spring, Van Hüllen (2012:
117) notes: "The degree of political liberalisation determines the fit between
the domestic political agenda and external demands for reforms. It reflects
different 'survival strategies' between political inclusion and exclusion and
is therefore a scope condition for rather than the result of cooperation and
change." Governments view "governance" as the simultaneous "stage managing" of political reform and concrete adoption of economic marketization as
simply an act of survival. Girod and Walters (2012), for instance, show how
the "stage managing" of democracy can be used to incentivize greater foreign
aid – one which allows elites to ignore and repress popular opinion.

Structurally, state power is expanded then for the ostensible purpose of
ensuring "good governance" and a stable sociopolitical environment for
marketization. "Unlike earlier governance programs identified with structural
adjustment," argue Jayasuriya and Hewison (2004: 272), "this new governance envisages a more active role for the state as a regulator of civil society
seeking to promote the disciplines of the market." This enhanced power of
governments is enshrined in policy initiatives, aimed at educating populations
as to how to better adapt and take advantage of neoliberalism. Tellingly, these
initiatives signify "a distinctly political project that uses the liberal language of
participation and empowerment as a strategy of 'antipolitics' that marginalizes
political contestation" (2004: 571).

A vital function of the state then is to preserve order for the sake of furthering neoliberalism within its borders. This includes the empowerment of gov-

ernments to deal with "regional and global security issues" that benefit more developed countries – such as the EU supporting Arab autocrats to coercively repress the increase of immigration from their countries into Europe (Hollis, 2012). All threats to such stability, whether political or economic, are solved through recourse to greater political authoritarianism. In 2001, the financial crisis in Turkey led to what Aybar and Lapavitsas (2001) refer to as "free market authoritarianism," a term that seemed progressively apt in the next decade-and-a-half of Turkish neoliberal politics. Such repression highlights a deeper authoritarian "self-disciplining" logic associated with the transition to neoliberalism. For instance, a structural adjustment program, "by creating critical problems of legitimacy for African regimes, erodes their political capacity to govern. This encourages regimes, some of which already exhibit dictatorial and authoritarian tendencies, to resort to even more repressive measures in carrying through adjustment reforms" (Ibhawoh, 1999: 158). Illuminated is the affective legitimization of political authoritarianism for protecting economic marketization and development. According to Brownlee (2007), "durable dictatorships" are the result of a powerful political party able to include elites and marginalize grassroots opposition. This extends to the political "policing" of neoliberalism generally. At stake is the moral and economic demand for governments to ensure their countries act "responsibly," leading to ever further repression and control by the "self-disciplining" capitalist state.

DISCIPLINING THE "IRRESPONSIBLE STATE"

The rise of the "self-disciplining" capitalist state highlights the political authoritarianism central to the spread of economic marketization. This authoritarian logic, however, is not confined to the state. It also extends to IFIs and foreign actors. Even more so, their enhanced power to intervene and shape national agendas is similarly connected to the need to ensure "good governance" in these contexts. Specifically, their legitimization stems from having to externally discipline governments that refuse to be "self-disciplined." They are the last line of defense against "economic irresponsibility," using their global influence to force countries into accepting greater marketization, whether or not it is in their interests.

The History from Less Government to Better Governments

Marketization is commonly portrayed as either apolitical or anti-political. The "freeing" of the economy is largely seen as distinct from issues of political power. Instead, it is presented as a policy aimed at simply improving competitiveness and productivity. Its politics, in this respect, is principally one of implementation rather than deliberation. When it is politicized, these policies are presented as challenging and reforming entrenched power structures. Traditionally, this has translated into a direct assault on governments, whereby the public sector is, if not the enemy, then at the very least a profound threat to economic growth and development. Nevertheless, the creation and maintenance of markets always involves the allocation and reallocation of sociopolitical power (Bardhan, 1989). The "history" of international efforts to encourage and impose capitalist reforms reflects the authoritarian politics vital to this project.

The end of the Second World War brought with it elite desires to establish some form of global economic governance. The creation of the World Bank and IMF symbolized the attempt to prevent future military conflict through fostering shared economic development and cooperation. Concretely, these organizations advised and formally monitored countries' economic strategies and policies, guiding and coercing them through loan conditions into accepting market-driven structural adjustment programs. Ostensibly, these measures were explicitly economically and not politically focused, outside of a general criticism of government regulation and central planning. Yet, "equally important to the financial and economic consequences of stabilization were the social and political effects. As was the case in Brazil and Argentina during the 1960s, the Bolivian stabilization plan aggravated social tensions, resulted in a more uneven income distribution, and precipitated authoritarianism in a fragile democracy" (Kofas, 1995: 214).

At the level of global governance, international organizations took a rather laissez-faire attitude to both economics and politics. Economically, the emphasis was on nurturing "free markets" as much as possible. Politically, whether or not a country was formally authoritarian or democratic was less important than the degree to which it successfully implemented marketization reforms. International power, as such, was one of disciplining countries to embrace capitalism ideologically and marketization in practice, regardless of the form of their national politics. As Lindenberg and Devarajan (1993: 180) write:

> Between 1973 and 1988, democratic developing countries grew more rapidly, restructured their exports more substantially, and improved their external balances more decisively than their nondemocratic counterparts ... They were as likely as authoritarian regimes to administer strong economic medicine – structural adjustment programs – and were no more likely to be overthrown as a result.

However, new perspectives in the 1980s stressing the crucial function of the state for economic development forced these international actors to become more political in their focus. The "East Asian Miracle" directly questioned dominant understandings of government interventions as impeding economic progress. These challenges to accepted knowledge gave birth to global power struggles for influence between emerging economic powers and these international organizations. Notably, Japan promoted "state-centric" development in part to increase its own influence in the East Asian region over and against the Western-backed World Bank and IMF (Wade, 1996). In response, the World Bank successfully sought to co-opt these discourses into the "dominant liberal narrative of progress and in facilitating the wider reinvention of liberalism in the post-1945 period" (Berger and Beeson, 1998: 487).

While it was able to lessen the impact of these alternative visions of development, the World Bank and the IMF were nonetheless forced to better account for the role of the state within its policies. It was no longer able to simply dismiss public regulation and intervention as unnecessary at best and counterproductive at worst. By contrast, it progressively concentrated on the construction of a "market-friendly" state. In 1989, the World Bank publicly declared the need for "not just less government but better government – government that concentrates its efforts less on direct interventions and more on enabling others to be productive" (World Bank, 1989: 5). This set the stage for these organizations to proscribe for countries not only their economics but also their politics.

Vital to this new state discourse was the positive ability of governments to establish stability, specifically for the purpose of enacting and protecting capitalist rights. "Not just less government but better government" became a prevailing mantra for restructuring society in line with neoliberal values. While "good governance" is a notoriously ambiguous term, international organizations exclusively associated it with successful market transformations. To this end, the World Bank distinguished six main dimensions of good governance (Kaufmann et al., 1999):

1. voice and accountability, which includes civil liberties and political stability;
2. government effectiveness, which includes the quality of policy-making and public service delivery;
3. the lack of regulatory burden;
4. the rule of law, which includes the protection of property rights;
5. independence of the judiciary; and
6. control of corruption.

Just as significantly, it opened the way for these international organizations to take up a more explicitly authoritarian role in introducing these governance "reforms." By defining what "good governance" is, it gave them greater legitimacy in policing nations who deviated from such internationally approved standards. In the name of ensuring "better governments," international actors gave themselves the enhanced right to discipline the "irresponsible state."

Disciplining the Irresponsible State

International actors such as the World Bank and IMF traditionally presented themselves as apolitical. Their concentration was fixated firmly on countries' economic policies and development. The growing emphasis placed on "good governance" starting in the 1990s shifted their attention to themes of sovereignty. Namely, what political institutions and practices are required to effectively introduce and maintain economic strategies for enhancing marketization? However, its concern with sovereignty extended beyond guiding contemporary governance and governments, often in quite authoritarian directions. It also became a regulatory, and if need be coercive, sovereign force for spreading and preserving capitalism.

Crucially, the rise of "good governance" ideals were borne out of a sovereign power struggle for hegemony between IFIs and other potential knowledge sources for guiding development. In particular, the failure of neoliberal reforms to provide for mass welfare, despite impressive gains in economic growth, challenged the authority of the global organizations most associated with these reforms. The previously discussed success of East Asian countries exemplified this broader questioning of these organizations' legitimacy. According to Kapur and Webb (2000: 18), "For the IFIs, the new mandate is a boost to their importance, but one fraught with peril ... The new mission arrived at a moment when growing doubts regarding the purpose and effectiveness of the IFIs seemed to threaten their funding, and even their continued existence." During the 1980s, the World Bank emerged as the dominant actor in "aid regimes" using its power as a means for "firmly tying ongoing project aid to policy reforms" (Gibbon, 1993: 40).

This re-establishing of their sovereignty also entailed an expansion of their political power. As Hyden (2008: 267) notes, "by channeling direct budget support to partner governments the DPs [development partners] are forced to think about governance as an integral part of their modus operandi." For creditor countries, it meant that their DPs could progressively dictate what they could and could not do politically. Democratic self-determination shifted increasingly upward, as IFIs maintained the right to force donor countries to adopt neoliberalism economically and politically. Institutionally, while the World Bank sustained its "non-political" mandate, practically it "accepted the role of secretariat for the consultative meetings of various donor consortia, which stipulated what political conditions would need to be met." In doing so, "this placed the Bank in the strategic position of being able to convey political conditions set by the respective consortia for the recipient countries concerned, and subsequently to monitor their implementation, without directly compromising its own non-political mandate" (Doornbos, 2003: 8).

Through this greater political authority, IFIs were able to make authoritarian demands on creditor nations. Capitalist "good governance" was transformed from a strong suggestion to a dictatorial condition for receiving loans and being included in the global marketplace. Therefore, "the Bank does not just lend money and produce ideas: it packages the ideas and the money together," combining lending with conditionality (Gilbert et al., 1999: F610). These new governance conditions not coincidentally coincided with "the substantial decrease of North–South redistribution by means of official development funding. It coincided as well with the international compliance of the left with the position that free markets are the primary tool for the development of what were once known as the Second and Third Worlds" (Demmers et al., 2004: 1).

Accordingly, the more neoliberalism was depoliticized economically, the greater the political authority – and authoritarianism – of IFIs was legitimized. This shift "impacted not only transitional states in East Central Europe but also more generally in the way democracy promotion was being conceptualized and instituted: liberal market democracy became the end point being worked toward" (Hobson and Kurki, 2012: 2). Politically, it reversed the traditional relation of "politics–policy" (whereby political decisions determined policies) into one of "policy–politics." This reflected what Leftwich (1994: 364) calls a "technicist fallacy" of neoliberals, where development issues can be solved by an "administrative or managerial fix." The power of IFIs to not only make but also enforce these "good governance" conditions played into this transformation of politics as primarily one of management and conformity to predetermined neoliberal mandates.

The extended sovereignty of these international organizations, furthermore, shifted the burden of control from the "self-disciplining" state to directly and indirectly "disciplining" global actors. As observed, this upward drift of governance from the national to the transnational was fundamentally non-democratic and focused on empowering client governments to protect their overriding capitalist agenda. Indeed, "the (World) Bank's understanding of good governance continues to reflect a concern over the effectiveness of the state rather than the equity of the economic system and the legitimacy of the power structure" (Santiso, 2001: 4). Wood (1997: 553) thus characterizes globalization as "another step in the geographical extension of economic rationality and its emancipation from political jurisdiction."

Additionally, IFIs could use their influence to bypass governments by shaping the subjectivities and social rationalities of populations. Discussing the case of Cambodia, Springer (2010: 931) observes:

> As disciplinary rationalities, strategies, technologies, and techniques coagulate under neoliberal subjectivation in contemporary Cambodian society through the proliferation of particular discursive formations like good governance, the structural

inequalities of capital are increasingly misrecognized. This constitutes symbolic violence, which is wielded precisely inasmuch as one does not perceive it as such.

The increasing role of international organizations for "governing" neoliberalism is justified by, and contributes to, a broader global capitalist fantasy of authoritarian "good governance." Part of the "common sense rhetoric of good governance" (Springer, 2010) is the right and requirement of IFIs to coercively police "irresponsible" states for their own good as well as the preservation of the international financial order itself.

The Disciplining Capitalist Fantasy of Authoritarian Good Governance

The hegemony of international actors for determining national policies along capitalist lines is underpinned by an affective discourse presenting them as the actors best able to protect the stability of the global market. It reflects a similar authoritarian dynamic as found in the "self-disciplining" state. More precisely, international and regional actors must use their growing power to safeguard the world economic order and, as such, the prosperity of all its citizens. Accordingly, akin to states, international sovereignty is enhanced and made more authoritarian in direct correlation to the global expansion of economic marketization.

This capitalist fantasy of political authoritarianism draws upon the unpredictability of the international marketplace. The World Bank and IMF must be strengthened exactly due to the fact that international capitalism is so volatile. Hale exemplifies this view in a 1998 article, maintaining it is "precisely this turbulence in global financial markets [that] demonstrates why the world needs the IMF: no other organization can serve as lender of last resort to buffer extreme economic turmoil during market stress" (Hale, 1998). In this regard, the inherent threat of an economic downturn creates the need for the strong hand of an international sovereign.

Critically, the explanation for this volatility has been shifted from an inherent characteristic of a capitalist system to the actions of "bad" nations and governments. The 2008 financial crisis, in particular, was blamed on international financial actors and bankers. However, this has now been redirected to individuals and states that refuse to be economically "responsible" – a demonized figure ranging from the evicted homeowner who should never have taken out a mortgage they couldn't afford to profligate governments who refuse to cut public spending. This general redirecting of accountability shaped, in turn, the relation between IFIs and those nations they lent money to. The problem was now framed as a failure of "good governance" and the requirement of international lenders to be more active in resolving these issues. Good governance initiatives like the Extractive Industries Transparency Initiative in Sub-Saharan

Africa, despite their ineffectiveness on the policy level, reinforced ideas that development failures can be exclusively attributed to corruption and fiscal "irresponsibility" (Hilson and Maconachie, 2008).

More generally, it is argued that donors should use a range of incentive-based and regulative measures to ensure these universally accepted governance values are adopted (Gisselquist, 2012: 1). This reflects earlier "strong" globalization perspectives that see the shift from nations to transnational capitalist actors (Strange, 1996). This view risks, as discussed throughout this analysis, minimizing the strengthening of the state for spreading neoliberalism nationally. Yet it does point to the uptake of this capitalist authoritarian logic by IFIs. Tellingly, early official statements on "good governance" highlight the enhanced authority and coercive power it grants international organizations. Quoting from a 1992 World Bank report at length on the subject:

> Governance, in general, has three distinct aspects: (a) the form of political regime (parliamentary or presidential, military or civilian, and authoritarian or democratic); (b) the processes by which authority is exercised in the management of a country's economic and social resources; and (c) the capacity of governments to design, formulate, and implement policies, and, in general, to discharge government functions. The first aspect clearly falls outside the Bank's mandate. The Bank's focus is, therefore, on the second and third aspects. (World Bank, 1992: 58)

This affective discourse of "good governance" legitimizes economic marketization and political authoritarianism both nationally and internationally. De Angelis (1997: 43) argues that corporate globalization ideologically "naturalises the market and the economy, to such an extent that it presents the latter as [an] autonomous force to which we must bow." Yet this inevitability of neoliberalism globally is sustained by an acceptance of, and investment in, the sovereignty of international organizations. The widespread call for economic regulation in the wake of the 2008 financial crisis was soon translated into the need for the "reregulation" of "irresponsible" national economies by IFIs and if needed by regional authorities. "Discourses of capitalist development exist as a sequential trajectory to be followed by all countries," according to Sheppard and Leitner (2010: 185); they "legitimate expertise located in the first world, and global capitalist governance, irrespective of serial policy failures."

The contemporary sovereignty of international actors results in a reconfigured and, in some ways, enhanced form of political authoritarianism globally. More precisely, globalization is characterized by the regulative rule of international and regional organizations. Those countries that fail to conform to their neoliberal edicts must be punished politically and economically through such means as higher interest rates, lower credit ratings, and currency speculation (Andrews, 1994; Goodman and Pauly, 1993; Mishra, 1999; Stewart, 1994). Foreign direct investment largely goes to countries with "good policies" such as economic liberalization as well as the protection of property rights (Alesina and Dollar, 2000). Consequently, Krastev (2010: 117) notes, "the politics of normalization replaced deliberation with imitation"; an imitation enforced by the increasingly strong hand of IFIs.

In terms of national politics, this can often mean supporting oligarchy in the name of preserving "good government" – such as in the case of Indonesia in the 1990s (Robison and Rosser, 2003). Similarly, in Africa the World Bank framed development failures on the lack of "good governance" and the continued "neopatrimonial" regimes of former colonial nations – rather than open democracy and debate they want states to conform to economic orthodoxy (Olukoshi, 1998). Fundamentally, the introduction of market reforms is "best explained," according to Robison and Rosser (2003: 173), "not as technical arrangements defined by self-evident rationality but as political products defined by power and interests." More precisely, it represents a deeper power struggle between various actors and coalitions for power, one that often can result in "oligarchic capitalism." The overriding prioritization by IFIs of "good governance" in this sense has "obscured corruption of the political process and the subsequent repression of popular demand for distributive justice" (Thomas, 1999: 551).

The current case of Syriza exemplifies this international global tyranny. The electoral rejection of austerity by the Greek population produced an authoritarian response from the so-called international "Troika" (composed of the IMF, Germany, and the European Central Bank). Economically, the question of debt was almost exclusively framed as one of the Greeks needing to pay their loans back and do so by becoming more "economically responsible" through implementing austerity policies. This was despite the fact that Germany and France profited greatly from the Greek debt (Schultz, 2012), as well as the broader reality that austerity increased rather than decreased debt due to its recessionary effects (Krugman, 2015). Nevertheless, politically it was seen as a direct challenge not only to the ideology of neoliberalism but also the sovereign authority of its international protectors. As such, Syriza needed to be coerced, or in some views punished, for their failure to exercise their democracy "responsibly."

This is the international capitalist fantasy of authoritarian "good governance" on full display. It is the disciplining of nations and populations in order to safeguard marketization. It does so as linked to an affective promise of future development achievable as long as states do not act "irresponsibly." Their failure to do so, to be "self-disciplined," necessitates strong and often coercive sovereign measures by the international community. The political tyranny of neoliberalism extends, thus, beyond its borders, producing in its wake an authoritarian global order.

CONCLUSION

This chapter explored the international dimension of political authoritarianism in the age of globalization. More precisely, how internationally imposed conditions and governance led to the respective "self-disciplining" and "disciplining" of nations and populations to implement neoliberal "reforms." Globalization and its international governance structures invest the state with new powers to police itself to fulfill its international financial obligations. It also empowers supranational actors with the same authoritarian task. It is not only economic marketization that is now global but also the political authoritarianism needed to implement and enforce it. The affective promise of "good governance" is a sovereign reality of national and transnational capitalist regulation and coercion.

8. Fighting for oppression: the battle between popular authoritarianism and repressive democracy

In November 2016, most of the United States (US) and the world woke up in shock to the reality that former billionaire developer and reality television host Donald J. Trump had been narrowly elected president. Throughout his campaign he had invoked rhetoric that had been criticized for being racist, sexist, jingoistic, and offensive. He claimed that he would "Make America Great Again" (MAGA), a slogan that became an acronym for far-Right populist movements that resonated globally. Over the next four years while in office, the Trump administration weathered repeated scandals, charges of overt corruption, and actions bordering on treason. Yet, even after losing his re-election bid and spurring an attempted coup on the Washington capital, for many Trump remains an icon of resistance and national strength. Importantly, he represents the dangerous rise of "popular" authoritarian capitalism.

The last half decade has been witness to the growth of right-wing populism. This anti-establishment mass politics can be attributed to a range of growing "gaps" that encompass socioeconomic cleavages linked to geography (urban versus rural), age, education, and material security (see Laboure and Braunstein, 2017). This sense of disempowerment and social distance has fostered a growing political psychology rooted in a profound mistrust of authorities and others (Jay et al., 2019). Demagogues such as Trump have risen to power to fill this gap and help fuel it to their own political advantage, strongmen who combine racist and extreme nationalist discourses with a promise to take on "elites" in the name of the "people." As the noted discourse theorist Ruth Wodak (2019: 21) argues:

> Despite various context-dependent, socio-political and historical differences, the ideologies (and the accompanying discursive and material practices) share important ideological features, including the dichotomous view of society (a merger of anti-elitism with a nativist nationalistic anti-pluralism). Accordingly, protecting the fatherland (or heartland/homeland) implies belief in a common narrative of the past, where "we" were either heroes or victims of evil. Moreover, conspiracies are a salient part of the discursive construction of fear which frequently draws on traditional anti-Semitic and anti-elitist tropes. The discursive strategies of provocation,

calculated ambivalence, de-tabooization and scandalization have paved the way for a "post-truth politics," indeed for a "post-shame politics."

This movement is directly linked to groups who have felt "left behind" by corporate globalization and threatened by an increasingly multilateral and multicultural international order (Miller, 2019). While anti-elitist in sentiment, these movements remain fundamentally committed to capitalism ideologically and in practice. Their enemies include "socialists," "liberals," and "progressives" who threaten not only the "free market" but also the rights and privileges of "real citizens" (Kinnvall and Svensson, 2022; Leser and Spissinger, 2020).

The danger of this populist resurgence has led to widespread fears for the very future of democracy. These movements (even when democratically elected) embrace ideas of demagogues who are willing to use violence and repression to achieve their "popular" aims. It is not a coincidence that one of the main antagonists of MAGA supporters in the US was "Antifa," who were literally "anti-fascists." In this respect, new groups have emerged such as the Proud Boys that regularly flaunt their fascist and authoritarian ideologies (Stern, 2019).

This trend is mirrored in right-wing populist regimes and movements around the world from Brazil to the Philippines. It reflects what the political theorist Black Stewart (2020: 1213) calls a new "far right civilizationism" that "represents an alternative vision for capitalist world order" which "symbolizes a coherent and realizable break from an elite 'globalist' agenda which they view as dominant within the policymaking circles of advanced transatlantic liberal capitalist states." There have been, understandably, a wide range of attempts to historically compare this populism to right-wing authoritarian movements of the past. The most obvious and common was the original fascist parties of the 1920s and 1930s who rejected liberal democracy as ineffective for addressing the problems of the Great Depression (see Hermansson et al., 2020).

These comparisons are certainly not without merit. And indeed, they do point to how rampant inequality linked to unmitigated capitalism can create the conditions for virulent racism and political repression. In particular, they show the ways that the failures of liberalism to distinguish itself from the exploitation and inequality of neoliberalism philosophically and in practice has rendered it ill equipped for defending basic rights and liberties against this resurgent fascism (see Peters, 2020). However, these legitimate fears tend to construct a political narrative that ignores the contemporary discourses that these populist ideas and movements have drawn upon and helped weaponize to their own advantage. According to the sociologist William I. Robinson (2019: 155), "The former involved the fusion of reactionary political power with national capital, whereas the latter involves the fusion of transnational capital with reactionary and repressive political power – an expression of the dictatorship of transnational capital."

Specifically, it has evolved from fantasies of state-led market progress centered on "protecting" capitalism and people in a competitive global marketplace into a jingoistic and explicitly racialized authoritarian politics centered on "preserving" the rights and privileges of the "people" against global and establishment elites. It is an update, in this respect, from the "capitalist despot" who can best ensure that a nation can survive and win in a cut-throat hyper-capitalist world. Here, though, it is a populist demagogue who is fighting on behalf of "real" deserving people who feel angered by ineffective elites and internal "lesser" populations threatening their way of life. It is a new popular version of "authoritarian capitalism" as a response to corporate globalization, one that both challenges its fundamental democratic institutions and ironically reinforces its ideological commitment to the free market.

THE RISE OF ETHNO-CAPITALISM

The last decade has witnessed a supposed renewal of nationalism. Values of patriotism or the dominance of nation-states have been relative mainstays even in this age of rapid economic globalization. However, within most mainstream politics they were balanced against the need and inevitability of an international market and the realities of multinational corporations. Both far-Right and, to an extent, left-wing populists have turned against global elites and reasserted the importance of a nation-based politics.

The critique of globalization by those who claim to represent "those left behind" by its economic progress has created the conditions for what can be termed nationalist capitalism. The emphasis is on recalibrating transnational markets so that they better serve the needs of national populations. "Two trends have emerged as a consequence of the expansion of the neoliberal project of economic plunder and political repression," notes Berch Berberoglu (2020: 4) in the introduction to his influential recent book *The Global Rise of Authoritarianism in the 21st Century*:

> The first has always benefited the transnational corporations ... the second has emerged in response to the crisis and impact of neoliberalism and capitalist globalization on broad segments of the population across the world in the form of a populist reaction led by psuedo-nationalist forces that have mobilised the people under the banner of ultra-nationalism and xenophobia.

This political turn is not reserved wholly for the right, however. In Brazil, for instance, the election of the far-Right leader Bolsonaro was directly related to the "neopopulist" turn of the Partido dos Trabalhadores (Worker's Party) which preceded him and advocated for a progressive nationalism against global capital (see de Souza, 2020).

It is important to note, further, that while in many key ways it is substantially different than the "establishment" politics which preceded it, twenty-first-century populism continues to draw heavily from its underlying discourses and desires. Critically, both remain fixated on ensuring that nations do all they can to enhance their competitive advantage in a hyper-contentious world marketplace.

Specifically, policies of fiscal austerity:

> contributed to citizens' sense of scarcity of public goods and services, including in the areas of social housing, healthcare, and education. Nationalist political entrepreneurs found in this sense of scarcity an opportunity to scapegoat groups they define as falling outside the national community, simultaneously redirecting blame away from the project of austerity itself. (Crowley, 2020: 134)

This type of continuity between previous mainstream political discourses and the ethno-nationalism of the contemporary far-Right is witnessed in social democracies such as Sweden, whose previous Center-Left leadership still relied upon discourses of national exceptionalism and an "essentialized" notion of the nation that transcended cultural sharedness or historical evolution (Elgenius and Rydgren, 2019).

For those on the Right, this means being able to elect not just demagogic leaders but executive-styled strongmen who can make the "best deals" for the country on behalf of the nation as a whole (see Mendes, 2016). This followed in a long tradition in which the failures of the status quo and the perceived inadequacies of existing democracies give rise to tyrannical leaders who paradoxically are charged with restoring freedoms and liberties (see Signer, 2009). Likewise, but differently, for those on the Left it entails rebuilding national infrastructure and human capabilities through public investment in progressive priorities such as education and renewable energy (Birch, 2020; Dorrien, 2019). While presenting starkly different agendas, each of these movements is committed to a form of national renewal that is linked to enhancing its international competitiveness.

The heightened nationalism of these populist discourses represented, further, a more inward-oriented authoritarian capitalist politics. The railing against elites was complemented by a need to above all protect the nation against external and internal threats. These political currents were, of course, not fundamentally new and in many ways echoed the prevailing "War on Terror" that was so dominant at the beginning of the twenty-first century (Foot, 2008; Hetherington and Suhay, 2011). However, in its evolved populist form the question was who was most responsible for national decay and what were their global connections?

Progressives offered a legitimate critique of the oligarchy, one that presciently identified how economic and political elites were perpetuating domestic inequality as part of an international elite network of exploitation and influence. It was a progressive mixture of economic oligarchy and political ochlocracy or mob rule (Glassman, 2021).

By contrast, the Right placed its attention on "establishment" figures and internal "woke" enemies, all of whom were committed to destroying conventional values for the benefit of the perceived undeserving. These discourses could echo and co-opt quite traditionally left-wing ideas and ambitions. Marine Le Pen in France embraced a far-Right version of green politics "by emphasising environmental threats against the French nation, such as climate change, pollution, energy policies and resource depletion, Marine Le Pen illustrated her vision for a 'patriotic ecology' that would be based on the protection of public health and security as well as French territory, heritage and national identity" (Boukala and Tountasaki, 2019: 72).

At the heart of both of these, though in markedly opposed ways, was a commitment to politically representing and serving the interests of the "real" population. It was rooted in "populist messages that (a) stress the centrality of 'ordinary' people, (b) shift blame to the 'corrupt' elites, or (c) combine people centrality and antielitist cues on 3 dimensions of populist attitudes: anti-elitism, homogeneous people, and popular sovereignty" (Hameleers et al., 2021: 491). The emphasis on rooting out the corrupting power of elites was conjoined with a belief that there existed a "deserving" set of people who were being exploited and "left behind" by globalization. This idea was radically captured in the Occupy-inspired slogans of fighting the "1%" for the benefit of the "99%." Importantly, this fixation on the 99 percent implied a mass politics centered on the struggle of the aggrieved majority (see Fuchs, 2014; Yardley, 2011).

The implicit (and at times explicit) driving assumptions of these movements was that there was an exemplary population that needed to be protected. While global inequality has given rise to resurgent progressive movements, it has also fueled ethno-nationalist political identities. The Right framed issues of oligarchy in terms of "real" people inferring and increasingly asserting that this means those of the right type of ethnicity. To this extent, there is an idea that "America should be for Americans" and "Russia for Russians," etc. (Lippard, 2011; Triandafyllidou, 2020).

The imperative to protect first the nation and then the "people" in a hyper-competitive global marketplace is transforming into an ethno-centric worldview of preserving the rights and privileges of essentialized cultures in a fast-changing and threatening international order (Abidde and Matambo,

2021; Karim, 2012). Emerging is a form of ethno-nationalist capitalism. The nation-state is historically linked to socially constructed political communities based on imagined bonds of a shared culture and past. These national identifications have at times, to varying degrees of intensity, lent themselves to strong forms of ethnic and racially based politics. Fascism, of course, drew heavily on the idea of a racially pure nation linking national strength and progress to ideas of racial superiority and unity. In the present age, the need for a demagogue leader to protect "deserving" citizens from global elites becomes tied up with a resurgence in explicit and implicit racism. Here, the "people" that need to be defended are linked to a culturally homogenous vision of the national population often directly and indirectly associated with a dominant (and perceived to be majoritarian) ethnicity.

This type of ethno-capitalism provides new groundings for legitimizing the ideologies and techniques of authoritarian capitalism. At a cultural level, the society needs to be policed to root out subversive ideas that would jeopardize the strength of the dominant national culture. It also means that populist leaders can, when necessary, use a wider variety of repressive power to officially address these threats. In this respect, discourses of "securitization" are now deployed for protecting the "real" people against internal enemies and dangerous outside forces.

PROTECTING THE GLOBAL NATIVE

In one of modern history's most interesting ironies, the inevitable march of globalization did not produce global political subjects. Certainly, culturally there has been a sense of internationalization as the world increasingly shares entertainment and, to a certain extent, social media interactions (see Featherstone, 2020; Hancock, 2019). However, the integration of the world economy has generated a pronounced political backlash in which an attachment to nationalism and essentialist ethnic identities once more has become predominant. As far back as the early 1990s, commentators such as renowned sociologist Kevin Robins (1991: 21) argued that the loss of empire and multilateralism associated with globalization created a sense of "protective illusion" in which "traditional and spiritual values [are] again intended to restore the sense of British community and confidence that has collapsed in these modern or maybe postmodern times." Updated to the present, this need to "protect" and "preserve" the past was reflected in a sense of "globalization backlash" (Crouch, 2018; Walter, 2021). Yet just as paradoxically, this move toward nativism has itself become global. The world is now divided into national tribes, all of whom must to varying degrees seek to co-exist and defend their right to survive and thrive.

It may sound strange but the root of this ethno-nationalism can be traced in no small part to traditions of anti-colonial resistance. Globalization was progressively viewed as an external and colonizing force. This view was witnessed in the shifting attitudes of residents in Western European countries most impacted by globalization who were "systematically less supportive of democracy and liberal values, more in favor of unconstrained strong leaders, and particularly concerned with immigration, especially with the cultural threat posed by it" (Colantone and Stanig, 2018: 1). Populations shared a sense of unease and vulnerability as corporations appeared to control national politics and shape it to their profitable advantage. The infamous example of the Koch brothers and the power of Koch industries in the US reflected how deeply out of control and alienating capital and capitalist felt to people (Leonard, 2020). At the same time, it played into an emergent executive "language of leadership" (Learmonth and Morrell, 2019) where bosses and chief executive officers were progressively celebrated and seen as strong visionary figures who could save both organizations and countries (see Bloom and Rhodes, 2018).

Already at the very onset of the Cold War there were ominous warnings of a "new world order." What was once considered to be mere conspiracy theory now became a legitimate critique of a world that served the interest of economic oligarchs and their supportive (often seemingly hand-picked) political establishment. It had given rise to soon to be "AI superpowers" like China, the US, and technology oligarchs from Silicon Valley (Lee, 2018). Emerging in its wake was a "new world order" that at once promoted and showed the "limits" of democracy in line with existing global power relations and the ideological commitment to the free market (see Ake, 2019; Dupuy, 2019). What began to arise internationally was a populist backlash that appropriated and, in many ways genuinely reflected, a sense of anti-colonial resistance. The specter and realities of globalization were framed as a form of external exploitation by global elites. The refrain that it had "left behind" a growing percentage of the population strengthened the notion that it was being perpetuated by a distant cabal of economic technocrats and establishment politicians who had little care for the people they ultimately profited from (Mutz, 2018; Wuthnow, 2019).

The supposed decline of national power further reinforced a spreading belief that people had lost their ability to democratically determine their own destinies, that they were mere subjects to the will of an inevitable globalization (Barak, 2018; Lang, 2021). This anti-colonial backlash morphed into a contemporary identity of global nativism. Traditionally, this term refers to a type of ultra-nationalism based on a presumed shared ethnic identity against "foreign" others (Betz, 2017; Lippard, 2011). However, in the contemporary era it took on additional and ultimately critically troubling dimensions. Notably, it came to symbolize how globalization was "stealing the culture" of "real" citizens, conjuring up images of themselves as indigenous populations whose way of life was suddenly under existential threat (Kešić and Duyvendak, 2019; Leroux, 2019).

The literal and now infamous appropriation of Native American dress by one of the leaders of the assault on the Capitol was no coincidence. Rather, it was bringing to the surface a deep-seated connection with past populations whose life and beliefs were placed under threat and even exterminated by outside forces of "modernization" (Fukuyama, 2018). According to Roger Bromley (2013: 21), here the foreign other:

> The immigrant is mapped against an already existing, fixed, and (so the story goes) socially cohesive national culture ... the "People" is not just an arithmetic total of individuals but the qualitative composition of humans with the same biological and cultural heritage. At stake then is a struggle for recognition taking place which is deep, complex and, partly at the level of the unconscious. Claims of Britishness, Frenchness, or Danishness (the three countries where Right parties led the EU elections in 2014) form the basis on which refugee and migrant issues are used as organising principles for the social critique of other political issues.

Significantly, this new "native" was not confined by national borders. Rather, it was progressively international in scope. Far from the vision of early globalists of a shared international culture and identity, the new zeitgeist was that the world was made up of competing ethno-nationalist tribes (see Bloom, 2017; Taylor, 2019).

This discourse harkened back to earlier authoritarian capitalist ideas of nations vying for capitalist advantage in a competitive global market. What was now emerging, though, was that it was ethnic-based tribes at modern economic and, at times, military war with one another for their very survival. The state had taken on an important role for preserving and perpetuating this modern-day tribalism. Its responsibility was protecting "native" populations from internal subversive threats and an external cabal of global elites. Repeatedly in countries across the world there was a desire for a strong government or leader who could properly protect the "tribe" from global danger. Further, they were popularly tasked with preserving these perceived native cultures and traditional "ways of life" that seemed to be rapidly dissipating due to corporate globalization.

This responsibility of the state has translated into a renewed popular remit to protect its population against impure threats to its way of life and future prosperity. Right-wing populism has been criticized for promoting mob violence, from machismo-type threats by demagogues to actual conspiracy-fueled coup attempts. Less heralded but every bit, and indeed if not more, dangerous is the legitimacy it gives to official forms and practices of internal repression. This can take the form of attempting to restrict voting rights to justified state oppression against foreign "undesirables" or political subversives.

THE RESPECTABLE REACTION

The obvious and understandable response to this popular authoritarianism is to reassert the sacredness of democracy. Notably, to reinforce the importance of existing democratic institutions and norms against the rising tide of twenty-first-century fascism. Quoting one of the leading experts on historical and contemporary fascism, Carl Boggs (2018: xi):

> If talk of a potential American fascism seems rather outlandish, as it has in mainstream political cultures, it actually rests on careful analysis of domestic and global at work in the society since perhaps World War II, if not earlier. Many such tendencies – the elevated role of Wall Street, rising workplace repression, militarization of society, increasing civic violence, surveillance order, widening gulf between rich and poor, growth of reactionary populism, and spread of a propagandistic media culture – are now taken for granted by the mass population.

Yet underpinning this morally righteous rhetoric is a quite conservative and ironically repressive politics (Ross, 2019), one that seeks to bolster the very status quo that gave birth and continues to drive this resurgent authoritarianism. The popularity of Trump and other far-Right populists is as mentioned above premised on the need to protect the supposed imperiled native citizen. The flip side of this discourse is the respondent need to secure established democratic and liberal norms and processes. To some, such as the renowned political scientist Kurt Weyland (2021: 5), this is attributable to the strong institutions and constitutional foundations of mature democracies like the US:

> which withstood the unusual turbulence of 2020–2021, [and] corroborated my emphasis on the longstanding solidity of US institutions as reliable safeguards against populist suffocation. This fundamental institutional strength is anchored in an age-old, rarely amended constitution, which has survived all socioeconomic, demographic, ethno-racial, and cultural transformation ... This institutional strength played a crucial role in foiling Trump's typically populist attempts at self-perpetuation. Trump's sustained pressures put judicial, administrative, and political institutions to a distressingly serious test – yet, overall, they passed.

Nevertheless, scholars including Matthew David Ordoñez and Anthony Lawrence Borja (2018: 139) take a more structural view of this issue, contending:

> populism's challenge against the supposed global hegemony of liberal democracy can be traced back to the internal contradiction between liberal and populist principles underlying all modern democracies. The nature of this conflict depends upon liberalism's adaptation to endemic social conditions. The inherent fragility of existing institutions and constant calls for popular sovereignty account for the inevitable conflict between these two opposing ideas.

Drawing on the example of the Philippines under the populist leadership of the far-Right demagogue Rodrigo Duterte, they note convincingly that his appeal and overall discourse has its roots paradoxically in the precise liberalism which he was supposedly politically challenging. It is worth quoting them again at length on this point:

> First, the intolerance underlying Duterte's populism can be understood as an inevitable reaction to the universalism of liberal civic identity. The capacity to excuse, if not support Duterte's "War on Drugs," and his rhetoric of violence against the supposed enemies of the people is another result of the irresolvable paradox between inclusion and exclusion. The question of who to include is only valid if exclusion is recognized as a necessity. Moreover, this question is also subject to endemic normative frameworks that can range from simple nationalism to religio moral elitism. Second, the aforementioned intolerance can also be analyzed as a reaction to already-existing social stratifications ranging from class to political morality. (Ordoñez and Borja, 2018: 148)

What emerges then is a politics of liberal reaction, where the impulse for even basic reforms is superseded by the need to consolidate past democratic gains. This politics of democratic protectionism is also rooted in staving off both internal and external threats. Domestically, it is found in what then presidential candidate Hillary Clinton referred to as "deplorables" (see Gibson et al., 2020; Gökarıksel, 2020). Internationally, the very preservation of freedom and popular rule is endangered by foreign misinformation by evil autocrats, notably those like Putin in Russia or when it is convenient the explicitly authoritarian Chinese government (Noland, 2020; van Krieken, 2019). While the danger of these groups should not be underestimated, it also must be situated as part of a broader political fantasy. It is an idea of progress that revolves above all else around the elimination of an other. The threat to democracy is suddenly personalized, distracting from its deeper structural causes. All that is needed is to eliminate Putin or stop ignorant racists and suddenly all will be right in the world (Busby and Monten, 2018; Diesen, 2022).

This reflects an updated fantasy of reactionary democracy explored in more depth in Chapter 5 where repression was justified in the name of protecting democracies under threat. The right to oppressive progressive groups and those deemed to be dangerous to the current capitalist order was justified in the name of securing "democratization." Similarly, left-wing resistance movements were suddenly denigrated as at best "idealist" and at worst a direct populist threat to the very survival of democracy (Léger, 2022; Royer, 2022). These types of repressive fantasies relied on two interconnected logics, both of which explicitly worked against the expansion of democracy beyond the very limited limits of conventional liberalism. The first was highlighted above and rooted in a repressive politics where the symptoms of democratic decline, autocracy, racism, and ethno-nationalism are conveniently confused with its causes in economic inequality, social disempowerment, and political alienation all resulting from decades of capitalist intensification (Bonanno, 2020). Such a politics was part of a broader strategy of "authoritarian neoliberalism," whose

> practices include the repeated invocations of "the market" or "economic necessity" to justify a wide range of restructurings across various societal sites (e.g. states, households, workplaces, urban spaces), the growing tendency to prioritize constitutional and legal mechanisms rather than democratic debate and participation, the centralization of state powers by the executive branch at the expense of popular participation and other nodes of governance, the mobilization of state apparatuses for the repression of oppositional social forces at a range of scales, and the heightened pressures and responsibilities shifted onto households by repeated bouts of crisis and the restructuring of the state's redistributive mechanisms. (Bruff and Tansel, 2019: 233)

Just as significant was the conflation of the clear necessity to preserve democratic establishments with the viability and requirement to protect the established status quo. It was couched in the rhetoric of a "return to normalcy," in which the time before the far-Right disruptions was considered an almost golden age of political tranquility and democratic peace. Reflected is what Raoul Martinez (2019: 20) has called the "Centrist Delusion" in which "the centre ground is a social construction, commanding most loyalty from those whose privilege protects them from the ravages of the system they support." These sentiments were updated from the types of fantasies mobilized by elites to save the financial order after the great economic crash of 2008 (see Bloom, 2016). The supposed need to above all promote economic recovery was now being transferred and politically weaponized for the achievement of "democratic recovery." The overarching desire was a return to an illusionary era of normalcy and assured democratic progress. Hidden behind this "respectable" discourse was a program of official repression and democratic repression at home and abroad.

DEMOCRATIC AUTHORITARIANISM

The conservative desire to return to some type of democratic normalcy is deeply appealing and understandable as it evokes idyllic visions of a society that is at once tolerant and reformable. It is also based on a fundamental myth that these democratic norms were critically opposed to authoritarianism in practice. Contemporary politics is framed, in this respect, as an existential "either/or choice" between civilized liberal democracy and barbaric far-Right populist tyranny (see Derber and Magrass, 2018). It is, of course, by now a well-worn litany about the repressive aspects of even legitimate democratic regimes. However, they are worth repeating especially to highlight how fundamental authoritarian techniques have been to sustaining modern democracies. The US is a prime example of this profound political irony. Its contemporary history of race-based mass incarceration has been credibly and famously referred to as a "gulag" by the brilliant and insightful scholar Ruth Wilson Gilmore (2007).

This domestic repression is matched by the extensive history of Western democratic governments promoting explicitly authoritarian regimes abroad for their own political interest and economic profit. These illiberal and authoritarian underpinnings have not disappeared. The desire of a return to democratic normality is in a sense an embrace of a supposedly more legitimate and less severe form of authoritarian capitalism. The critical criminologist Judah Schept (2013) has undertaken incredible studies, for instance, of a proposed "justice campus" in the city of Bloomington, Indiana that represented a form of "progressive punishment," combining incarceration with liberal values of socioeconomic rehabilitation. Analogously, Birhanu O. Dirbaba and Penny O'Donnell (2012: 283) introduce the concept of "manipulative liberalism" to explain how, for instance, in Ethiopia "journalists have found it difficult to take advantage of the professional opportunities available to them in a more open media system due to the government's manipulative use of media-related laws and a broad range of media strategies designed to maintain its political control of the news media and the news agenda." Here, the introduction of liberal freedom was linked to the registration of journalists and the adherence to "War on Terror"-type restrictions on what could be reported upon. For this reason, Michael Wilkinson (2021) has referred to the present age specifically in Europe as one of "authoritarian liberalism" in which executive power and a conservative adherence to a depoliticized market and liberal democratic values are reified and preserved at all costs.

These have been rebooted and even to a certain degree expanded. This is particularly witnessed in the increase in a wide range of hi-tech surveillance practices against everyday citizens and workers. The use of sophisticated data collection and cameras is deployed in a diverse array of social, political, and economic settings. It reflects what Shoshana Zuboff calls "surveillance capitalism" (2019), which

> unliterally claims human experience as free raw material for translation into behavioural data. Although some of these data are applied to product or service improvement, the rest are declared as a proprietary behavioural surplus, fed into advanced manufacturing processes known as "machine intelligence," and fabricated into prediction products that anticipate what you will do now, soon, and later ... Surveillance capitalists have grown immensely wealthy from these trading operations, for many companies are eager to lay bets on future behaviour ... the

competitive dynamics of these new markets drive surveillance capitalists to acquire ever more predictive sources of behavioural surplus: our voices, personalities, and emotions.

It is not a coincidence that data privacy has become one of, if not the most important, twenty-first-century human rights issues and points of struggle (Feldstein, 2019; Xu, 2021). These surveillance strategies create even within otherwise credible democracies quite authoritarian everyday cultures. Politically, activist groups have been spied on digitally and infiltrated. In this respect, according to Inez Miyamoto (2020: 49), "The use of surveillance technologies against citizens challenges the existing political culture of democratic states – the fundamental beliefs, values, and norms that have long defined them. In other words, surveillance technologies conflict with the agreement between democratic governments and their citizens for privacy and civil liberty protections." Arising is a democratic political culture that not only tolerates but relies upon the hi-tech surveillance, monitoring, and smart disciplining of its population (see Ermoshina et al., 2022; Greitens, 2020).

Economically, employees have had to accept daily surveillance of their work (see Balica, 2019; Blumenfeld et al., 2020; Manokha, 2020). This has been intensified to reflect the more precarious character of the present-day workforce and the growing need to monitor employees working from home (Axtell et al., 2019; Garden, 2018; Woodcock, 2020). Internationally, this supposedly respectable democratic authoritarianism is found in the persistence of imperial anti-democratic actions across the world. It is important to note that two of the most obvious and egregious examples perpetuated by the US in supporting the right-wing oligarchic coup against a democratically elected Centre-Left government in Honduras and the disastrous invasion of Libya were done by the Centrist Obama regime, directed by then Secretary of State Hillary Clinton, not the far-Right Demagogue Donald Trump.

These authoritarian strategies are also witnessed with regard to the arguably more pernicious rise of "philanthro-capitalism." On the surface, the generosity of billionaires is seemingly laudatory and the epitome of twenty-first-century notions of good citizenship. Philanthropists such as Bill and Melinda Gates and their Gates Foundation have been praised for their efforts to eradicate global diseases such as polio and malaria (Mediavilla and Garcia-Arias, 2019; Sklair and Glucksberg, 2021). Yet, digging deeper, these actions reflect a strategy and culture that depends upon and perpetuates quite inscriptive and non-democratic beliefs and practices (McGoey, 2021; Thompson, 2018). At the macro level, they tend to accept and, at points, even encourage regimes – elected or otherwise – that are willing to subvert when necessary human rights for the sake of effectively delivering foreign aid programs (McGoey et al., 2018). More broadly, they foster an ideology in which governments are perceived to be inherently unable to provide basic public services and, there-fore, need to be supplemented and ultimately supplanted by the private sector and charitable foundations. The underlying danger is that this draws power away from democratically accountable public institutions and toward private conglomerates who principally must answer to their shareholders (Bloom and Rhodes, 2018).

Revealed is the rise of a rebooted form of "democratic authoritarianism," specifically, the spread and legitimization of political, economic, and social repression in the name of preserving democracy. This discursive strategy has been deployed by a wide range of actors from governments to corporations to philanthropists for justifying enhanced surveillance and behavior control over populations. The crisis of democracy driving far-Right populism has ironically become an opportunity for expanding the geographic scope and repressive possibilities of authoritarian democracies.

THE AUTHORITARIAN CHOICE OF A NEW GENERATION

This chapter has explored how "authoritarian capitalism" has evolved into new and expansive forms of populist and democratic authoritarian regimes and cultures. While substantially different, they both seek to protect and preserve the hegemony of global capitalism. Each further claims to be based on a mass politics of defending freedom and rights, with the former done in the name of the "people" and the latter for the sake of "citizens." Moreover, both are rooted in a nationalist politics of renewal and recovery in which the state either in the manifestation of a popular demagogue or established institutions is invested with fresh power for monitoring people and preserving entrenched power relations internationally.

Of course, while these are fundamentally similar, their degrees of difference are important. Within democratic regimes, there is still greater potential for expanding economic democracy and holding publicly accountable the oppres-sive power of the state. The role of social movements for political and econom-ically reimagining the present order is absolutely crucial in this regard. It is a question of whether democracy and freedom can be renewed and revitalized or will be trapped within a politics of populism on the one hand and carceral surveillance-based liberal democracy on the other.

Present is the authoritarian choice of a new generation. It is between a far-Right ethno-capitalism and a Centrist democratic authoritarianism. The crisis of liberal democracy has revitalized the popular appeal of both of these repressive alternatives and, in turn, has granted new life to the increasingly authoritarian status quo. The choice of the present era has become not one between democracy and tyranny but rather which type of authoritarianism one politically prefers.

9. Conclusion: breaking free from authoritarian capitalism

In 1848, Marx and Engels famously declared "there is a spectre haunting Europe – the spectre of communism." Today, if there is a specter it appears to be fascism. It seems to shadow contemporary politics, an ominous future that harkens back to a past of mass oppression, totalitarianism, and even social extermination. In the face of these fears is a parallel danger of genuine cynicism, a belief by those who traditionally embrace progressive values of inclusion and even equality that the possibility of truly transforming the world for the better is pure idealism. Rather, all that can be achieved is preserving previously won gains and an admittedly disappointing and even repressive democratic status quo.

The overriding aim of this book is to illuminate the positive relationship between political authoritarianism and economic marketization. Contemporary processes of globalization are conventionally trumpeted as a harbinger of universal democracy. Yet the reality is one of growing market despotism and illiberalism, one characterized by dictators for whom progress means marketization and their own continued monopoly on power, liberal democracies with militarized police forces and ruled by elected plutocracies, and international financial institutions that reserve the right to politically discipline economically "irresponsible" nations.

Key in this respect is how this more authoritarian mode of economic development sheds light on the deeper evolution of capitalism connected to globalization. Importantly, the current era is commonly depicted as a time when the free market is expanding both inwards and outwards. Internally, it is reshaping society, economics, and politics to reflect financial values of profitability and privatization. Externally, the reach of capitalism is extending to every corner of the globe.

Yet perhaps less heralded is another specter: the proclaimed faith that another world is indeed possible and that this is not the end of democratic history after all! This revolutionary promise is witnessed in the emergence of direct resistance to authoritarian capitalism in a wide variety of ways. Across the globe have arisen new movements for fundamental change, rejecting both modern-day fascism and an oligarchic liberal democracy.

These can be further witnessed in the growth of international movements against racially based police brutality and, more generally, state violence. Black Lives Matter began as an uprising against an increasingly militarized police force (especially in the United States (US)) and the stark realities of mass incarceration linked to systemic racism. It has evolved into a fresh vision of a society without police signaling the abolishment of daily exploitative cultures of discipline and punishment.

What this reflects is a different and freer future. It transcends the limits of repressive democracies and explicitly seeks to overcome the threat of far-Right populism. Required is a clear realization that capitalism inevitably inexorably leads to authoritarian realities and destinies. As capitalism spreads to every corner of the globe, in search of new markets and populations to discover, conquer, and extract profit from, so too will its oppressive methods for ensuring its interests are protected and served. Perhaps the biggest threat to authoritarian capitalism is that discourses and policies have come to dominate the entirety of what is considered politically possible, providing us only with a despairing choice between fascism and democratic repression.

THE AUTHORITARIAN EVOLUTION OF GLOBAL CAPITALISM

It is perhaps tempting to critically ascribe this authoritarianism to traditional forms of capitalist repression and colonial maneuverings. Undoubtedly, the present bears the weight of this past. The market has always been regulatory – dictating to an extent available politics and institutions. Profit has similarly always been imperial – rapacious, to quote Marx, in its spread and dependent on the exploitation of the weak by the strong. The future of the current world thus begins in its history. Yet while this era echoes what came before, it is not identical. It is a reflection, yes, but also an evolution. The question at the heart of this analysis is how present-day discourses and processes of globalization reinforce political authoritarianism.

There is not surprisingly a growing set of literature on precisely this concern. The seemingly ceaseless and unstoppable international expansion of capitalism has given rise to novel perspectives for understanding the politics and governance of this new world. These range from efforts to shift the focus from national governments to transnational governance to neoliberalism's need to coercively reshape the globe in its image.

Theories of hegemony, in particular, go a long way in shedding light on this relation. The global expansion of capitalism is supported by a range of ideological justifications. To this effect "any new historical bloc must have not only power in civil society and economy, it also needs persuasive ideas and arguments ... which build on and catalyse its political networks and organizations"

(Gill and Law, 1989: 94). The politics of hegemony involves the incorporation, co-option, and repackaging of past ideas to legitimate present-day material interests, power relations, and ideologies. As Gramsci (1971: 168) observes:

> An appropriate political initiative is always necessary to liberate the economic thrust from the dead weight of traditional policies (and ideas) – i.e. to change the political direction of certain forces which have to be absorbed if a new homogenous political-economic historic bloc, without internal contradictions, is to be success-fully formed.

There is a definite story of power to tell at this point. Economic and political elites must continually promote marketization as both necessary and desirable. In this respect: "ideas in the form of intersubjective meanings are accepted as part of the global political economy itself. This is significant because ideas, developed, for example, by key organic intellectuals, can play a crucial role in forging a hegemonic project in times of structural crisis" (Bieler and Morton, 2003: 480).

The market does not only sell things. It must also be sold and resold within a dynamic and diverse geopolitical marketplace. Crucial to this international selling of enhanced capitalism are clear and inspiring stories of market progress.

Modernization theory stands as one such narrative. The belief that markets lead to democracy was a powerful global myth. It elegantly connected so-called economic freedom with political freedom. It was a tale of prosperity and liberalism that could be applied and embraced all countries and popula-tions. It bridged cultural differences into a shared pursuit of upward economic and political development, providing the modern world with a discourse to look past bloody histories of colonialism for a present of common purpose and toward a future of universal progress.

The fall of the Soviet Union was supposed to herald an "end of history" in just such a direction. However, a strange thing happened on the way to moder-nity. Markets were not paving a road to genuine democracies. Instead, history appeared to be arriving at a destination of authoritarianism; one that combined capitalism with illiberalism, marketization with oppression, economic reforms with growing political despotism. It is a historical development that "has con-founded the expectation that authoritarianism was merely a transitional phase before democracy, proving under certain conditions autocracies can last ... As democracy flourished in unexpected territories, political scientists forecast the downfall of many remaining autocracies ... The remainder is a tale of authori-tarianism in the age of democratization" (Brownlee, 2007: 2).

The contradiction between triumphant expectation and troubling reality represents a profound crisis for contemporary capitalism and globalization.

If democracy, and indeed economic prosperity, were not on the horizon, was this not simply domination and imperialism updated for the new millennium? This ideological tension was exacerbated, as it usually is, by a structural crisis of capitalism. The 2008 financial crash put in stark relief these issues, raising questions over the desirability of markets and financial capitalism. Even the traditionally conservative *Wall Street Journal* admitted in late 2009 that the "crisis compels economists to reach for a new paradigm" (Whitehouse, 2009).

Required was a new story of capitalism. A tale that could reinforce today's marketization as a harbinger of a better tomorrow for everyone, in every nation. As French President Nicolas Sarkozy declared (Phillips, 2009: 1): "either we re-found capitalism or we destroy it." This was a theme reinforced in the January 2009 Paris summit, tellingly entitled "New World, New Capitalism." That same year, newly inaugurated US President Barack Obama proclaimed at the G20 London Summit that world leaders had "made enormous strides in committing ourselves to comprehensive reform of a failed regulatory system," enabling them to "put an end to the bubble-and-bust economy that has stood in the way of sustained growth and enabled abusive risk-taking that endangers our prosperity" (Obama, 2009). This cycle of instability and recovery echoes scholarly perspectives linking the success of capitalism to its ability politically to strengthen itself in the face of crisis. At stake is the reconfiguration of alliances and beliefs to reflect a changing and often unpredictable sociopolitical climate.

The fantasy of authoritarian capitalism reveals these tensions in full. It highlights efforts to infuse marketization with fresh legitimacy. It refocuses attention on the capacity of governments and international institutions to properly guide markets for the global betterment of society as a whole. More precisely, it reaffirms the ideological correctness of capitalism for directing development. Yet it now retells this narrative of coming prosperity as involving, indeed needing, a strong national and supranational sovereign to correctly manage this process, protecting this blueprint for progress from internal and external modern-day threats.

Significantly, it transforms narratives of development from a story of inevitability to a contemporary morality tale. Citizens and governments, across contexts all around the world, must be "fiscally responsible." It is their moral obligation to pay their debts, resist today's temptation for spending in order to save for the future. Obviously, the sin of going against this market orthodoxy can be quite alluring. Populations and states can so easily fall prey to "irresponsible" investments in social welfare or expanding public ownership and services. That is why a strong sovereign is needed to ensure that citizens and government do not go astray from their financial obligations; a twenty-first-century "big brother," always watching just in case individually or collectively we fail to perform our moral duties as market subjects.

THE GLOBAL "AUTHORITIZATION" OF CAPITALISM

The "free market" is rapidly becoming a universal principle for organizing global socioeconomic relations. It is extending into all areas of cultural and economic life. It is also spreading outward to every part of the globe. Present is the almost total reconfiguration of society to reflect capitalist values. This comprehensive transformation points to the multifaceted and complex nature of this modern "capitalist societalization" (Jessop, 1990: 7). Marketization is joining with and redirecting a range of other social forces – from human rights, to public services, to gender equality – with the purpose of deepening its cultural and economic influence. Whereas traditional capitalist features such as class remain important, they by no means exhaust the ways it is shaping contemporary sociopolitical relations. Vital in this respect to the strengthening and survival of global marketization is the increasing "authoritarianization" of politics and society.

Authoritarianism in the present age is specifically aimed at coercively molding society into this capitalist image. The advancement of the "free market" promotes the liberty of the individual and the power of private enterprise. Yet it still requires protection, as it must be defended from those who question its values, practices, and interests. A crucial tension, then, is how to combine forms of decentered self-governance with broader types of disciplining sovereign control. This issue was apparent as early as 1990 at the very dawn of the "end of history." In the words of one commentator: "The challenge of the approaching decade will be to link more complex pressures and demands, which can only be catered for by new forms of structural decentralization, with ever new sophisticated forms of strategic monitoring and control at the macro level" (Cerny, 1990: xiv).

The passage into the twenty-first century has only heightened these concerns. The current capitalist era is often referred to as "neoliberalism." In contrast to past eras, it represents a more orthodox and enhanced commitment to market ideologies and practices for ordering the social. More precisely, neoliberalism, in principle, is defined by "The priority of the price mechanism, the free enterprise, the system of competition and a strong and impartial state" (Mirowski and Plehwe, 2009: 13–14). The state in this equation is commonly perceived to be close to non-existent or, at the very least, substantially weakened. However, as will be shown, instead it has been reconfigured and in many ways transformed with dramatic authoritarian consequences.

It is worth, therefore, better understanding the function of the state within neoliberalism in order to begin to clarify how it contributes to contemporary political authoritarianism. Contrary to the belief that the state or governments are merely "impartial" actors in the proliferation of hyper-marketization strategies, as expressed in the quote above, the public sector plays an important part in the spread and maintenance of neoliberalism. First and foremost, the state exists to protect and defend this increasingly privatized socioeconomic system. In this respect:

> The role of the state is to create and preserve an institutional framework appropriate to such practices. The state has to guarantee, for example, the quality and integrity of money. It must also set up those military, defence, police and legal structures and functions required to secure private property rights and to guarantee, by force if need be, the proper functioning of markets. (Harvey, 2005: 2)

Nevertheless, the state also takes on a more proactive role. It must do more than simply preserve the market where it is already present. It also helps expand it to areas of social life where it has not yet ventured. Hence, "if markets do not exist (in areas such as land, water, education, health care, social security, or environmental pollution) then they must be created, by state action if necessary" (Harvey, 2005: 2).

Still the exact form and limits of this state intervention is by no means completely agreed upon by advocates of neoliberalism. Indeed, the principle of a reduced public sphere runs up against its structural necessity in the implementation and reproduction of this system. As such, the ideal level of involvement of the state for neoliberal thinkers and supporters

> ranges over a wide expanse in regard to ethical foundations as well as to normative conclusions. At the one end of the line is "anarcho-liberalism," arguing for a complete laissez-faire, and the abolishment of all government. At the other end is "classical liberalism," demanding a government with functions exceeding those of the so-called night-watchman state. (Blomgren, 1997: 224)

Accordingly, the state, far from taking a backseat within neoliberalism, can be viewed as a leader in the forefront of its initiation and survival. Whereas traditional liberalism assumed that the individual "rational market subject" was the "natural condition" of humanity, neoliberals have, somewhat unexpectedly, a more socialized perspective. Namely, that it is society that must foster these values, both individually and collectively. Otherwise, communities could return to inefficient and dangerous group-based ideologies, such as communism. Required, thus, is "a programme of deliberate intervention by government in order to encourage particular types of entrepreneurial, competitive and commercial behaviour in its citizens" (Gilbert, 2013: 9).

A crucial but relatively less acknowledged leadership function of the state is to ensure the necessary political stability for these economic changes to be successful and long-standing. In this sense, there is a certain paradox central to neoliberalism: as the economic power of the state decreases its political power increases. Governments are granted augmented power to ensure social order, to "police society." Accordingly, they must spearhead a "deliberate" strategy of government intervention to secure public order and deal with threats to this order. Central to neoliberalism, therefore, is a distinct rationale for political authoritarianism – the promotion of a "strong state" to be a vigilant "night watchman" to guarantee not only the public's safety but also the orderly creation and reinforcing of economic marketization.

Indeed, in the new millennium the "night watchman" role of the state has evolved significantly. Notably, it has done so to better reflect prevailing market values and capitalist interests. The very meaning of the "order" that must be protected has changed. It is no longer just or even primarily "public order." It is now principally the "financial order." The state must be ready and willing to defend the global market economy against any and all threats. This includes those who would endanger the world's present wellbeing and future progress due to their intentional, or unintentional, economic "irresponsibility." The rallying cry of the "War on Terror" has shifted, likewise, from fighting those whose violence and extremism destroy accepted liberal freedoms to new international battles against "economic terrorists." National governments, hence, must be empowered to safeguard marketization and global capitalism wherever and whenever it is in jeopardy.

Significantly, this "authoritization" does not end at the level of the state. Just as capitalism is "global," so too is its progressively repressive form of sovereignty. Individuals and civil society groups are not the only ones potentially guilty of economic "irresponsibility" and "terrorism." Governments can also be a danger to international stability, through promoting "misinformed," "shortsighted," "risky," and "selfish" policies that question or directly oppose marketization. Needed, therefore, are transnational "night watchmen" who are willing to enforce these often unpopular but necessary "economic reforms." International financial institutions as well as powerful donor countries serve to keep market dissidents in line globally. Revealed is a growing authoritarian new world market order.

IN THE GLOBAL "GRIP" OF AUTHORITARIAN CAPITALISM

The structural mandate for a disciplining capitalist sovereignty has produced, and to an extent is produced by, new normative legitimizations for authoritarianism. Democracy and the need for democratization remain dominant political ideals rhetorically. Nevertheless, the requirement for states and international organizations to make sure that citizens and institutions are fiscally "responsible" requires novel ethical and affective justifications for this repressive regulation. The increased portrayal of capitalism as a moral duty is coupled with an enhanced moralization of its structurally necessary authoritarian politics.

Current processes and discourses of globalization, significantly, shift governance away from democratic decision making in favor of a more technocratic, and in practice despotic and illiberal, sovereignty. The emphasis on good governance grants states the right to "self-discipline" national institutions and groups to facilitate enhanced marketization. It provides them with an ethical and appealing rationale for not just defending but implicitly and explicitly promoting such authoritarianism.

Modern-day Ethiopia exemplifies this legitimization of authoritarian capitalism. After a generation of famines and economic underdevelopment, much publicized and broadcast throughout the world, the country has achieved impressive growth rates of over 10 percent for the past decade (World Bank, 2013). Its success has led some economists to refer to it as an "African Lion," linking it to the so-called "Asian Tigers" of the 1990s. Tellingly, while the policies that have made this "economic miracle" possible are market driven, most of the accolades have gone to the country's state for implementing, guiding, and when necessary enforcing this agenda. According to Dereje Feyissa Dori, African Research Director at the International Law and Policy Institute, who is based in the capital Addis Ababa, "The idea is a state with a sense of mission. It is building capitalism from above" (quoted in Kushkush, 2015).

Undoubtedly, the regime has much to be proud of based on its efforts. Extreme poverty has been reduced from 38.7 percent in 2004–2005 to 29.6 percent in 2012–2013. Poverty overall has declined to 33 percent since the beginning of the new millennium, dropping from 44 percent in 2000. Furthermore, hospitals are being built with foreign aid in rural areas and new construction projects litter the urban centers, especially the capital. Nevertheless, despite the triumphant rhetoric, these impressive results are not driven solely, or necessarily principally, by marketization strategies. Instead, as Leary and Woodeneh admit:

> Since 2005, agricultural growth has been responsible for a reduction in poverty of 4 percent a year, suggesting that the agricultural growth strategy pursued by the Government of Ethiopia has paid off. High food prices and good weather ensured that increased use of fertilizer was translated into higher incomes for poor farmers with access to markets. Government spending on basic services and effective rural safety nets has also helped the least well-off in Ethiopia. The Productive Safety Net Program alone has pushed 1.5 million people out of poverty. (Leary and Woodeneh, 2015)

Moreover, this state-driven capitalist development has come with a high political and human cost. While the country's government has become increasingly federalized, in contrast to the centralized rule marking most of the twentieth century, this has not meant that its authoritarianism has been substantially weakened or abandoned. The Ethiopian People's Revolutionary Democratic Front has governed Ethiopia since 1991, monopolizing power through state violence and the manipulation of elections. Additionally, it has wielded this power in the name of advancing a market agenda against any and all opposition. The regime has been criticized for a wide range of human rights offenses, many of which are done to protect its market-based "development" strategy from internal threats.

Yet these "costs" of development are put aside in favor of a triumphant narrative of authoritarian capitalist progress. According to Obang Metho, Executive Director of the advocacy group Solidarity Movement for a New Ethiopia, "When a society is not free, development is not as sustainable. It is not investment in building the human capacity of the people, but only in infrastructure and opportunities that mostly benefit the narrow interests of regime cronies" (quoted in Kushkush, 2015). Still, the international community has largely ignored such concerns, trumpeting instead the ability of a strong marketization state for creating a "middle-income country." Quoting one gushing BBC Africa correspondent, "if you're looking for results, then this vast climate-change challenged country, led by a hugely ambitious and severely authoritarian government, is worth a visit" (Harding, 2015).

Vital, in this regard, is how this renewed ethical justification for authoritarianism expands established legitimizations for state power within a capitalist society. The extension of enhanced sovereign policing builds on previous normative arguments for the proper role of governments within a market system. Specifically, it takes from and extends upon both libertarian and liberal legitimizations of state power.

For market libertarians, on the right side of anarchy so to speak, government power is limited to that of the "night watchman." They are charged with maintaining public order and safety. The aim is to allow the private economy to operate as free from state interference as is safely possible. In the new millennium this once singular task of the government has grown substantially. It is now asked, as discussed above, to maintain not only civic order but also fiscal order. Put differently, governments increasingly take as their right the need to protect society from those who threaten marketization and as such "economic health."

The promotion of governments as modern-day "night watchmen" exists both as a structural necessity and an affective discourse legitimizing state power and repression. It unites the population against "dangers to development" and "financial irresponsibility," providing capitalism a secure environment in which to operate effectively and spread. Far from minimizing the state, it is expected to regulate the social and cultural sphere in order to preserve a "responsible fiscal order." This can range in practice from anti-corruption campaigns, the spearheading and policing of "good governance," reducing the rights of employees, and directly repressing civil protests.

Yet, the logic of authoritarian capitalism has also captured more critical perspectives of marketization and globalization. Under a conventional liberal paradigm, governments are invested with the power to help deal with the problems and inefficiencies produced by a market economy. Lessening inequality, building infrastructure, investing in research and technology development – all to varying degrees, depending on context – rely on a strong public sector. However, in the current era, this liberal rationale has been reconfigured. Presently, the state is turned to in order to properly "guide marketization" to best fit specific national and cultural conditions.

Crucially, the state once again becomes a focal point for "leading" development. It is put forth as a primary, if not the primary, force for ensuring that countries properly follow the "marketization" blueprint for achieving and retaining economic prosperity. This state promotion goes hand in hand with a resurgent fantasy of authoritarian capitalism. Governments must do whatever is necessary to guarantee that policy and populations do not deviate from these "correct" market proscriptions.

Similar to almost all tyrannical appeals, the story of authoritarian capitalism is composed of a potent mixture of hope and fear. The hope that with "good governance" and a willingness to stay the present course, capitalism will deliver socioeconomic progress. The belief that across contexts, nationalities, cultures, and histories, marketization will pave the way for a brighter tomorrow for everyone. The fear that this straight path to progress will be blocked by those who would sacrifice future wellbeing for short-term gains. Those who challenge this internationally accepted model for growth would do so for their own corrupt personal profit. Without the strong arm of the state and international financial institutions, these threats could easily derail marketization and therefore national development.

Just as importantly, this despotic market narrative has gone global. It transcends the fate of individual nations and regions. It now involves all of us, universally as part of a shared, and vulnerable, international financial order. The world's survival and advancement depend on protecting the global marketplace. Authoritarian measures, both by national and transnational sovereigns, are required to deal with those who intentionally or unintentionally would put this fragile but necessary order in jeopardy. This includes terrorists and the "economically irresponsible" alike. In the contemporary age of globalization, those who fail to be good global market citizens impact not just their own welfare but potentially the entire world's.

Thus, being "economically responsible" transcends the narrow limits of self-interest. It is a global moral duty that individuals, groups, and countries have to those who also reside on earth. The failure to adopt austerity or pay back your debts can have ripple effects, creating waves of instability that will wash up on and destroy the shores of your international neighbors living oceans away from you. To refuse to conform to these market-oriented ethical mandates is to selfishly put the world and its collective wellbeing in danger.

The fantasy of global economic marketization therefore demands political authoritarianism. It is more than a structural necessity. It is a popular desire. It plays into the hopes and fears of an international populace raised to believe that their present survival and future wellbeing depend on the stability of the international financial order. It is for exactly this reason that strong, and if necessary oppressive, capitalist sovereigns are supposedly required to protect this vulnerable global market and the continued economic development of the world's population.

THE GLOBAL SHIFT FROM LIBERAL DEMOCRACY TO CAPITALIST SOVEREIGNTY

An ongoing and vital question for the study of capitalism and globalization is the respective roles of the state and sovereignty. This concern can be, and has been, approached from a number of different analytical perspectives. Perhaps not completely surprisingly, the most dominant line of inquiry has been largely normative in nature. What should the function and scope of governments be within a private economy? These discussions of "ought" highlight the tension of reconciling an ideological commitment to marketization with the structural necessity of a relatively active state. Conversely, critical theories, notably Marxism, seek to theoretically describe the ways governments have historically supported and perpetuated capitalism. This present analysis similarly highlights within the modern setting how globalization creates the structural and discursive conditions for political authoritarianism.

A hoped for key advancement, in this regard, is to illustrate the role of the state as primarily one of capitalist disciplining. It is not meant merely to sustain basic social order, invest in vital services, or regulate the market. Nor is it simply one of advancing the interests of class domination. Rather, it is to empower individuals and institutions to be fiscally responsible. Such disciplining then is by no means singular in the forms it can and does take. It encompasses activities ranging from education to punishment. Central, though, is the requirement above all else to ultimately ensure that actors embrace and follow this market agenda whatever the cost.

This helps resolve a significant structural tension central to marketization. Namely, how to teach people to be "good" capitalists and employees. And once they learn, how to guarantee that they continue to follow such lessons. The idea that actors are naturally economically rational belies a complex social reality where individuals, and states for that matter, must be continually educated on how to act efficiently and successfully as market subjects. This structural concern is especially heightened in the contemporary context. As the logic of the market has spread into new societal spheres, increasingly coming to define any and all areas of cultural life, so too has the need to cultivate "responsible" capitalist citizens.

Sovereignty is, hence, primarily linked to disciplining. On the one hand, actors have the supposed power and moral duty to be "self-disciplining." They must resist temptations to act fiscally "irresponsibly." This echoes ideas within economics of "responsible autonomy," in which employees are given increased freedom with the aim that they will use it to improve their efficiency and productivity (see Friedman, 1977). Such an ethos has expanded to encompass what it means to be a modern citizen. Freedom, in this context, connotes a "choice, autonomy, selfresponsibility and the obligation to maximize one's life as a kind of enterprise" (Rose et al., 2006: 91).

Foucault's description of contemporary power as "disciplinary" in character further sheds light on this phenomenon. Specifically, "discipline may be identified neither with an institution nor with an apparatus; it is a type of power, a modality for its exercise, comprising a whole set of instruments, techniques, procedures, levels of application, targets; it is a 'physics' or an 'anatomy' of power, a technology" (Foucault, 1977: 215). This evolution of power has given rise to a type of "self-disciplining governmentality." Here, the traditional sovereign power of the ruler is supplanted by an "ensemble formed by the institutions, procedures, analyses and reflections, the calculations and tactics that allow the exercise of this very specific albeit complex form of power, which has as its target population, as its principal form of knowledge political economy, and as its essential technical means apparatuses of security" (Foucault, 1991: 102–3).

Yet sovereignty does not disappear in this new disciplinary regime. It is reconfigured and transformed, transplanted at least partly to individual agents who must employ their freedom to self-modulate their beliefs and practices. Foucault (2008) gestures to this type of both top-down and bottom-up power in his theorization of "etatization" of power linked to the historical development of neoliberalism. Here, the rationality of the state, premised on hierarchy and authority, becomes insinuated in all facets of social life. Building on this insight Latham introduces the idea of a "social sovereignty" to shed light on the continued modern prevalence of sovereignty within present-day social institutions and relations, observing that "social sovereignty offers us a way to understand how in later modernity, both the state and diverse range of non-state actors of interest to Foucault (such as professionals and experts) can both be central to the governance of an increasingly wide range of social domains" (Latham, 2000: 2).

Particularly relevant to issues of authoritarian capitalism and globalization, the inevitable failure of this sovereign "self-disciplining" invites the strong response of a higher authority. Coercive measures are expected and indeed demanded to protect undisciplined actors not only from themselves but also from harming the social and economic order as a whole. Consequently, both these interconnected types of sovereignty lend themselves to authoritarianism in the present era of globalization. At the level of "self-discipline," states can use this rationale to justify repressing dissent within their borders and reordering social institutions to reflect capitalist values. Pressures from the international community to be a responsible economic member fuel such oppression.

Furthermore, in the absence of such "self-disciplining," a larger authority, notably states to citizens and international financial institutions to states, must actively and coercively intervene. The current global context is organized from the top down and the bottom up around this multilevel authoritarian sovereignty. Higher-level sovereigns must constantly monitor and police those below them – citizens must be disciplined by states, who in turn must be disciplined by international and transnational institutions.

THE END OF DEMOCRATIC HISTORY?

The twentieth century bore witness to both the global spread of democracy and the rise of new totalizing forms of authoritarianism. It is telling that its three major global conflicts – First World War, Second World War, and Cold War – were all fought and won in the name of "democracy" (Bouchet, 2015; Pee, 2018; Pee and Schmidli, 2018). In the midst of the "War on Terror" and in the immediate aftermath of the Iraqi Invasion, US scholar Michael McFaul (2004: 147) referred to "democracy promotion as a world value," arguing that "The promotion of democracy, even when embraced and, according to many, tainted by the most powerful country in the international system, has also become an international norm." Yet the ongoing and quite militant desire to spread democracy brought with it both renewed possibilities for progress and freedom and justifications for enhanced political repression. This included most recently the ongoing detainment and torture of individuals without trial suspected of terrorism to new forms of hi-tech surveillance for encouraging "good behavior" (see Fitzpatrick, 2003; Herman, 2011; Wilson, 2005). Just as the fight for democracy was perceived to be global, so too was the pervasiveness of the illiberal methods to supposedly achieve this high-minded goal. Here the ability to engage in repressive activities was justified within a wide range of international contexts as necessary to defeat democracy's terrorist enemies. In the case of Kenya, for instance, it was reported that its government was:

> committed to countering terrorism. However it seems as if Kenya is more con-
> cerned about achieving peace and stability rather than protecting human rights.
> Human rights are often portrayed as a potential barrier to effective protection from
> terrorists' acts rather than a prerequisite for genuine security ... as disappearances,
> extrajudicial killings, inhuman treatment, and punishment of alleged terrorists are
> all tactics used. (Sempijja and Nkosi, 2019: 447)

Reflected is an enduring democratic paradox that its very defense is precisely that which can create new opportunities for updating and expanding author-itarianism. An absolutely crucial and urgent question then for the present era is whether the current attempts to combat authoritarianism are leading to the renewal of democracy or simply newer and more sophisticated forms of repression. The last several decades have revealed in stark detail the failures of liberal democracy to deliver upon its promised global peace or basic human rights. There are a range of issues accounting for this failure. However, one factor that is often underexplored or even completely ignored is the role of increased economic competition for exacerbating these contradictions and conflicts.

This book has sought to show how the intensification of national market competition has led, in turn, to the legitimization of and need for increasingly politically repressive measures. Further, and in a sense even more troubling, is that this oppressive governance is increasingly framed in a way that attracts a broad range of mass support. Early in the twenty-first century, influential scholars such as Levitsky and Way (2002: 52) had already begun to highlight the existence of "competitive authoritarianism," denoting regimes where "formal democratic institutions are widely viewed as the principal means of obtaining and exercising political authority. Incumbents violate those rules so often and to such an extent, however, that the regime fails to meet conventional minimum standards for democracy." Their explanation for these "hybrid" forms of rule was that in the wake of the Cold War, "A large number of transi-tions took place in countries with high levels of poverty, inequality, and illiter-acy; weak states and civil societies; institutional instability; contested national borders; and – in parts of the former communist world – continued domination by the state of the economy, major religious institutions, and other areas of social activity" (2002: 61). Yet the proceeding decades have born witness to the pervasive and insidious role that neoliberalism has played in advancing authoritarianism at the expense of democracy (see Biebricher, 2020). The failure of hyper-capitalist policies to deal with the structural issues identified by Levitsky and Way replacing corrupted state power for the oligarchy of cor-porations has only intensified these problems. Indeed, it was increasingly clear that widespread revolts in nations like Syria had their roots in the growing "organic relationship between Westernized merchant classes and authoritarian forces" (Dahi and Munif, 2012: 323).

The Liberal vision, of course, is that democracy will ensure that both economic and political competition can be regulated by law and a commitment to shared democratic and rights-based principles in doing so preventing the outbreak of violence at its source (see McNair, 2000). In practice, it has intensified existing conflicts and power differentials while giving rise to virulent new ones. In its place, the theorist Adrian Pabst (2021) has proposed what he terms a "postliberal politics" based on principles of trust, community, and local transformation at the expense of free market globalization that has eroded trust in democratic institutions. These developments give fresh and troubling meaning to the once heralded end of history proclaimed at the start of the new millennium. It now no longer signals the final death knell of tyranny but the proposed demise of democracy itself, as corporations are engaged in what Hertz (2002) referred to as a "silent takeover" of popular rule. While ultimately optimistic, the scholar John Keane (2009) shares these fears, proclaiming that:

> The vexing thought that democracy as we now know it in all its geographic and historical variations might not survive indefinitely, that it could slit its own throat or quietly take its own life in an act of "democide," even that it could be overpowered and killed off by an outside force that escape its attention, runs counter, of course, to much recent optimism about the global triumph of democracy.

To a certain extent, the very notion that history as we know it was politically at its termination point was always a contradiction in terms when it came to democracy. For popular rule to be democratic it must be constantly growing, expanding, changing, updating. What it proposed instead was not just the supposed absence of authoritarianism but the vital limits of its own democratic progress. What it missed, furthermore, is that the resistance against capitalism in global markets has been a major source of its regeneration and long-term vitality. It spurred novel policies for encouraging mass participation and welfare, for instance. If capitalism was the handmaiden to modern democracy, it was as its antagonist as much if not more than its ally. The attempt to make the relationship purely complementary and intertwined without change robbed democracy of its ability to grow and, in no small part, its actual structural purpose.

It is not surprising that a hallmark of the contemporary age is a much lamented democratic deficit (see Norris, 2011). Replacing a genuine civic culture is "commercial democracy" driven by corporate public relations techniques and goals (Cronin, 2018). The realities of democratic decline are exacerbated by free-market development strategies like those associated with the International Monetary Fund which rely upon an ineffective and largely "non-responsive" government to put through its socially and economically devastating "reforms" (see Lang, 2021). It is then not surprising that around the world, voting rates were in rapid decline and cynicism abounded regarding the power of elections and elected officials for making actual change. At the heart of this decline was a widely shared loss of faith in democracy as it currently existed to reign in the power of economic elites or address the human, social, and ecological costs of their insatiable appetite for ever greater wealth. "Capitalism has always fostered change, which has had political implications. The development of social welfare states to channel and moderate that change was important after World War II," notes Helen Milner (2021: 1107). "But today the inequality, insecurity, and interdependence it is breeding are creating serious political problems for democracies. No longer is democracy seen by many as the only game in town; more autocratic forms of government are being considered, especially with the successful example of China's rise." This has led to the rise of explicitly "authoritarian capitalist" regimes such as Hungary (Scheiring, 2020) or ineffectual "technocratic" solutions (Frahm et al., 2022).

This feeling of mass political disempowerment has catalyzed a deeper and more profound collective existential crisis that systemic transformation was utopian and, therefore, practically unachievable. Following the 2008 financial crash and its decade-long aftermath, there have been new challenges to existing free-market orthodoxies including bringing into the relative mainstream once unimaginable and dismissed ideas such as Universal Basic Income and the need to "rethink" economic wholesale (see Hunt and Stanley, 2019). At the very least, this has fostered a new era where people are exploring different "varieties of capitalism," questioning the dogmatic adherence of elites to a neoliberal Washington Consensus (Palley, 2022). Yet these emerging "alternatives" place existing democracies in a rather difficult situation in which they must at once assert their ability to be the sole and best way to represent the interests of "the people" while repressing demands for systemic change. It is the contradiction that has allowed far-Right populist and authoritarian regimes to claim the mantle as the supposed "genuine" forces of change against the status quo.

This deepening democratic alienation sowed the seeds for authoritarian fantasies to fill this democratic gap. In particular, the corporate executive and supposed "visionary" tech entrepreneur became idealized as the best and really only source for enacting genuine transformation (see Fridell and Konings, 2013; Larson, 2020). Democracy itself was labelled inefficient, a necessary but outdated mode of decision making that was far outstripped by the energy and sheer power of private enterprise (Bloom and Rhodes, 2017). These economic arguments were transplanted into the political realm with the full-blown advent of neoliberalism in the 1980s. It is of course revealing that the actual introduction of these hyper-capitalist policies in the 1970s was ushered in by the actual Chilean dictator Augusto Pinochet (Drake and Frank, 2004; Taylor, 2006). As the last decades of the century progressed, there was a prevailing proclaimed need to make the public sector and democratic systems generally more productive by imitating and adopting mindsets and practices most usually associated with corporations rather than elected governments.

These strategies reflected a vision of the strong executive leader, able to cut through red tape and bypass democratic gridlock. It is not a far stretch for this to evolve as it has done so into a populist call for a capitalist demagogue, the strong executive leader par excellence. The only genuine democratic counter to this authoritarianism was to try to entrench whatever elected and deliberative rights and norms that had not been completely eroded. The brilliant but tragically departed critical theorist Mark Fisher (2009; also see Shonkwiler and La Berge, 2014) refered to the start of the new millennium as one defined by a sense of "capitalist realism." Similarly, the present condition is too often one of "democratic realism" it points to the acceptance that democracy can never expand beyond its liberal limits. As such, the best that can be hoped for is piece-meal reform and minor improvements. Reflected is the resignation with democratic status quo and a passionate commitment to defending it regardless of how hollow its ideals and ritualistic its practices have become.

A WORLD BEYOND AUTHORITARIAN CAPITALISM

Democracy finds itself at a historical crossroads, two paths of which lead equally to its prospective final termination. One road heads toward a world dominated by explicitly authoritarian ethno-capitalist regimes. The other to a political reality marked by ever more repressive democracies. Indeed, scholars have noted the fact that expectations for democracy are so low that people overestimate its presence believing it exists when it is clearly absent (Kruse et al., 2019). Even more troubling is that populations now increasingly associate democracy and its achievement with explicitly authoritarian values that support the "obedience to the 'guardianship' of 'wise' rulers whose authority defies constitutional checks, public criticism and electoral contestation (or at least fair contestation)" while rejecting basic liberal norms protecting individual liberties (Kirsch and Welzel, 2019: 60). These observations echo fears over the rise of "top-down democracy" (Mobrand, 2019) and "illiberal democracy" (Plattner, 2019) spreading throughout the world.

In the best-case scenario we have reached the end of democratic history, the limits of what is deemed possible being a society based on collective popular rule and individual freedoms. The focus is now squarely on preserving past gains and stopping the creep of resurgent fascism in its present tracks.

However, the real future of democracy lies in its ability to free itself from the grip of authoritarian capitalism.

Given these circumstances, is it even possible to think, act, and organize beyond authoritarian capitalism? The answer, thankfully, is a clear and definite yes. The world abounds with rising experiments showing what a revitalized post-capitalist democratic society can and could be. These have contributed, in part, to fresh radical "narratives of hope" that envision a world beyond capitalism and currently narrow liberal consumerist understandings of democracy and freedom (Blühdorn, 2017). By "liberating the macro economy from the imperative of endless growth, and at the micro economic/workplace level liberating production from capitalist productivity," declares John Barry (2020: 67), "could simultaneously enhance human freedom and flourishing and ecological sustainability." Required, then, is a combination of what now appears to be almost utopian visions of a post-capitalist society with the democratization of communities and workplaces "from below" to realize these principles in practice (Alexander, 2020). Suddenly opened up is the potential to create a vision of "life after capitalism" (Frase, 2016) that includes democratic relations based on "sustainable consumption" (Dermody et al., 2021) and a "workless society" (Little, 2016). These also now encompass "concrete utopias" that seek to move beyond even ideas of "post-work" societies for the possibility of collectively shared "post-capitalist" societies rooted in contemporary struggles like Unemployed Workers Organizations in Argentina that "creates the capacity to reshape the relationship between individuals, society and the rule of money, value, and the capitalist state rather than reinforce it" (Dinerstein and Pitts, 2018: 471).

Notably, there has also been the re-emergence of workers' struggles across the world. Recently, Amazon employees made global headlines in establishing their first successful union against the digital behemoth. The *LA Times* proclaimed: "The union victory at Amazon's JFK8 facility in Staten Island was truly remarkable. A majority of the employees there voted last week for union representation despite the company's hard-nosed union avoidance tactics, marking the first successful US organizing effort in the company's history" (Duff, 2022: n.p.). This historic victory reflects a progressive "human technology reconfiguration" based on "how digital technology facilitates the exploitation of labour, and how workers and their representatives react to digital technologies that management introduces into the labour process" (Fuchs et al., 2022: 30). Crucially, it democratically highlights how "working conditions and labour relations are not only predetermined and produced by Amazon, but that the production of knowledge can also be influenced by workers" (Ibid: 30). These movements can also give rise to new identities based on the democratization of precarious platform work, providing the foundation for challenging the authoritarian character of governance of the digital economy (see della Porta et al., 2022; Heiland and Schaupp, 2021; Johnstone and Pernicka, 2021). These forms of platform organizing, in this respect, allow for the building of innovative democratic institutions and power relations (Woodcock and Cant, 2022).

Critical to this struggle was the ability to challenge and overcome corporate surveillance and propaganda explicitly trying to undermine these efforts (see Mikell, 2021; Vgontzas, 2022). It resonates with similar attempts to reassert and update economic democracy to reflect contemporary conditions. This democratization against authoritarian capitalism in the workplace includes erotic dancers (Barbagallo and Cruz, 2021; Chateauvert, cited in Gall, 2018), Starbucks baristas (see Gruenberg, 2022), precarious service workers (Chakraborty, 2019), health workers (see Wexler et al., 2020), and domestic workers (see Hepburn, 2019). Importantly, these attempts to revive economic democracy are showing what is similarly possible politically. Non-profit and public workers, for instance, are now increasingly claiming that "it would be foolish to pretend that our jobs aren't political" (Zelnick et al., 2022: 5), revealing how demands for workers' rights also translate into broader desires for public control over resources and services.

Even more radically, arguably, has been the resurgence of worker- and community-owned cooperatives the world over (Gall, 2020; Kirsanova et al., 2021). They not only echo the revolutionary democratic expansions of the past but have also integrated traditionally capitalist values such as "individualism" and "flexibility" into a fresh vision of smart freedom and collectivity (Katsabian, 2021). These efforts bring to the fore the explicit challenges that capitalism brings to resuscitating and expanding present-day democracy. "Platform cooperativism aims to foster social change by creating a People's Internet and replacing corporate-owned platforms with user-owned co-operatives," notes Marisol Sandoval (2020: 801). "It yokes social activism with business enterprise. As a result, the movement is shaped by tensions and contradiction between politics and enterprise, democracy and the market, commons and commercialisation, activism and entrepreneurship." At the level of individual subjectivity, it provides new modes of experiencing and making sense of the world rooted in principles of equality and shared decision making that challenge and transcend the hegemony of "cognitive capitalism" entrenched in the need for hierarchy and executive authority (see Zygmuntowski, 2018). Moreover, it promotes alternative development models based on these radical democratic principles providing different frameworks of public administration, planning, and governance that combine the enhanced participation and power of individuals and communities with values of sustainability and material wellbeing (see Berry and Bell, 2018; Cameron, 2022; Hodson et al., 2020; Monticelli, 2018; Sutton, 2019).

Driving these movements are economic theories and ideologies promising the possibility of democracy, material equality, and a sustainable planet. Ideas of common ownership have been revived, linked to new technologies such as 3D printing, foretelling the potential for overcoming the artificial scarcity of capitalism (see Frankel, 2022; Götz, 2019; Reed, 2020; Savvides, 2019; Schröter, 2020; Smith, 2020). These also offer the opportunity to link modern democracies to cooperative principles such as "open source" design and the digital commons (see Kostakis et al., 2018; Troxler, 2019). These have been coupled with post-growth and degrowth perspectives (Banerjee et al., 2021; Rammelt and Gupta, 2021). Significantly, "post-growth initiatives and practices should not be seen as blueprints for a no-growth, non-capitalist future (being) but as prefiguration of alternatives in a non-linear process of transformation (becoming) which is riddled with tensions and contractions and uncertain outcomes" (Savini et al., 2022).

It is precisely this combination of genuine hope and uncertainty, alternatives and unpredictability, that still makes democracy so vital to the realization of these futures. It is about a type of planning that asks people to decide together how these radical values can best meet their collective needs based on their particular circumstances. This change will not happen all at once, in one place, with clear central planning. Rather:

> A post-growth future will be highly geographically and temporally heterogeneous. Various post-growth trends and drivers of change will unfold at different rates and to varying extents in different world regions. In particular, there will be pronounced differences in drivers between the developed and developing nations due to clear contrasts in their priorities, prevailing conditions, and external dependencies (social, political and economic). (Crownshaw et al., 2019: 123)

It also presages the reconfiguration of the state for this purpose, combining bottom-up power with shared institutional action for putting in place radical policies for achieving these goals (D'Alisa and Kallis, 2020). Consequently, a major task of the present era is to channel popular disappointment with the status quo into fresh movements for reinventing and reviving democracy. "In times like these, when populism has become mainstream," notes Raquel Neyra (2019: 563), "we should turn from its politics of resentment and racism to the alternative leftist populism of a politics of hope with a new vision of society." In doing so, it becomes possible to conceive of the fresh and urgent paradigms such as degrowth as part of a democratic transition beyond "the confines of a liberal parliamentary democracy" (Asara et al., 2013: 217). The success of "democratic degrowth," though, depends on its ability to "connect to real social processes and to the emotions of the large part of the population" (Romano, 2012: 582). Required, in turn, is to transform these from emerging shared hopes and desires into "commons" democratic norms, institutions, processes, and realities based on the principles of popular participation, civic equality, and the possibility of grassroots-led global change (see Fuchs, 2021; Gastil and Richards, 2017; Papadimitropoulos, 2017; Reid and Taylor, 2010).

Fundamental to this radical democracy sea change is directly challenging the most repressive aspects of authoritarian capitalism, a task taken up by the popularization and contemporary revival of abolitionist traditions (see Carrier and Piché, 2015; Phelps and Frazier, 2021; Thompson, 2018). These movements against systemic racism, police brutality, and mass incarceration are:

> articulating a vision of democracy that centers the lived experiences of people, particularly marginalized communities. Requiring more than legal standing and a secure right to vote, the abolitionist view of democracy calls for economic and civic standing, community self-determination, and equality. This view starkly contrasts with the dominant concept of democracy in the legal field most attentive to democratic concerns – the law of democracy, which defines democracy largely according to electoral rules and processes. (Bass, 2020: 1901)

This vision seeks to at once abolish the policing of populations alongside the capitalist interests which profit from them and those they protect (see Davis, 2011; Ellerman, 2021; Gimbel and Muhammad, 2018; Hooker, 2015; McLeod, 2018).

What is ever more clear is that authoritarian capitalism is becoming increasingly virulent in the face of its own crisis. At present, the dominant political landscape remains limited to two ultimately authoritarian options: ethno-capitalist fascism and repressive capitalist democracy. This moment, though, is also an opportunity to reinvent democracy in order not to succumb to a fate of market tyranny. It calls for bold thinking, experimentation, and movements that can imagine and struggle to implement a society beyond authoritarian capitalism.

CONCLUSION: AUTHORITARIAN CAPITALISM IN THE AGE OF GLOBALIZATION

This book explores how political authoritarianism is emerging as an affective discourse for justifying deepening economic marketization globally. In particular, it reflects a reconfigured modernization discourse updated for the new millennium. The traditional assumption that markets will lead to democracy has been transformed into a twenty-first-century story of authoritarian progress, where a fiscally self-disciplining state and disciplining international institutions will use their power to ensure that countries around the world develop and prosper. Required is not democracy, deliberation, debate, experimentation, or a rethinking of core values. Instead, all that is needed is for governments and international financial institutions to rule populations with a firm and "responsible" hand.

This attractive narrative of authoritarian capitalism represents the fundamental political fantasy of present-day economic capitalism. It drives and is adaptable to a diverse range of contexts, all of which are marshaling oppressive state power in the name of extending marketization. Market despots such as Russia and China trumpet themselves as the only actors capable of profitably leading their nations within a competitive and dangerous global marketplace. Developmental states like Singapore and Mexico justify the repression of anti-market dissent in the name of protecting vulnerable economic gains and political democracy, respectively. Established liberal democracies, including the US, legitimize the enhanced policing and incarceration of their populations for the sake of preserving social order, safe for a modern fiscal economy.

Reflected is a paradox at the heart of contemporary globalization. Its international expansion is made possible by the increased repressive "responsibility" granted to nations. Significantly, the more capitalism grows globally the more it relies on the power of governments for its survival. This structural dependence on the state is met by a renewed affective investment in the agency of national leaders to effectively negotiate and meet the demands of a global market. Put differently, whereas markets and corporations may be the prime drivers of the world, it remains the nation-state's job to successfully manage and maintain it. A crucial component of neoliberalism is the channeling of this agency into an authoritarian mandate for governments to police themselves and their citizens in line with capitalist values.

This fantasy reveals, furthermore, something potentially fundamental about the relation of sovereignty and capitalism. It introduces the concept of "capitalist sovereignty." Here, it is not that capitalists are rulers or even fully in control of those who do rule. Instead, it is that the primary aim of government and governance is to regulate citizens and economies to "responsibly" conform to capitalist prerogatives and ideologies. This differs, or more precisely evolves, from previous forms of "state capitalism" in which national governments acted principally to foster favorable conditions for the advancement of the private economy as well as publicly deal with its excesses. Conversely, capitalist sovereignty empowers individuals and states to be fiscally "self-disciplined" with the expectation that they can be "disciplined" by a higher authority if they fail to fulfill this moral capitalist obligation.

Witnessed is the rise of authoritarian capitalism in the age of globalization. The inevitable march of marketization globally goes hand in hand with the destruction of democracy and the promotion of legitimated repression. At a deeper level, it creates a new capitalist subject – spanning from the international to the state to the individual – whose primary responsibility is to do their market duty or suffer the consequences. A vital concern for the twenty-first century is whether we can, thus, break free from the global "grip" of authoritarian capitalism.

The new millennium has been marked by the rise of authoritarian capitalism. Politics is, by and large, a fatal choice between the return of fascism and the smart repression of a stagnant liberal democracy. The declared lesson of the twentieth century was that the fate of popular rule and freedom depended on the global spread of the free market. The emerging truth of the twenty-first century is that the biggest threat to democracy is in fact capitalism itself. New movements and political ideologies are required that can serve as a blueprint for a world free from the grip of authoritarian capitalism.

References

Abernethy, L. (2015). Singapore teenager charged over critical Lee Kuan Yew video. *The Guardian*, March 31. Available at: www.theguardian.com/world/2015/mar/31/ singapore-teenager-amos-yee-pangsang-charged-critical-lee-kuan-yew-video

Abidde, S. O. and Matambo, E. K. (2021). *Xenophobia, Nativism and Pan-Africanism in 21st Century Africa.* Cham: Springer Nature Switzerland AG.

Abrahamsen, R. (2000). *Disciplining Democracy: Development Discourse and Good Governance in Africa.* London: Zed Books.

Adas, M. (2009). *Dominance by Design: Technological Imperatives and America's Civilizing Mission.* Boston, MA: Harvard University Press.

Adorno, T. W., Frenkel-Brunswik, E., Levinson, D. J. and Sanford, R. N. (1950). *The Authoritarian Personality.* New York: Harper and Row.

Ahrne, G., Rydgren, J. and Sörbom, A. (2005). *Politics and Globalization: Bringing Parties In.* Stockholm: SCORE (Stockholms centrum för forskning om offentlig sektor).

Ake, C. (2019). The new world order: A view from Africa. In H. Henrik Holm (ed.), *Whose World Order?* (pp. 19–42). New York: Routledge.

Alesina, A. and Dollar, D. (2000). Who gives foreign aid to whom and why? *Journal of Economic Growth*, 5(1), 33–63.

Alexander, S. (2020). Post-capitalism by design not disaster. *The Ecological Citizen*, 3(Suppl B), 13–21.

Alford, R. R. and Friedland, R. (1985). *Powers of Theory: Capitalism, the State, and Democracy.* Cambridge: Cambridge University Press.

Alvarez, R. (1988). Defensa de la legalidad y el diálogo, propuso Cárdenas en el Zócalo. *La Jornada*, July 8, 15.

Ambrosio, T. (2009). *Authoritarian Backlash: Russian Resistance to Democratization in the Former Soviet Union.* London: Ashgate Publishing.

Amin, S. (1997). *Capitalism in the Age of Globalization: The Management of Contemporary Society.* London: Zed Books.

Amnesty International (2011). Annual report: Mexico. Amnesty International. Available at: www.amnestyusa.org/research/reports/annual-report-mexico-2011

Andrews, D. M. (1994). Capital mobility and state autonomy: Toward a structural theory of international monetary relations. *International Studies Quarterly*, 38(2), 193–218.

Andrews, D. M. (2008). *Orderly Change: International Monetary Relations since Bretton Woods.* Ithaca, NY: Cornell University Press.

Anghie, A. (2000). Civilization and commerce: The concept of governance in historical perspective. *Villanova Legal Review*, 45(5), 887–912.

Annan, K. (1998). *Secretary General of the United Nations: Annual Report to the General Assembly on the Work of the Organisation.* New York: United Nations.

Anon (2015). Mexico: World report 2015. Human Rights Watch. Available at: www .hrw.org/world-report/2015/country-chapters/mexico

Apcar, L. M., Arnold, W. and Mydans, S. (2007). Excerpts from an interview with Lee Kuan Yew. *International Herald Tribune*, August 29.

Araujo, O. and Sirvent, C. (2005). *Instituciones electorales y partidos políticos en México*. Mexico: Jorale Editores.

Arellano-López, S. and Petras, J. F. (1994). Non-governmental organizations and poverty alleviation in Bolivia. *Development and Change*, 25(3), 555–68.

Armijo, L. E. and Faucher, P. (2002). "We have a consensus": Explaining political support for market reforms in Latin America. *Latin American Politics and Society*, 44(2), 1–40.

Asara, V., Profumi, E. and Kallis, G. (2013). Degrowth, democracy and autonomy. *Environmental Values*, 22(2), 217–39.

Asher, M. G. (1995). *Compulsory Savings in Singapore: An Alternative to the Welfare State*. Dallas: National Center for Policy Analysis.

Aslund, A. (2007). *Russia's Capitalist Revolution: Why Market Reform Succeeded and Democracy Failed*. Washington, DC: Peterson Institute.

Atabaki, T. and Zurcher, E. J. (2004). *Men of Order: Authoritarian Modernization under Atatürk and Reza Shah*. New York: Palgrave Macmillan.

Avigur-Eshel, A. (2013). The promise-discipline politics of neoliberalism: Israel, Chile and their respective 2011 popular protests. In: *APSA 2013 Annual Meeting Paper*. Available at: http://papers.ssrn.com/sol3/papers.cfm?abstract_id=2303135

Avritzer, L. (2006). New public spheres in Brazil: Local democracy and deliberative politics. *International Journal of Urban and Regional Research*, 30(3), 623–37.

Axtell, C., Taylor, M. and Wessels, B. (2019). Big Data and employee wellbeing: Walking the tightrope between utopia and dystopia. *Social Sciences*, 8(12), 321.

Aybar, S. and Lapavitsas, C. (2001). The recent Turkish crisis: Another step toward free market authoritarianism. *Historical Materialism*, 8(1), 297–308.

Azuela, A. et al. (1988). El compromiso por la democratización. *La Jornada*, August 15, 9.

Babb, S. L. and Babb, S. (2004). *Managing Mexico: Economists from Nationalism to Neoliberalism*. Princeton, NJ: Princeton University Press.

Bacevich, A. J. (2003). *The Imperial Tense Prospects and Problems of American Empire*. Chicago, IL: Ivan R Dee Publisher.

Bai, E. (2015). Putin's Orthodox conservatives vs. Russia's unorthodox liberals. *Russia Direct*, January 20. Available at: www.russiadirect.org/analysis/putins-orthodox -conservatives-vs-russias-unorthodoxliberals

Baker, G. (1999). The taming of the idea of civil society. *Democratization*, 6(3), 1–29.

Balica, R. (2019). Automated data analysis in organizations: Sensory algorith-mic devices, intrusive workplace monitoring, and employee surveillance. *Psychosociological Issues in Human Resource Management*, 7(2), 61–6.

Balogh, B. (2009). *A Government Out of Sight: The Mystery of National Authority in Nineteenth-Century America*. Cambridge: Cambridge University Press.

Banerjee, S. B. and Linstead, S. (2001). Globalization, multiculturalism and other fic-tions: Colonialism for the new millennium? *Organization*, 8(4), 683–722.

Banerjee, S. B., Jermier, J. M., Peredo, A. M., Perey, R. and Reichel, A. (2021). Theoretical perspectives on organizations and organizing in a post-growth era. *Organization*, 28(3), 337–57.

Bangura, Y. (1991). *Authoritarian Rule and Democracy in Africa: A Theoretical Discourse*. Geneva: United Nations Research Institute for Social Development.

Barak, O. (2018). Security networks, deep states, and the democratic deficit in the Middle East. *Middle East Journal*, 72(3), 447–65.

Barbagallo, C. and Cruz, K. (2021). Dancers win at work: Unionization and Nowak v Chandler Bars Group Ltd. *Studies in Political Economy*, 102(3), 354–75.

Barber, B. R. (1992). Jihad vs. McWorld: How globalism and tribalism are shaping the world. *The Atlantic*, March, 53–63.

Bardhan, P. (1989). The new institutional economics and development theory: A brief critical assessment. *World Development*, 17(9), 1389–95.

Barry, J. (2020). Green republican political economy: Towards the liberation from economic growth and work as disutility. *Citizen*, 3(Suppl B), 67–76.

Bass, K. (2020). Beyond elections: Abolitionist lessons for the law of democracy. *University of Pennsylvania Law Review*, 169, 1901.

BBC News (2008). World leaders grapple with crisis. BBC News, November 15. Available at: http://news.bbc.co.uk/1/hi/business/7730763.stm

Beckett, K. (2000). *Making Crime Pay: Law and Order in Contemporary American Politics*. Oxford: Oxford University Press.

Beckett, K. and Western, B. (2001). Governing social marginality welfare, incarceration, and the transformation of state policy. *Punishment and Society*, 3(1), 43–59.

Beeson, M. (2010). The coming of environmental authoritarianism. *Environmental Politics*, 19(2), 276–94.

Bell, D., Brown, D., Jayasuriya, K. and Jones, D. M. (1995). *Towards Illiberal Democracy in Pacific Asia*. London: Macmillan.

Bell, J. (2011). Upbeat Chinese not primed for a jasmine revolution. Pew Research Center, March 31. Available at: www.pewglobal.org/2011/03/31/upbeat-chinese-public-may-not-be-primed-for-a-jasminerevolution/#fn-14115-1

Bell, P. and Cleaver, H. (1982). Marx's crisis theory as a theory of class struggle. *Research in Political Economy*, 5(5), 189–261.

Bellows, T. J. (1970). *The People's Action Party of Singapore: Emergence of a Dominant Party System*. New Haven, CT: Yale University Southeast Asia Studies.

Beng-Huat, C. (1985). Pragmatism of the People's Action Party government in Singapore: A critical assessment. *Asian Journal of Social Science*, 13(1), 29–46.

Berberoglu, B. (ed.) (2020). *The Global Rise of Authoritarianism in the 21st Century: Crisis of Neoliberal Globalization and the Nationalist Response*. New York: Routledge.

Berezin, M. (2009). *Illiberal Politics in Neoliberal Times*. Cambridge: Cambridge University Press.

Berger, M. T. and Beeson, M. (1998). Lineages of liberalism and miracles of modernisation: The World Bank, the East Asian trajectory and the international development debate. *Third World Quarterly*, 19(3), 487–504.

Berman, G. and Dar, A. (2013). Prison population statistics. London: House of Commons Library. Available at: http://researchbriefings.parliament.uk/ResearchBriefing/Summary/SN04334#fullreport

Bernhard, M. (2011). The leadership secrets of Bismarck: Imperial Germany and competitive authoritarianism. *Foreign Affairs*, 90(6), 150–4.

Berry, D. and Bell, M. P. (2018). Worker cooperatives: Alternative governance for caring and precarious work. *Equality, Diversity and Inclusion: An International Journal*, 37(4), 376–91.

Betz, H. G. (2017). Nativism across time and space. *Swiss Political Science Review*, 23(4), 335–53.

Bevir, M. (2003). A decentred theory of governance. In H. P. Bang (ed.), *Governance as Social and Political Communication*. Manchester: Manchester University Press.

Bialer, S. (1982). *Stalin's Successors: Leadership, Stability and Change in the Soviet Union*. Cambridge: Cambridge University Press.

Biebricher, T. (2020). Neoliberalism and authoritarianism. *Global Perspectives*, 1(1).

Bieler, A. and Morton, A. D. (2003). Globalisation, the state and class struggle: A "Critical Economy" engagement with open Marxism. *British Journal of Politics and International Relations*, 5(4), 467–99.

Biersteker, T. J. (1990). Reducing the role of the state in the economy: A conceptual exploration of IMF and World Bank prescriptions. *International Studies Quarterly*, 34(4), 477–92.

Bigo, G. and Tsoukala, A. (2008). Understanding (in)security. In G. Bigo and A. Tsoukala (eds), *Terror, Insecurity and Liberty: Illiberal Practices of Liberal Regimes after 9/11*. London: Routledge.

Birch, J. (2020). The rise of socialism in the United States: American "exceptionalism" and the Left after 2016. In C. Brundenius (ed.), *Reflections on Socialism in the Twenty-First Century* (pp. 103–30). Cham: Springer.

Bittner, E. (1967). The police on skid-row: A study of peace keeping. *American Sociological Review*, 32(5), 699–715.

Blomgren, A.-M. (1997). *Nyliberal politisk filosofi. En kritisk analys av Milton Friedman, Robert Nozick och F. A. Hayek*. Nora: Bokförlaget Nya Doxa.

Bloom, P. (2011). China's shifting capitalism: The role of norms in China's market transition. *Organization*, 18(1), 129–37.

Bloom, P. (2013). Fight for your alienation: The fantasy of employability and the ironic struggle for self-exploitation. *Ephemera: Theory and Politics in Organization*, 13(4), 785–807.

Bloom, P. (2014). Back to the capitalist future: Fantasy and the paradox of crisis. *Culture and Organization*, 22(2), 158–77.

Bloom, P. (2015). The "real" enemy: Fantasizing the liberal final solution. *Library of Social Science*. Available at: http://oro.open.ac.uk/44986/

Bloom, P. (2016). Back to the capitalist future: Fantasy and the paradox of crisis. *Culture and Organization*, 22(2), 158–77.

Bloom, P. (2017). How to resist the rise of the global nativist. *The Conversation*, March 17.

Bloom, P. and Cederstrom, C. (2009). The sky's the limit: Fantasy in the age of market rationality. *Journal of Organizational Change Management*, 22(2), 159–80.

Bloom, P. and Rhodes, C. (2017). *CEO Society: The Corporate Takeover of Everyday Life*. London: Bloomsbury Publishing.

Bloom, P. and Rhodes, C. (2018). The trouble with charitable billionaires. *The Guardian*, May 24.

Blühdorn, I. (2017). Post-capitalism, post-growth, post-consumerism? Eco-political hopes beyond sustainability. *Global Discourse*, 7(1), 42–61.

Blumenfeld, S., Anderson, G. and Hooper, V. (2020). Covid-19 and employee surveillance. *New Zealand Journal of Employment Relations*, 45(2), 42–56.

Bøås, M. and McNeill, D. (eds) (2004). *Global Institutions and Development: Framing the World?* London: Routledge.

Bobo, L., Kluegel, J. R. and Smith, R. A. (1997). Laissez-faire racism: The crystallization of a kinder, gentler, antiblack ideology. In S. A. Tuch and J. K. Martin (eds), *Racial Attitudes in the 1990s: Continuity and Change* (pp. 23–5). New Haven, CT: Greenwood Publishing.

Boetsch, R. L. (2005). Neoliberalism and democracy. *Privredna izgradnja*, 48(1–2), 17–30.

Bogaards, M. (2009). How to classify hybrid regimes? Defective democracy and electoral authoritarianism. *Democratization*, 16(2), 399–423.

Boggs, C. (2018). *Fascism Old and New: American Politics at the Crossroads*. New York: Routledge.

Boltanski, L. and Chiapello, È. (2007). *The New Spirit of Capitalism* (trans. by Gregory Elliott). London: Verso.

Bonanno, A. (2020). The crisis of neoliberalism, populist reaction, and the rise of authoritarian capitalism. In B. Berberoglu (ed.), *The Global Rise of Authoritarianism in the 21st Century: Crisis of Neoliberal Globalization and the Nationalist Response* (pp. 15–30). New York: Routledge.

Bonefeld, W. (1992). Social constitution and the form of the capitalist state. In W. Bonefeld, R. Gunn and K. Psychopedis (eds), *Open Marxism: Dialectics and History*. London: Pluto Press.

Boot, M. (2003). American imperialism? No need to run away from label. *USA Today*, May 6.

Booth, R. (2011). Anarchists should be reported, advises Westminster anti-terror police. *The Guardian*, July 11. Available at: www.theguardian.com/uk/2011/jul/31/westminster-police-anarchist-whistle blower-advice

Börzel, T. A. (2015). The noble west and the dirty rest? Western democracy promoters and illiberal regional powers. *Democratization*, 22(3), 519–35.

Bouchet, N. (2015). *Democracy Promotion as US Foreign Policy: Bill Clinton and Democratic Enlargement*. New York: Routledge.

Boukala, S. and Tountasaki, E. (2019). From black to green: Analysing Le Front National's "patriotic ecology." In B. Forchtner (ed.), *The Far Right and the Environment* (pp. 72–87). Abingdon: Routledge.

Bowles, P. (2005). Globalization and neoliberalism: A taxonomy and some implications for anti-globalization. *Canadian Journal of Development Studies/Revue canadienne d'études du développement*, 26(1), 67–87.

Bowornwathana, B. (2004). Thaksin's model of government reform: Prime ministerialisation through "a country is my company" approach. *Asian Journal of Political Science*, 12(1), 135–53.

Box, R. C., Marshall, G. S., Reed, B. J. and Reed, C. M. (2001). New public management and substantive democracy. *Public Administration Review*, 61(5), 608–19.

Bratton, M. (1989). Beyond the state: Civil society and associational life in Africa. *World Politics*, 41(3), 407–30.

Bremmer, I. (2009). State capitalism comes of age. *Foreign Affairs*, 88(3), 40–55.

Bremmer, I. (2010). *The End of the Free Market: Who Wins the War between States and Corporations?* New York: Penguin Publishing.

Brenner, N. (1997). Global, fragmented, hierarchical: Henri Lefebvre's geographies of globalization. *Public Culture*, 10(1), 135–67.

Brenner, N. (1999). Beyond state-centrism? Space, territoriality, and geographical scale in globalization studies. *Theory and Society*, 28(1), 39–78.

Brenner, N. and Theodore, N. (2002). Cities and the geographies of "actually existing neoliberalism." *Antipode*, 34(3), 349–79.

Bromley, R. (2013). The long baking process of history: Changing narratives of the nation. *Ceasefire*, September 29.

Brouwer, I. (2000). Weak democracy and civil society promotion: The cases of Egypt and Palestine. In M. Ottaway and T. Carothers (eds), *Funding Virtue: Civil Society Aid and Democracy Promotion* (pp. 21–48). Washington, DC: Carnegie Endowment.

Brown, W. (2004). America from Abu Ghraib. In B. Van Eekelen, J. Gonzalez, B. Stotzer and A. Tsing (eds), *Shock and Awe: War on Words*. Santa Cruz, CA: New Pacific Press.

Brown, W. (2015). *Undoing the Demos: Neoliberalism's Stealth Revolution*. Boston, MA: MIT Press.

Brownlee, J. (2005). Ruling parties and regime persistence: Explaining durable authoritarianism in the third wave era. Unpublished paper. Available at: www.researchgate .net/profile/Jason_Brownlee2/publication/228467400_Ruling_Parties_and_Regime _Persistence_Explaining_Durable_Authoritarianism_in_the_Third_Wave_Era/ links/0046353bab10e383bb000000.pdf

Brownlee, J. (2007). *Authoritarianism in an Age of Democratization*. Cambridge: Cambridge University Press.

Brownlee, J. (2009). Portents of pluralism: How hybrid regimes affect democratic transitions. *American Journal of Political Science*, 53(3), 515–32.

Bruff, I. and Tansel, C. B. (2019). Authoritarian neoliberalism: Trajectories of knowledge production and praxis. *Globalizations*, 16(3), 233–44.

Bruhn, K. (2010). *Taking on Goliath: The Emergence of a New Left Party and the Struggle for Democracy in Mexico*. University Park, PA: Penn State Press.

Brumberg, D. (2002). The trap of liberalized autocracy. *Journal of Democracy*, 13(4), 56–68.

Bryson, J. M., Crosby, B. C. and Bloomberg, L. (2014). Public value governance: Moving beyond traditional public administration and the new public management. *Public Administration Review*, 74(4), 445–56.

Bullock, P. and Yaffe, D. (1975). Inflation, the crisis and the post-war boom. *Revolutionary Communist*, 3(4), 5–45.

Bunce, V. (2003). Rethinking recent democratization. *World Politics*, 55(2), 167–92.

Burnham, P. (1994). Open Marxism and vulgar international political economy. *Review of International Political Economy*, 1(2), 221–31.

Busby, J. and Monten, J. (2018). Has liberal internationalism been Trumped? In R. Jervis, F. J. Gavin, J. Rovner and D. Labrosse (eds), *Chaos in the Liberal Order* (pp. 49–60). New York: Columbia University Press.

Bush, G. W. (2002). State of the Union Address. January 30. Available at: http:// georgewbush-whitehouse.archives.gov/news/releases/2002/01/20020129-11.html

Busvine, D. (2012). Analysis: Putin disavows, but won't ditch, state capitalism. Reuters, June 23. Available at: www.reuters.com/article/2012/06/23/us-russia-privatisation -idUSBRE85M0BG20120623

Butler, J. (1997). *The Psychic Life of Power: Theories in Subjection*. Stanford, CA: Stanford University Press.

Cacho, L. M. (2000). The people of California are suffering: The ideology of white injury in discourses of immigration. *Journal for Cultural Research*, 4(4), 389–418.

Cameron, A. and Palan, R. (1999). The national economy in the contemporary global system. In M. Shaw (ed.), *Politics and Globalisation: Knowledge, Ethics and Agency* (pp. 37–54). London: Routledge.

Cameron, J. (2022). Post-capitalism now: A community economies approach. In S. Alexander, S. Chandrashekeran and B. Gleeson (eds), *Post-Capitalist Futures* (pp. 41–52). Singapore: Palgrave Macmillan.

Cammack, P. (1998). Globalisation and the death of liberal democracy. *European Review*, 6, 249–63.

Cammack, P. (2012). Risk, social protection and the world market. *Journal of Contemporary Asia*, 42(3), 359–77.

Campbell, C. (2015). Highlights from China's new defense white paper, "China's military strategy." US–China Economic and Security Review Commission, June 1.

Canak, W. L. (1984). The peripheral state debate: State capitalist and bureaucratic-authoritarian regimes in Latin America. *Latin American Research Review*, 19(1), 3–36.

Canetti-Nisim, D. (2004). The effect of religiosity on endorsement of democratic values: The mediating influence of authoritarianism. *Political Behavior*, 26(4), 377–98.

Cansino, C. (2000). *La transición mexicana, 1997–2000*. México: Centro de Estudios de Política Comparada.

Canterbury, D. C. (2005). *Neoliberal Democratization and New Authoritarianism*. Burlington, VT: Ashgate.

Carapico, S. (2002). Foreign aid for promoting democracy in the Arab world. *The Middle East Journal*, 56(3), 379–95.

Cárdenas, C. and Ledo, P. M. (1987). Documento de Trabajo número 2. In J. Fonseca (ed.), *Corriente Democrática. Alternativa frente a la crisis*. México: Costa-Amic Editores.

Carmin, H. A. and Meyer, L. (1998). *A la sombra de la Revolución Mexicana*. Mexico, DF: Cal y Arena.

Carothers, T. (2002). The end of the transition paradigm. *Journal of Democracy*, 13(1), 5–21.

Carothers, T. (2003). Promoting democracy and fighting terror. *Foreign Affairs*, 82(1), 84–97.

Carrier, N. and Piché, J. (2015). The state of abolitionism. *Champ pénal/Penal field*, 12.

Carroll, T. and Jarvis, D. S. (eds) (2014). *The Politics of Marketising Asia*. London: Palgrave Macmillan.

Caryl, C. (2015). The new model dictator. *Foreign Policy*, February 13. Available at: http://foreignpolicy.com/2015/02/13/new-model-dictator-putin-sisi-erdogan/

Cassiday, J. A. and Johnson, E. D. (2010). Putin, Putiniana and the question of a post-Soviet cult of personality. *Slavonic and East European Review*, 88(4), 681–707.

Castañeda, J. G. (2006). Latin America's left turn. *Foreign Affairs*, 85(3), 28.

Castillo, H. (1988). Discurso de Heberto Castillo en el Zócalo. *El Universal*, June 25.

Castro, H. (1988). Llama Cárdenas a defender el voto y llegar hasta donde el pueblo quiera. *La Jornada*, July 22.

Cavatorta, F. and Haugbølle, R. H. (2012). The end of authoritarian rule and the mythology of Tunisia under Ben Ali. *Mediterranean Politics*, 17(2), 179–95.

Cerny, P. G. (1990). *The Changing Architecture of Politics: Structure, Agency and the Future of the State*. London: Sage.

Cerny, P. G. (1997). Paradoxes of the competition state: The dynamics of political globalization. *Government and Opposition*, 32(2), 251–74.

Chakraborty, I. (2019). Narratives of precarious work and social struggle: Women support service workers in India's information technology sector. *TRAVAIL, capital et société*, 49(1).

Chan, H. C. (1975). *Politics in an Administrative State: Where Has the Politics Gone?* Singapore: University of Singapore Publishing.

Chandler, D. (2004). The responsibility to protect? Imposing the "liberal peace." *International Peacekeeping*, 11(1), 59–81.

Chang, D. O. (2002). Korean labour relations in transition: Authoritarian flexibility? *Labour, Capital and Society*, 35(1), 10–40.

Chee, C. H. and Evers, H. D. (1978). National identity and nation building in Singapore. In P. Chen and H. Evers (eds), *Studies in ASEAN Sociology: Urban Society and Social Change*. Singapore: Chopmen Enterprises.

Cherniavsky, M. (1961). *Tsar and People: Studies in Russian Myths*. New Haven, CT: Yale University Press.

Chesnais, F. (1984). Marx's crisis theory today. In C. Freeman (ed.), *Design, Innovation and Long Cycles in Economic Development* (2nd edn; pp. 186–93). London: Frances Pinter.

Choudhary, K. (2007). Globalisation, governance reforms and development: An introduction. In K. Choudhary (ed.), *Globalisation, Governance Reforms and Development in India*. London: Sage.

Christensen, S. (2012). Higher education and entrepreneurial citizenship in Singapore. *Learning and Teaching*, 5(3), 39–55.

Christensen, T. and Lægreid, P. (2002). New public management: Puzzles of democracy and the influence of citizens. *Journal of Political Philosophy*, 10(3), 267–95.

Chua, B. H. (1995). *Communitarian Ideology and Democracy in Singapore*. London: Routledge.

Clarke, G. (1998). Non-governmental organizations (NGOs) and politics in the developing world. *Political Studies*, 46(1), 36–52.

Clarke, J. and Newman, J. (2012). The alchemy of austerity. *Critical Social Policy*, 32(3), 299–319.

Clarke, M. (2008). China's "War on Terror" in Xinjiang: Human security and the causes of violent Uighur separatism. *Terrorism and Political Violence*, 20(2), 271–301.

Clarke, S. (1994). *Marx's Theory of Crisis*. New York: Macmillan.

Clarke, S. (1998). *Structural Adjustment without Mass Unemployment? Lessons from Russia*. Cheltenham, UK and Northampton, MA, USA: Edward Elgar Publishing.

Clarke, S. (2004). The neoliberal theory of society. In A. Saad Filho and D. Johnston (eds), *Neoliberalism: A Critical Reader*. London: Pluto Press.

Cleaver, H. (1992). The inversion of class perspective in Marxian theory: From valorisation to self-valorisation. *Open Marxism*, 2, 106–44.

Cohen, J. (2015). Xi's crackdown on corruption has hit the obvious targets. Financial Times, January 1. Available at: www.ft.com/cms/s/0/32b90fd8-8129-11e4-b956 -00144feabdc0.html#axzz3isjMlmzs

Colantone, I. and Stanig, P. (2018). The economic determinants of the "cultural backlash": Globalization and attitudes in Western Europe. BAFFI CAREFIN Centre Research Paper (2018-91).

Coles, R. L. (2002). Manifest destiny adapted for 1990s' war discourse: Mission and destiny intertwined. *Sociology of Religion*, 63(4), 403–26.

Collier, D. (1979). Overview of the bureaucratic-authoritarian model. In D. Collier (ed.), *The New Authoritarianism in Latin America* (pp. 1–4). Princeton, NJ: Princeton University Press.

Comaroff, J. and Comaroff, J. L. (2002). Alien-nation: Zombies, immigrants, and millennial capitalism. *The South Atlantic Quarterly*, 101(4), 779–805.

Congressional-Executive Commission on China (2014). Annual report: 2014. US Congress, October 9. Available at: www.cecc.gov/sites/chinacommission.house .gov/files/2014%20annual%20report_0.PDF

Conklin, A. L. (1997). *A Mission to Civilize: The Republican Idea of Empire in France and West Africa, 1895–1930*. Stanford, CA: Stanford University Press.

Contu, A. and Grey, C. (2003). Against learning. *Human Relations*, 56(8), 931–52.

Cooke, B. and Kothari, U. (eds) (2001). *Participation: The New Tyranny?* London: Zed Books.

Cooper, F. and Stoler, A. L. (1997). *Tensions of Empire: Colonial Cultures in a Bourgeois World*. Los Angeles, CA: University of California Press.

Cooper, H. L. (2015). War on drugs policing and police brutality. *Substance Use and Misuse*, 50(8–9), 1–7.

Cooper, R. (2002). The new liberal imperialism. *The Observer*, February 7.

Córdova, A. (1979). *La formación del poder político en México*. Mexico, DF: Era.

Cornwall, A. and Coelho, V. S. (eds) (2007). *Spaces for Change? The Politics of Citizen Participation in New Democratic Arenas*. London: Zed Books.

Courpasson, D. and Clegg, S. (2006). Dissolving the iron cages? Tocqueville, Michels, bureaucracy and the perpetuation of elite power. *Organization*, 13(3), 319–43.

Courpasson, D. and Reed, M. (2004). Introduction: Bureaucracy in the age of enterprise. *Organization*, 11(1), 5–12.

Cox, R. W. (1987). *Production, Power and World Order: Social Forces in the Making of History*. New York: Columbia University Press.

Cox, R. W. (1996). Globalization, multilateralism, and democracy. In R. W. Cox and T. J. Sinclair (eds), *Approaches to World Order* (pp. 524–36). Cambridge: Cambridge University Press.

Cremin, C. (2011). *Capitalism's New Clothes, Enterprise, Ethics and Enjoyment in Times of Crisis*. London: Pluto Press.

Cronin, A. M. (2018). *Public Relations Capitalism: Promotional Culture, Publics and Commercial Democracy*. New York: Springer.

Crossette, B. (2000). Globalization tops 3-day agenda for World Leaders. *New York Times*, September 3.

Crouch, C. (2018). *The Globalization Backlash*. Chichester: John Wiley & Sons.

Crowley, N. (2020). Austerity and ethno-nationalism. In A. Ron and M. Nadesan (eds), *Mapping Populism: Approaches and Methods* (pp. 134–45). Abingdon: Routledge.

Crownshaw, T., Morgan, C., Adams, A., Sers, M., Britto dos Santos, N., Damiano, A. … and Horen Greenford, D. (2019). Over the horizon: Exploring the conditions of a post-growth world. *The Anthropocene Review*, 6(1–2), 117–41.

Cunningham, E. (2015). Moscow's sphinx meets with Egypt's new czar. *Washington Post*, February 9. Available at: www.washingtonpost.com/news/worldviews/wp/2015/02/09/moscows-sphinxmeets-with-egypts-new-czar/

Cypher, J. M. (2013). Neodevelopmentalism vs. neoliberalism: Differential evolutionary institutional structures and policy response in Brazil and Mexico. *Journal of Economic Issues*, 47(2), 391–400.

D'Alisa, G. and Kallis, G. (2020). Degrowth and the state. *Ecological Economics*, 169, 106486.

Dahi, O. S. and Munif, Y. (2012). Revolts in Syria: Tracking the convergence between authoritarianism and neoliberalism. *Journal of Asian and African Studies*, 47(4), 323–32.

Dahl, A. and Soss, J. (2014). Neoliberalism for the common good? Public value governance and the downsizing of democracy. *Public Administration Review*, 74(4), 496–504.

Dahl, R. A. (1989). *Democracy and Its Critics*. New Haven, CT: Yale University Press.

Dalacoura, K. (2005). US democracy promotion in the Arab Middle East since 11 September 2001: A critique. *International Affairs*, 81(5), 963–79.

Dalmasso, E. (2012). Surfing the democratic tsunami in Morocco: A political society and the reconfiguration of a sustainable authoritarian regime. *Mediterranean Politics*, 17(2), 217–32.

David, M. (2014). One nation, one voice: Press control and propaganda in Putin's Russia. *The Conversation*, April 14. Available at: https://theconversation.com/one-nation-one-voice-press-control-and-propagandain-putins-russia-25551

Davidson, J. (2012). Humanitarian intervention as liberal imperialism: A force for good. *POLIS Journal*, 7 (Summer), 128–64.

Davis, A. Y. (2011). *Abolition Democracy: Beyond Empire, Prisons, and Torture*. New York: Seven Stories Press.

De Alcantara, C. H. (1998). Uses and abuses of the concept of governance. *International Social Science Journal*, 50(155), 105–14.

De Angelis, M. (1997). The autonomy of the economy and globalisation, *Common Sense*, 21, 41–59.

de Souza, M. L. (2020). The land of the past? Neo-populism, neo-fascism, and the failure of the left in Brazil. *Political Geography*, 83, 102186.

Dean, M. (2002). Liberal government and authoritarianism. *Economy and Society*, 31(1), 37–61.

della Porta, D., Chesta, R. E. and Cini, L. (2022). Mobilizing against the odds: Solidarity in action in the platform economy. *Berliner Journal für Soziologie*, 1–29.

Demmers, J., Jilberto, A. E. F. and Hogenboom, B. (2004). *Good Governance in the Era of Global Neoliberalism*. London: Routledge.

Demo, A. (2005). Sovereignty discourse and contemporary immigration politics. *Quarterly Journal of Speech*, 91(3), 291–311.

Deng Xiaoping (1978). Emancipate the mind and seek truth from facts and united as one in looking to the future. *People's Daily*, December 13.

Deng Xiaoping (1980). To build socialism we must first build the productive forces. *People's Daily*, May 5. Available at: http://english.peopledaily.com.cn/dengxp/vol2/text/b1430.html

Deng Xiaoping (1984a). Building a socialism with a specifically Chinese character. *People's Daily*, June 30. Available at: http://en.people.cn/dengxp/vol3/text/c1220.html

Deng Xiaoping (1984b). Speech at the ceremony celebrating the 35th anniversary of the founding of the People's Republic of China. *People's Daily*, October 1. Available at: http://english.peopledaily.com.cn/dengxp/vol3/text/c1240.html

Deng Xiaoping (1985). Unity depends on ideals and discipline. *People's Daily*, March 7. Available at: http://english.peopledaily.com.cn/dengxp/vol3/text/c1350.html

Deng Xiaoping (1989). First priority should always be given to national sovereignty and security. *People's Daily*, December 1. Available at: http://english.peopledaily.com.cn/dengxp/vol3/text/d1100.html

Derber, C. and Magrass, Y. R. (2018). *Moving Beyond Fear: Upending the Security Tales in Capitalism, Fascism, and Democracy*. New York: Routledge.

Dermody, J., Koenig-Lewis, N., Zhao, A. L. and Hanmer-Lloyd, S. (2021). Critiquing a utopian idea of sustainable consumption: a post-capitalism perspective. *Journal of Macromarketing*, 41(4), 626–45.

Desch, M. C. (2008). America's liberal illiberalism: The ideological origins of overreaction in US foreign policy. *International Security*, 32(3): 7–43.

Deudney, D. and Ikenberry, G. J. (2009). The myth of the autocratic revival. *Foreign Affairs*, 88(1), 77–93.

Diamond, L. J. (1994). Toward democratic consolidation. *Journal of Democracy*, 5(3), 4–17.

Diamond, L. J. (1999). *Developing Democracy: Toward Consolidation*. Baltimore, MD: Johns Hopkins University Press.

Diamond, L. J. (2002). Thinking about hybrid regimes. *Journal of Democracy*, 13(2), 21–35.

Diamond, L. J. (2010). Why are there no Arab democracies? *Journal of Democracy*, 21(1), 93–112.

Dicklitch, S. (1998). *The Elusive Promise of NGOs in Africa: Lessons from Uganda*. London: Palgrave Macmillan.

Diefenbach, T. (2007). The managerialistic ideology of organisational change management. *Journal of Organizational Change Management*, 20(1), 126–44.

Diesen, G. (2022). Russiagate: Russophobia against the Political Opposition. In A. P. Tsygankov (ed.), *Russophobia* (pp. 175–200). Singapore: Palgrave Macmillan.

Dinerstein, A. C. and Pitts, F. H. (2018). From post-work to post-capitalism? Discussing the basic income and struggles for alternative forms of social reproduction. *Journal of Labor and Society*, 21(4), 471–91.

Dirbaba, B. O. and O'Donnell, P. (2012). The double talk of manipulative liberalism in Ethiopia: An example of new strategies of media repression. *African Communication Research*, 5(3), 283–312.

Dirlik, A. (1997). Critical reflections on "Chinese capitalism" as paradigm. *Identities: Global Studies in Culture and Power*, 3(3), 303–30.

Dodge, T. (2002). *Bringing the Bourgeoisie Back In: Globalisation and the Birth of Liberal Authoritarianism in the Middle East*. Washington, DC: Brookings Institute Press.

Dominiczak, P. and Prince, P. (2015). David Cameron to fast-track tough anti-terror laws. *The Telegraph*, May 13. Available at: www.telegraph.co.uk/news/uknews/terrorism-in-the-uk/11600927/DavidCameron-to-fast-track-tough-anti-terror-laws.html

Doorenspleet, R. (2000). Reassessing the three waves of democratization. *World Politics*, 52(3), 384–406.

Doorewaard, H. and Benschop, Y. (2003). HRM and organizational change: An emotional endeavor. *Journal of Organizational Change Management*, 16(3), 272–86.

Doornbos, M. (2003). Good governance: The metamorphosis of a policy metaphor. *Journal of International Affairs*, 57(1), 3.

Dore, R., Lazonick, W. and O'Sullivan, M. (1999). Varieties of capitalism in the twentieth century. *Oxford Review of Economic Policy*, 15(4), 102–20.

Dorrien, G. (2019). *Social Democracy in the Making*. New Haven, CT: Yale University Press.

Drake, P. W. (1998). The international causes of democratization, 1974–1990. In P. W. Drake and M. D. McCubbins (eds), *The Origins of Liberty: Political and Economic Liberalization in the Modern World*. Princeton, NJ: Princeton University Press, 70–91.

Drake, P. W. and Frank, V. K. (2004). *Victims of the Chilean Miracle: Workers and Neoliberalism in the Pinochet Era, 1973–2002*. Durham, NC: Duke University Press.

Duff, M. (2022). Amazon workers scored a huge union victory but face a tough road ahead. *Los Angeles Times*, April 8.

Duffield, M. (1998). Post-modern conflict: Warlords, post-adjustment states and private protection. *Civil Wars*, 1(1), 65–102.

Duggan, L. (2012). *The Twilight of Equality? Neoliberalism, Cultural Politics, and the Attack on Democracy*. Boston, MA: Beacon Press.

Dunning, T. (2004). Conditioning the effects of aid: Cold War politics, donor credibility, and democracy in Africa. *International Organization*, 58(2), 409–23.

Dupuy, A. (2019). *Haiti in the New World Order: The Limits of the Democratic Revolution*. New York: Routledge.

Dutkiewicz, P., Bichler, S. and Nitzan, J. (2013). Capitalism as a mode of power: Shimshon Bichler and Jonathan Nitzan interviewed by Piotr Dutkiewicz. In P. Dutkiewicz and R. Sakwa (eds), *22 Ideas to Fix the World: Conversations with the World's Foremost Thinkers* (pp. 326–54). New York: New York University Press.

Easton, S. T. and Walker, M. A. (1997). Income, growth, and economic freedom. *American Economic Review*, 87(2), 328–32.

The Economist (2015). How Vladimir Putin tries to stay strong. *The Economist*, April 18. Available at: www.economist.com/news/europe/21648678-russias-president-trapped-his-own-strident-anti-westernrhetoric-how-vladimir-putin-tries

Edwards, M. and Hulme, D. (1996). Too close for comfort? The impact of official aid on nongovernmental organizations. *World Development*, 24(6), 961–73.

Ekman, J. (2009). Political participation and regime stability: A framework for analyzing hybrid regimes. *International Political Science Review*, 30(1), 7–31.

El-Mahdi, R. (2011). *Empowered Participation or Political Manipulation? State, Civil Society and Social Funds in Egypt and Bolivia*. Boston, MA: Brill Publishing.

Elgenius, G. and Rydgren, J. (2019). Frames of nostalgia and belonging: The resurgence of ethno-nationalism in Sweden. *European Societies*, 21(4), 583–602.

Ellerman, D. (2021). *Neo-Abolitionism*. Springer International Publishing.

Encarnación, O. G. (2005). The follies of democratic imperialism. *World Policy Journal*, 22(1), 47–60.

Enck-Wanzer, D. (2011). Barack Obama, the Tea Party, and the threat of race: On racial neoliberalism and born again racism. *Communication, Culture and Critique*, 4(1), 23–30.

Engberg, J. and Ersson, S. (1999). Illiberal democracy in the Third World: An empirical enquiry. Paper presented for the workshop "Democracy in the Third World: What should be done?" ECPR Joint sessions of workshops, Mannheim, March 26–31.

Epstein, B. (1994). Anti-communism, homophobia, and the construction of masculinity in the postwar US. *Critical Sociology*, 20(3), 21–44.

Ermoshina, K., Loveluck, B. and Musiani, F. (2022). A market of black boxes: The political economy of Internet surveillance and censorship in Russia. *Journal of Information Technology and Politics*, 19(1), 18–33.

Escobar, A. (2004). Beyond the Third World: Imperial globality, global coloniality and anti-globalisation social movements. *Third World Quarterly*, 25(1), 207–30.

Ethier, D. (2003). Is democracy promotion effective? Comparing conditionality and incentives. *Democratization*, 10(1), 99–120.

Fairclough, N. (2007). *Language and Globalization*. London: Routledge.

Farr, K. W., Lord, R. A. and Wolfenbarger, J. L. (1998). Economic freedom, political freedom, and economic well-being: A causality analysis. *Cato Journal*, 18(2), 247–62.

Farrell, T. (2000). America's misguided mission. *International Affairs*, 76(3), 583–92.

Farrington, J. and Bebbington, A. (1993). *Reluctant Partners? Nongovernmental Organizations, the State and Sustainable Agricultural Development*. London: Psychology Press.

Featherstone, M. (2020). Problematizing the global: An Introduction to global culture revisited. *Theory, Culture and Society*, 37(7–8), 157–67.

Feldstein, S. (2019). *The Global Expansion of AI Surveillance* (Vol. 17). Washington, DC: Carnegie Endowment for International Peace.

Figes, O. (1997). *A People's Tragedy: The Russian Revolution, 1891–1924*. New York: Random House.

Fisher, M. (2009). Capitalist Realism: Is There No Alternative? John Hunt Publishing.

Fisher, W. F. (1997). Doing good? The politics and antipolitics of NGO practices. *Annual Review of Anthropology*, 26, 439–64.

Fiss, P. C. and Hirsch, P. M. (2005). The discourse of globalization: Framing and sensemaking of an emerging concept. *American Sociological Review*, 70(1), 29–52.

Fitzpatrick, J. (2003). Speaking law to power: The war against terrorism and human rights. *European Journal of International Law*, 14(2), 241–64.

Fligstein, N. (2001). *The Architecture of Markets: An Economic Sociology of Twenty-First-Century Capitalist Societies*. Princeton, NJ: Princeton University Press.

Foner, E. (1999). *The Story of American Freedom*. New York: W. W. Norton and Company.

Foot, R. (2008). Exceptionalism again: The Bush administration, the "global war on terror" and human rights. *Law and History Review*, 26(3), 707–25.

Foster, J. B. (2003). *Class Struggle and the Industrial Revolution: Early Industrial Capitalism in Three English Towns*. London: Routledge.

Foster, J. B. and McChesney, R. W. (2003). Kipling, the "White Man's Burden," and US imperialism. *Monthly Review*, 55(3), 1–11.

Foucault, M. (1977). *Discipline and Punish: The Birth of the Prison*. New York: Vintage Press.

Foucault, M. (1991). Governmentality. In G. Burchell, C. Gordon and P. Miller (eds), *The Foucault Effect: Studies in Governmentality*. Chicago, IL: University of Chicago Press.

Foucault, M. (2008). *The Birth of Biopolitics: Lectures at the Collège de France, 1978–1979*. London: Palgrave Macmillan.

Foweraker, J. (1989). Popular movements and the transformation of the system. In W. A. Cornelius, J. Gentleman and P. H. Smith (eds), *Mexico's Alternative Political Futures* (pp. 109–29). San Diego, CA: Center for US–Mexican Studies.

Fowler, A. (1991). The role of NGOs in changing state–society relations: Perspectives from Eastern and Southern Africa. *Development Policy Review*, 9(1), 53–84.

Fox, V. and Allyn, R. (2007). *Revolution of Hope*. New York: Viking Penguin.

Foxley, A. (1983). *Latin American Experiments in Neoconservative Economics*. Los Angeles, CA: University of California Press.

Frahm, N., Doezema, T. and Pfotenhauer, S. (2022). Fixing technology with society: The coproduction of democratic deficits and responsible innovation at the OECD and the European Commission. *Science, Technology, and Human Values*, 47(1), 174–216.

Franck, T. M. (1992). The emerging right to democratic governance. *American Journal of International Law*, 86(1), 46–91.

Frankel, B. (2022). From technological utopianism to universal basic services. In S. Alexander, S. Chandrashekeran and B. Gleeson (eds), *Post-Capitalist Futures* (pp. 77–86). Singapore: Palgrave Macmillan.

Frase, P. (2016). *Four Futures: Life after Capitalism*. London: Verso.

Freeden, M. (1996). *Ideologies and Political Theory: A Conceptual Approach*. Oxford: Oxford University Press.

Frenkel, R. and O'Donnell, G. (1979). The "stabilization programs" of the International Monetary Fund and their internal impacts. In R. R. Fagen and C. Arnson (eds), *Capitalism and the State in US–Latin American Relations* (pp. 171–203). Stanford, CA: Stanford University Press.

Fridell, G. and Konings, M. (2013). *Age of Icons: Exploring Philanthrocapitalism in the Contemporary World*. Toronto: University of Toronto Press.

Friedman, A. (1977). Responsible autonomy versus direct control over the labour process. *Capital and Class*, 1(1), 43–57.

Friedman, M. (1962). *Capitalism and Freedom*. Chicago, IL: University of Chicago Press.

Fu, H. and Chu, Y. H. (1996). Neo-authoritarianism, polarized conflict and populism in a newly democratizing regime: Taiwan's emerging mass politics. *Journal of Contemporary China*, 5(11), 23–41.

Fuchs, C. (2014). *OccupyMedia! The Occupy Movement and Social Media in Crisis Capitalism*. Winchester: John Hunt Publishing.

Fuchs, C. (2021). The digital commons and the digital public sphere: How to advance digital democracy today. *Westminster Papers in Communication and Culture*, 16(1).

Fuchs, M., Dannenberg, P. and Wiedemann, C. (2022). Big Tech and labour resistance at Amazon. *Science as Culture*, 31(1), 29–43.

Fukuyama, F. (1989). The end of history? *The National Interest*, Summer, 3–18.

Fukuyama, F. (1992). Asia's soft authoritarian alternative. *New Perspectives Quarterly*, 9(2), 60–1.

Fukuyama, F. (2018). Against identity politics: the new tribalism and the crisis of democracy. *Foreign Affairs*, 97, 90.

Fung, A., Wright, E. O. and Abers, R. (2003). *Deepening Democracy: Institutional Innovations in Empowered Participatory Governance*. London: Verso.

G20 (2008). Washington Declaration. Washington Summit, November 15. Available at: www.g20.org/Documents/g20_summit_declaration.pdf

Gabennesch, H. (1972). Authoritarianism as world view. *American Journal of Sociology*, 77(5), 857–75.

Gall, G. (2018). *Sex Worker Unionization: Global Developments, Challenges, and Possibilities*. Basingstoke: Palgrave Macmillan.

Gall, G. (2020). Emerging forms of worker collectivism among the precariat: When will capital's "gig" be up? *Capital and Class*, 44(4), 485–92.

Galpin, T. J. (1983). The democratic roots of Athenian imperialism in the fifth century BC. *Classical Journal*, 79(2), 100–9.

Gamble, A. (1979). The free economy and the strong state. *Socialist Register*, 16(16), 1–25.

Garden, C. (2018). Labor organizing in the age of surveillance. *Saint Louis University Law Journal*, 63, 55.

Gastil, J. and Richards, R. C. (2017). Embracing digital democracy: A call for building an online civic commons. *PS: Political Science and Politics*, 50(3), 758–63.

Gat, A. (2007). The return of the authoritarian capitalists. *New York Times*, June 14.

Gathii, J. T. (1999). Good governance as a counter insurgency agenda to oppositional and transformative social projects in international law. *Buffalo Human Rights Legal Review*, 5, 107.

Gavrov, S. (2007). Is the transition to authoritarianism irreversible? *Russian Politics and Law*, 45(1), 20–30.

George, C. (2007). Consolidating authoritarian rule: Calibrated coercion in Singapore. *The Pacific Review*, 20(2), 127–45.

Gerber, T. P. and Hout, M. (2004). Tightening up: Declining class mobility during Russia's market transition. *American Sociological Review*, 69(5), 677–703.

Gertler, M. S. (1997). Globality and locality: The future of "geography" and the nation-state. In P. J. Rimmer (ed.), *Pacific Rim Development: Integration and Globalisation in the Asia-Pacific Economy*. Sydney: Allen and Unwin, 12–33.

Giannone, D. (2015). Suspending democracy? The governance of the EU's political and economic crisis as a process of neoliberal restructuring. In K. Demetriou (ed.), *The European Union in Crisis: Exploration in Representation and Democratic Legitimacy*. London: Springer International Publishing.

Giavazzi, F. and Tabellini, G. (2005). Economic and political liberalizations. *Journal of Monetary Economics*, 52(7), 1297–330.

Gibbon, P. (1993). The World Bank and the new politics of aid. *European Journal of Development Research*, 5(1), 35–62.

Gibson, J., Claassen, C. and Barceló, J. (2020). Deplorables: Emotions, political sophistication, and political intolerance. *American Politics Research*, 48 (2), 252–62.

Giddens, A. (2020). Modernity and self-identity: Self and society in the late modern age. In S. Seidman and J. C. Alexander (eds), *The New Social Theory Reader* (pp. 354–61). Abingdon: Routledge.

Gideon, J. (1998). The politics of social service provision through NGOs: A study of Latin America. *Bulletin of Latin American Research*, 17(3), 303–21.

Gilbert, A. (1992). Must global politics constrain democracy? Realism, regimes, and democratic internationalism. *Political Theory*, 20(1), 8–37.

Gilbert, C., Powell, A. and Vines, D. (1999). Positioning the World Bank. *Economic Journal*, F598–F633.

Gilbert, J. (2013). What kind of thing is "neoliberalism"? *New Formations: A Journal of Culture/Theory/Politics*, 80, 7–22.

Gill, S. R. and Law, D. (1989). Global hegemony and the structural power of capital. *International Studies Quarterly*, 33(4), 475–99.

Gillham, P. F., Edwards, B. and Noakes, J. A. (2013). Strategic incapacitation and the policing of "Occupy Wall Street" protests in New York City, 2011. *Policing and Society*, 23(1), 81–102.

Gills, B. K. (2000). The crisis of postwar East Asian capitalism: American power, democracy and the vicissitudes of globalization. *Review of International Studies*, 26(3), 381–403.

Gilman, N. (2003). Modernization theory, the highest state of American intellectual history. In D. C. Engerman (ed.), *Staging Growth: Modernization, Development, and the Global Cold War* (pp. 47–89). Boston, MA: University of Massachusetts Press.

Gilmore, R. W. (2007). *Golden Gulag*. Los Angeles, CA: University of California Press.

Gimbel, V. N. and Muhammad, C. (2018). Are police obsolete? Breaking cycles of violence through abolition democracy. *Cardozo Law Review*, 40, 1453.

Girod, D. M. and Walters, M. R. (2012). Elite-led democratisation in aid-dependent states: The case of Mauritania. *Journal of North African Studies*, 17(2), 181–93.

Giroux, H. A. (2004). *The Terror of Neoliberalism: Authoritarianism and the Eclipse of Democracy*. Boulder, CO: Paradigm Publisher.

Giroux, H. A. (2007). The emerging authoritarianism in the United States: Political culture under the Bush/Cheney administration. *Symploke*, 14(1), 98–151.

Gisselquist, R. M. (2012). Good governance as a concept, and why this matters for development policy (No. 2012/30). WIDER Working Paper. Helsinki: United Nations University World Institute for Development Economics Research.

Glassman, R. M. (2021). *Can Democracy Survive in the 21st Century? Oligarchy, Tyranny, and Ochlocracy in the Age of Global Capitalism*. Berlin: Springer Nature.

Glynos, J. and Stavrakakis, Y. (2004). Sussing out the limits of Laclau's embrace of Lacan. In S. Critchley and O. Marchart (eds), *Laclau: A Critical Reader* (p. 201). London: Psychology Press.

Gökarıksel, S. (2020). Antifascist strategy today: Lineages of anticommunism and "militant democracy" in Eastern Europe. In J. Rayner, S. Falls, G. Souvlis and T. C. Nelms (eds), *Back to the '30s?* (pp. 215–34). Cham: Palgrave Macmillan.

Goldman, M. I. (2004). Putin and the oligarchs. *Foreign Affairs*, 83(6), 33–44.

Good, K. (1996). Authoritarian liberalism: A defining characteristic of Botswana. *Journal of Contemporary African Studies*, 14(1), 29–51.

Goodman, J. B. and Pauly, L. W. (1993). The obsolescence of capital controls? Economic management in an age of global markets. *World Politics*, 46(1), 50–82.

Gordon, T. (2005). The political economy of law-and-order policies: Policing, class struggle, and neoliberal restructuring. *Studies in Political Economy*, 75(Spring), 55–77.

Gore, C. (2000). The rise and fall of the Washington Consensus as a paradigm for developing countries. *World Development*, 28(5), 789–804.

Gortari, C. S. (1988). *Juntos enfrentaremos los retos*. Mexico, DF: Partido Revolucionario Institucional, Comité Ejecutivo Nacional, Secretaría de Información y Propaganda.

Götz, M. (2019). Unpacking the provision of the industrial commons in Industry 4.0 cluster. *Economics and Business Review*, 5(4), 23–48.

Gramsci, A. (1971). *Selections from the Prison Notebook*. London: Smith, Lawrence and Wishart.

Grant, D., Hardy, C., Oswick, C. and Putnam, L. L. (2004). *The Sage Handbook of Organizational Discourse*. London: Sage.

Gray, J. (1996). *After Social Democracy: Politics, Capitalism and the Common Life*. London: Demos.

Green, D. (2005). Liberal imperialism as global-governance perspective. In M. J. Hoffmann and A. D. Ba (eds), *Contending Perspectives on Global Governance: Coherence, Contestation and World Order* (pp. 231–48). London: Routledge.

Greenfeld, L. (1990). The formation of the Russian national identity: The role of status insecurity and ressentiment. *Comparative Studies in Society and History*, 32(3), 549–91.

Greitens, S. C. (2020). Surveillance, security, and liberal democracy in the post-COVID world. *International Organization*, 74(S1), E169–E190.

Grindle, M. S. (2007). *Going Local: Decentralization, Democratization, and the Promise of Good Governance*. Princeton, NJ: Princeton University Press.

Grossman, H. (1992). *The Law of Accumulation and Breakdown of the Capitalist System*. London: Pluto.

Gruenberg, M. (2022). Starbucks unionising drive accelerating, as is retaliation. *The Guardian*, February 28.

Grugel, J. and Riggirozzi, P. (2012). Post-neoliberalism in Latin America: Rebuilding and reclaiming the state after crisis. *Development and Change*, 43(1), 1–21.

Gualmini, E. and Schmidt, V. A. (2013). State transformation in Italy and France: Technocratic versus political leadership on the road from non-liberalism to neo-liberalism. In V. A. Schmidt and M. Thatcher (eds), *Resilient Liberalism in Europe's Political Economy* (pp. 346–73). Cambridge: Cambridge University Press.

Guild, E. and Groenendijk, C. A. (2009). Understanding the contest of community: Illiberal practices in the EU? In E. Guild, C. A. Groenendijk and S. Carrera (eds), *Illiberal Liberal States: Immigration, Citizenship and Integration in the EU* (pp. 1–28). Farnham: Ashgate.

Guilhot, N. (2005). *The Democracy Makers: Human Rights and International Order.* New York: Columbia University Press.

Haas, R. (2006). Rethinking Sovereignty. Project Syndicate, February 14. Available at: https://www.project-syndicate.org/commentary/rethinking-sovereignty

Habermas, J. (1991). *The Structural Transformation of the Public Sphere: An Inquiry into a Category of Bourgeois Society.* Boston, MA: MIT Press.

Hadiz, V. R. (2004). The rise of neo-Third Worldism? The Indonesian trajectory and the consolidation of illiberal democracy. *Third World Quarterly*, 25(1), 55–71.

Hadiz, V. R. and Robison, R. (2005). Neo-liberal reforms and illiberal consolidations: The Indonesian paradox. *Journal of Development Studies*, 41(2), 220–41.

Haggard, S. and Webb, S. B. (1993). What do we know about the political economy of economic policy reform? *World Bank Research Observer*, 8(2), 143–68.

Haggard, S. and Webb, S. B. (eds) (1994). *Voting for Reform: Democracy, Political Liberalization and Economic Adjustment.* New York: Oxford University Press.

Hale, D. (1998). The IMF, now more than ever: The case for financial peacekeeping. *Foreign Affairs*, 77(6), 7–13.

Hall, D. T. (1976). *Careers in Organizations.* Tucson, AZ: Goodyear.

Hall, P. A. and Soskice, D. (2004). *Varieties of Capitalism and Institutional Complementarities.* Boston, MA: Springer Press.

Hall, S. (1978). *Policing the Crisis: Mugging, the State and Law and Order.* London: Macmillan.

Hall, S. (2011). The march of the neoliberals. *The Guardian*, September 12.

Halonen, T. (2003). Globalisation needs Chydenius' perspective. Speech at Anders Chydenius Jubilee Year in Kokkola, March 1. Available at: www.chydenius.net/eng/news/uutinen.asp?id=601&referer=2&pages=2

Hameleers, M., Schmuck, D., Schulz, A., Wirz, D. S., Matthes, J., Bos, L. et al. (2021). The effects of populist identity framing on populist attitudes across Europe: Evidence from a 15-country comparative experiment. *International Journal of Public Opinion Research*, 33(3), 491–510.

Hamilton-Hart, N. (2000). The Singapore state revisited. *The Pacific Review*, 13(2), 195–216.

Han, J. and Ling, L. H. M. (1998). Authoritarianism in the hypermasculinized state: Hybridity, patriarchy, and capitalism in Korea. *International Studies Quarterly*, 42(1), 53–78.

Hancock, J. H. (2019). Fashion, style and global culture with sneakers uniting us. *Fashion, Style and Popular Culture*, 6(1), 3–6.

Handelman, S. (1995). *Comrade Criminal: Russia's New Mafiya.* New Haven, CT: Yale University Press.

Hanson, S. E. (2007). The uncertain future of Russia's weak state authoritarianism. *East European Politics and Societies*, 21(1), 67–81.

Harding, A. (2015). The Ethiopians who predict an end to international aid. BBC News, July 13. Available at: www.bbc.co.uk/news/world-africa-33505312

Hardt, M. (1999). Affective labor. *Boundary 2*, 89–100.

Harvey, D. (2003). *The New Imperialism.* Oxford: Oxford University Press.

Harvey, D. (2005). *A Brief History of Neoliberalism*. Oxford: Oxford University Press.
Harvey, D. (2007a). In what ways is "the new imperialism" really new? *Historical Materialism*, 15(3), 57–70.
Harvey, D. (2007b). Neoliberalism as creative destruction. *Annals of the American Academy of Political and Social Science*, 610(1), 21–44.
Hawthorne, A. (2001). The "democracy dilemma" in the Arab World: How do you promote reform without undermining key United States Interests? *Foreign Service Journal*, February.
Hawthorne, A. (2004). *Middle Eastern Democracy: Is Civil Society the Answer?* Washington, DC: Carnegie Endowment for International Peace.
Hay, C. and Marsh, D. (2000). *Demystifying Globalization*. Basingstoke: Macmillan.
Hay, C. and Rosamond, B. (2002). Globalization, European integration and the discursive construction of economic imperatives. *Journal of European Public Policy*, 9(2), 147–67.
Heale, M. J. (1990). *American Anti-Communism: Combating the Enemy Within, 1830–1970*. Baltimore, MD: Johns Hopkins University Press.
Heiland, H. and Schaupp, S. (2021). Breaking digital atomization: Resistant cultures of solidarity in platform-based courier work. In P. V. Moore and J. Woodcock (eds), *Augmented Exploitation: Artificial Intelligence, Automation and Work* (pp. 138–48). London: Pluto Press.
Held, D., McGrew, A., Goldblatt, D. and Perraton, J. (eds) (1999). *Global Transformations: Politics, Economics, Culture*. Cambridge: Polity Press.
Henry, P. J., Sidanius, J., Levin, S. and Pratto, F. (2005). Social dominance orientation, authoritarianism, and support for intergroup violence between the Middle East and America. *Political Psychology*, 26(4), 569–84.
Hepburn, S. (2019). Service and solidarity: Domestic workers, informal organising and the limits of unionisation in Zambia. *Journal of Southern African Studies*, 45(1), 31–47.
Herman, S. N. (2011). *Taking Liberties: The War on Terror and the Erosion of American Democracy*. Oxford: Oxford University Press.
Hermansson, P., Lawrence, D., Mulhall, J. and Murdoch, S. (2020). *The International Alt-Right: Fascism for the 21st Century?* New York: Routledge.
Hertz, N. (2002). *The Silent Takeover: Global Capitalism and the Death of Democracy*. New York: Simon and Schuster.
Heryanto, A. (1999). Where communism never dies: Violence, trauma and narration in the last Cold War capitalist authoritarian state. *International Journal of Cultural Studies*, 2(2), 147–77.
Hetherington, M. J. and Suhay, E. (2011). Authoritarianism, threat, and Americans' support for the war on terror. *American Journal of Political Science*, 55(3), 546–60.
Hetherington, M. J. and Weiler, J. D. (2009). *Authoritarianism and Polarization in American Politics*. Cambridge: Cambridge University Press.
Hibou, B., Meddeb, H. and Hamdi, M. (2011). *Tunisia after 14 January and Its Social and Political Economy*. Copenhagen: EuroMediterranean Human Rights Network.
Hill, D. and Kumar, R. (2008). Neoliberalism and its impacts. In D. Hill and R. Kumar (eds), *Global Neoliberalism and Education and Its Consequences*. London: Routledge.
Hill, M. and Lian, K. F. (2013). *The Politics of Nation Building and Citizenship in Singapore*. London: Routledge Press.
Hill, R. J. and Cappelli, O. (2013). *Putin and Putinism*. London: Routledge Press.

Hilson, G. and Maconachie, R. (2008). "Good governance" and the extractive industries in Sub-Saharan Africa. *Mineral Processing and Extractive Metallurgy Review*, 30(1), 52–100.

Hinnebusch, R. (2006). Authoritarian persistence, democratization theory and the Middle East: An overview and critique. *Democratization*, 13(3), 373–95.

Hinnebusch, R. (2015). Globalization, democratization, and the Arab uprising: The international factor in MENA's failed democratization. *Democratization*, 22(2), 335–57.

Hiriart, P. and Alvarez, R. (1988). La oposición debe de fundamentar sus quejas, demanda. *Bartlet. La Jornada*, July 7.

Hobson, C. and Kurki, M. (eds) (2012). *The Conceptual Politics of Democracy Promotion*. London: Routledge Press.

Hodges, D. C., Gandy, D. R. and Gandy, R. (2002). *Mexico Under Siege: Popular Resistance to Presidential Despotism*. London: Zed Books.

Hodson, M., Kasmire, J., McMeekin, A., Stehlin, J. G. and Ward, K. (eds) (2020). *Urban Platforms and the Future City: Transformations in Infrastructure, Governance, Knowledge and Everyday Life*. New York: Routledge.

Holliday, I. (2000). Productivist welfare capitalism: Social policy in East Asia. *Political Studies*, 48(4), 706–23.

Hollis, R. (2012). No friend of democratization: Europe's role in the genesis of the "Arab Spring." *International Affairs*, 88(1), 81–94.

Hood, S. J. (1998). The myth of Asian-style democracy. *Asian Survey*, 38(9), 853–66.

Hooker, J. (2015). Black politics after Ferguson: From democratic sacrifice/suffering to abolition democracy. Paper delivered at the Annual Meeting of the Western Political Science Association (pp. 1–4).

Horcasitas, J. F. M. (1993). *El tiempo de la legitimidad. Elecciones, autoritarismo y democracia en México*. Mexico, DF: Cal y Arena.

Hout, W. (1996). Development strategies and economic performance in Third World countries, 1965–92. *Third World Quarterly*, 17(4), 603–24.

Howarth, D. (2000). *Discourse*. London: Open University Press.

Human Rights Watch (2014a). World report 2014: China. New York: Human Rights Watch. Available at: www.hrw.org/world-report/2014/country-chapters/china-and-tibet

Human Rights Watch (2014b). World report 2014: Chile. New York: Human Rights Watch. Available at: www.hrw.org/world-report/2014/country-chapters/chile

Human Rights Watch (2015). World report 2015: Mexico. New York: Human Rights Watch. Available at: www.hrw.org/world-report/2015/country-chapters/Mexico

Hunt, T. and Stanley, L. (2019). From "there is no alternative" to "maybe there are alternatives": Five challenges to economic orthodoxy after the crash. *The Political Quarterly*, 90(3), 479–87.

Huntington, S. P. (1991). Democracy's third wave. *Journal of Democracy*, 2(2), 12–34.

Hurst, L. (2015). Greece signs reform deal with OECD to avoid Troika "blackmail." *Newsweek*, March 12. Available at: http://europe.newsweek.com/greece-signs-reform-deal-oecd-troika-blackmail-313399

Hyden, G. (2008). After the Paris Declaration: Taking on the issue of power. *Development Policy Review*, 26(3), 259–74.

Ibhawoh, B. (1999). Structural adjustment, authoritarianism and human rights in Africa. *Comparative Studies of South Asia, Africa and the Middle East*, 19(1), 158–67.

Ignatieff, M. (2003). The burden. *New York Times Magazine*, January 5. Available at: www.nytimes.com/2003/01/05/magazine/05EMPIRE.html

Im, H. B. (1987). The rise of bureaucratic authoritarianism in South Korea. *World Politics*, 39(2), 231–57.

Inglehart, R. and Welzel, C. (2005). *Modernization, Cultural Change, and Democracy: The Human Development Sequence*. Cambridge: Cambridge University Press.

Inglehart, R. and Welzel, C. (2009). How development leads to democracy. *Foreign Affairs*, 88(2), 33–48.

Jackson, B. (2010). At the origins of neo-liberalism: The free economy and the strong state, 1930–1947. *The Historical Journal*, 53(1), 129–51.

Jackson, R. (2007). Constructing enemies: "Islamic terrorism" in political and academic discourse. *Government and Opposition*, 42(3), 394–26.

Jay, S., Batruch, A., Jetten, J., McGarty, C. and Muldoon, O. T. (2019). Economic inequality and the rise of far-right populism: A social psychological analysis. *Journal of Community and Applied Social Psychology*, 29(5), 418–28.

Jayal, N. G. (2007). A democratic deficit: Citizenship and governance in the era of globalisation. In K. Choudhary (ed.), *Globalisation, Governance Reforms and Development in India* (pp. 97–112). London: Sage.

Jayasuriya, K. and Hewison, K. (2004). The antipolitics of good governance: From global social policy to a global populism? *Critical Asian Studies*, 36(4), 571–90.

Jenkins, R. (1991). The political economy of industrialization: A comparison of Latin American and East Asian newly industrializing countries. *Development and Change*, 22(2), 197–231.

Jessop, B. (1982). *The Capitalist State: Marxist Theories and Methods*. Oxford: Martin Robertson.

Jessop, B. (1990). *State Theory: Putting the Capitalist State in Its Place*. Cambridge: Polity Press.

Jessop, B. (1998). The rise of governance and the risks of failure: The case of economic development. *International Social Science Journal*, 50(155), 29–45.

Jha, U. K. (2004). Democratic deficits in a globalizing world: Thy way out. *Indian Journal of Political Science*, 65(4), 531–40.

Jiang, S. (2015). Xi Jinping's 2015 hit list: Corruption, cleavage. CNN, January 13. Available at: http://edition.cnn.com/2015/01/12/china/china-2015-look-ahead/

Johnston, H. and Pernicka, S. (2021). Struggles over the power and meaning of digital labour platforms: A comparison of the Vienna, Berlin, New York and Los Angeles taxi markets. In J. Drahokoupil and K. Vandaele (eds), *A Modern Guide to Labour and the Platform Economy*. Cheltenham, UK and Northampton, MA, USA: Edward Elgar Publishing.

Jones, B. R. J. (2000). *The World Turned Upside Down? Globalization and the Future of the State*. New York: St Martin's Press.

Jones, D. M. and Brown, D. (1994). Singapore and the myth of the liberalizing middle class. *The Pacific Review*, 7(1), 79–87.

Jose, J. (2007). Reframing the "governance" story. *Australian Journal of Political Science*, 42(3), 455–70.

Kapur, D. and Webb, R. (2000). *Governance-Related Conditionalities of the International Financial Institutions*. New York: United Nations.

Karim, S. (2012). The co-existence of globalism and tribalism: A review of the literature. *Journal of Research in International Education*, 11(2), 137–51.

Katsabian, T. (2021). Collective action in the digital reality: The case of platform-based workers. *Modern Law Review*, 84(5), 1005–40.

Kaufman, R. R. (1979). Industrial change and authoritarian rule in Latin America: A concrete review of the bureaucratic-authoritarian model. In D. Collier (ed.), *The*

New Authoritarianism in Latin America (pp. 165–254). Princeton, NJ: Princeton University Press.

Kaufman, R. R. (1985). Democratic and authoritarian responses to the debt issue: Argentina, Brazil, Mexico. *International Organization*, 39(3), 473–503.

Kaufmann, D., Kraay, A. and Zoido, P. (1999). Governance matters. Available at: https://papers.ssrn.com/sol3/papers.cfm?abstract_id=188568

Kavka, M. (2008). *Reality Television, Affect and Intimacy: Reality Matters*. London: Palgrave Macmillan.

Kaylan, M. (2014). Kremlin values: Putin's strategic conservatism. *World Affairs Journal*, 177(1), 9–17.

Keane, J. (2009). *The Life and Death of Democracy*. New York: Simon and Schuster.

Kellner, D. (1998). Globalization and the postmodern turn. In R. Axtmann (ed.), *Globalization and Europe* (pp. 23–42). London: Pinter.

Kelly, P. F. (1999). The geographies and politics of globalization. *Progress in Human Geography*, 23(3), 379–400.

Kenny, K., Whittle, A. and Willmott, H. (2011). *Understanding Identity and Organizations*. London: Sage.

Kešić, J. and Duyvendak, J. W. (2019). The nation under threat: Secularist, racial and populist nativism in the Netherlands. *Patterns of Prejudice*, 53(5), 441–63.

Kesselman, M., Krieger, J. and Joseph, W. (2009). *Introduction to Comparative Politics*. London: Cengage Learning.

Keynes, J. M. (1926). *The End of Laissez-Faire*. London: Hogarth Press.

Kiely, R. (1998). Neo liberalism revised? A critical account of World Bank concepts of good governance and market friendly intervention. *Capital and Class*, 22(1), 63–88.

Kim, D. (2013). Modernization or betrayal: Neoliberalism in Mexico. *Constellations*, 4(1), 221–31.

King, D. (1999). *In the Name of Liberalism: Illiberal Social Policy in the United States and Britain*. Oxford: Oxford University Press.

Kinnvall, C. and Svensson, T. (2022). Exploring the populist "mind": Anxiety, fantasy, and everyday populism. *British Journal of Politics and International Relations*. 13691481221075925.

Kirkpatrick, J. J. (1982). *Dictatorships and Double Standards: Rationalism and Reason in Politics*. New York: Simon and Schuster.

Kirsanova, E. V., Mokhirev, A. I., Sokolov, A. M., Suvorova, E. V. and Zikirova, S. S. (2021). Platform cooperativism: A new model in the knowledge economy. In A. Bogoviz, A. Suglobov, A. Maloletko, O. Kaurova and S. Lobova (eds), *Frontier Information Technology and Systems Research in Cooperative Economics* (pp. 141–7). Cham: Springer.

Kirsch, H. and Welzel, C. (2019). Democracy misunderstood: Authoritarian notions of democracy around the globe. *Social Forces*, 98(1), 59–92.

Klebnikov, P. (2000). *Godfather of the Kremlin: Boris Berezovsky and the Looting of Russia*. Boston, MA: Houghton Mifflin.

Klein, N. (2007). *The Shock Doctrine: The Rise of Disaster Capitalism*. London: Palgrave Macmillan.

Klesner, J. (2004). The structure of the Mexican electorate: Social, attitudinal, and partisan bases of Vicente Fox's victory. In J. I. Domínguez and C. H. Lawson (eds), *Mexico's Pivotal Democratic Election: Candidates, Voters, and the Presidential Campaign of 2000* (pp. 91–122). Stanford, CA: Stanford University Press.

Knack, S. (2004). Does foreign aid promote democracy? *International Studies Quarterly*, 48(1), 251–66.

Knight, N. (1986). The Marxism of Mao Zedong: Empiricism and discourse in the field of Mao studies. *Australian Journal of Chinese Affairs*, 16(July), 7–22.

Kofas, J. V. (1995). The politics of austerity: The IMF and US foreign policy in Bolivia, 1956–1964. *Journal of Developing Areas*, 29(2), 213–36.

Kooiman, J. (1994). *Modern Governance: New Government–Society Interactions*. London: Sage.

Kornberger, M., Clegg, S. R. and Carter, C. (2006). Rethinking the polyphonic organization: Managing as discursive practice. *Scandinavian Journal of Management*, 22(1), 3–30.

Kostakis, V., Latoufis, K., Liarokapis, M. and Bauwens, M. (2018). The convergence of digital commons with local manufacturing from a degrowth perspective: Two illustrative cases. *Journal of Cleaner Production*, 197, 1684–93.

Kraar, L. (1974). Singapore: Country run like a corporation. *Fortune*, 90(1), 85.

Kraska, P. B. and Kappeler, V. E. (1997). Militarizing American police: The rise and normalization of paramilitary units. *Social Problems*, 44(1), 1–18.

Krastev, I. (2010). Deepening dissatisfaction. *Journal of Democracy*, 21(1), 113–19.

Krastev, I. (2012). Authoritarian capitalism versus democracy. *Policy Review*, 172, 47.

Krugman, P. (2015). Ending Greece's nightmare. *New York Times*, January 26.

Kruse, S., Ravlik, M. and Welzel, C. (2019). Democracy confused: When people mistake the absence of democracy for its presence. *Journal of Cross-Cultural Psychology*, 50(3), 315–35.

Kumi, E., Arhin, A. A. and Yeboah, T. (2014). Can post-2015 sustainable development goals survive neoliberalism? A critical examination of the sustainable development–neoliberalism nexus in developing countries. *Environment, Development and Sustainability*, 16(3), 539–54.

Kupchan, C. A. (2012). Democratic malaise: Globalization and the threat to the West. *Foreign Affairs*, 90(1), 62–7.

Kuromiya, H. (2014). Inventing the enemy: Denunciation and terror in Stalin's Russia. *Social History*, 39(4), 596–8.

Kurtz, S. (2003). Democratic imperialism: A blueprint. *Policy Review*, 3.

Kurzman, C. (1998). Waves of democratization. *Studies in Comparative International Development*, 33(1), 42–64.

Kushkush, I. (2015). Ethiopia long mired in poverty rides an economic boon. *New York Times*, March 3.

Kyung-Sup, C. (1999). Compressed modernity and its discontents: South Korean society in transition. *Economy and Society*, 28(1), 30–55.

Laboure, M. and Braunstein, J. (2017). The gaps of nations and the rise of far-Right populism. *Euro Crisis in the Press*, March 23.

Laclau, E. and Mouffe, C. (1986). *Hegemony and Socialist Strategy: Towards a Radical Democratic Politics*. London: Verso.

Lane, D. (2008). From chaotic to state-led capitalism. *New Political Economy*, 13(2), 177–84.

Lang, V. (2021). The economics of the democratic deficit: The effect of IMF programs on inequality. *Review of International Organizations*, 16(3), 599–623.

Larner, W. (2000). Neo-liberalism: Policy, ideology, governmentality. *Studies in Political Economy*, 63(Autumn), 5–25.

Larson, R. (2020). *Bit Tyrants: The Political Economy of Silicon Valley*. Chicago, IL: Haymarket Books.

Latham, M. E. (2000). *Modernization as Ideology: American Social Science and "Nation Building" in the Kennedy Era*. Chapel Hill, NC: University of North Carolina Press.

Latham, M. E. (2011). *The Right Kind of Revolution: Modernization, Development, and US Foreign Policy from the Cold War to the Present*. Ithaca, NY: Cornell University Press.

Latham, R. (2000). Social sovereignty. *Theory, Culture and Society*, 17(4), 1–18.

Learmonth, M. and Morrell, K. (2019). *Critical Perspectives on Leadership: The Language of Corporate Power*. New York: Routledge.

Leary, M. and Woodeneh, G. (2015). Poverty in Ethiopia down 33 percent since 2000. World Bank, January 20.

Ledgister, F. S. J. (1998). *Class Alliances and the Liberal Authoritarian State: The Roots of Post-Colonial Democracy in Jamaica, Trinidad and Tobago, and Surinam*. Trenton, NJ: Africa World Press.

Lee, K. F. (2018). *AI Superpowers: China, Silicon Valley, and the New World Order*. Boston, MA: Houghton Mifflin.

Lee, W. O. (2004). Emerging concepts of citizenship in the Asian context. In W. Lee, D. Grossman, K. J. Kennedy and G. P. Fairbrother (eds), *Citizenship Education in Asia and the Pacific: Concepts and Issues*. New York: Springer Science and Business Media.

Lee, W. O. (2013). The development of a future-oriented citizenship curriculum in Singapore: Convergence of character and citizenship education and curriculum 2015. In Z. Deng, S. Gopinathan, C. Kim-Eng Lee (eds), *Globalization and the Singapore Curriculum: From Policy to Classroom* (pp. 241–60). New York: Springer.

Lee, Y. J. and Ku, Y. W. (2007). East Asian welfare regimes: Testing the hypothesis of the developmental welfare state. *Social Policy and Administration*, 41(2), 197–212.

Leffler, M. P. (2003). 9/11 and the past and future of American foreign policy. *International Affairs*, 79(5), 1045–63.

Leftwich, A. (1993). Governance, democracy and development in the Third World. *Third World Quarterly*, 14(3), 605–24.

Leftwich, A. (1994). Governance, the state and the politics of development. *Development and Change*, 25(2), 363–86.

Léger, M. J. (2022). Bernie beats Trump, Clinton and Obama beat Bernie. In M. Léger (ed.), *Bernie Bros Gone Woke* (pp. 59–96). Leiden: Brill.

Leiva, F. I. (2008). Toward a critique of Latin American neostructuralism. *Latin American Politics and Society*, 50(4), 1–25.

Leonard, C. (2020). *Kochland: The Secret History of Koch Industries and Corporate Power in America*. New York: Simon and Schuster.

Leroux, D. (2019). *Distorted Descent: White Claims to Indigenous Identity*. Manitoba: University of Manitoba Press.

Leser, J. and Spissinger, F. (2020). The functionality of affects: Conceptualising far-right populist politics beyond negative emotions. *Global Discourse: An Interdisciplinary journal of Current Affairs*, 10(2), 325–42.

Levitsky, S. and Way, L. A. (2002). The rise of competitive authoritarianism. *Journal of Democracy*, 13(2), 51–65.

Levitsky, S. and Way, L. A. (2010). *Competitive Authoritarianism: Hybrid Regimes after the Cold War*. Cambridge: Cambridge University Press.

Leys, C. (2003). *Market-Driven Politics: Neoliberal Democracy and the Public Interest*. London: Verso.

Leyva, M. A. L. (2007). *La encrucijada: entre la protesta social y la participación electoral (1988)*. Mexico, DF: FLACSO.

Lindenberg, M. and Devarajan, S. (1993). Prescribing strong economic medicine: Revisiting the myths about structural adjustment, democracy, and economic performance in developing countries. *Comparative Politics*, 25(2), 169–82.

Lingle, C. (1996a). The end of the beginning of the "Pacific century"? Confucian corporatism and authoritarian capitalism in East Asia. *The Pacific Review*, 9(3), 389–409.

Lingle, C. (1996b). *Singapore's Authoritarian Capitalism: Asian Values, Free Market Illusions, and Political Dependency*. Fairfax, VA: The Locke Institute.

Linz, J. J. (2000). *Totalitarian and Authoritarian Regimes*. Boulder, CO: Lynne Rienner.

Lipset, S. M. (1959). Some social requisites of democracy: Economic development and political legitimacy. *American Political Science Review*, 53(1), 69–105.

Lippard, C. D. (2011). Racist nativism in the 21st century. *Sociology Compass*, 5(7), 591–606.

Little, B. (2016). Post-capitalism and the workless society. *Soundings: A Journal of Politics and Culture*, 62(1), 156–60.

Lynch, M. (2012). Theorizing the role of the "war on drugs" in US punishment. *Theoretical Criminology*, 16(2), 175–99.

Ma, L. J. (2009). Viewpoint: China's authoritarian capitalism: Growth, elitism and legitimacy. *International Development Planning Review*, 31(1), i–xii.

MacEwan, A. (2005). Neoliberalism and democracy: Market power versus democratic power. In A. Saad Filho and D. Johnston (eds), *Neoliberalism: A Critical Reader* (pp. 170–83). London: Pluto Press.

MacFarquhar, R. and Schoenhals, M. (2006). *Mao's Last Revolution*. Cambridge: Cambridge University Press.

Mahbubani, K. (2005). *Beyond the Age of Innocence: Rebuilding Trust between America and the World*. New York: Public Affairs.

Mahbubani, K. (2009). *The New Asian Hemisphere: The Irresistible Shift of Global Power to the East*. New York: Public Affairs.

Mann, M. (1996). Authoritarian and liberal militarism: A contribution from comparative and historical sociology. In S. Smith, K. Booth and M. Zalewski (eds), *International Theory: Positivism and Beyond* (pp. 221–39). Cambridge: Cambridge University Press.

Manokha, I. (2020). The implications of digital employee monitoring and people analytics for power relations in the workplace. *Surveillance and Society*, 18(4), 540–54.

Mao Zedong (1955). In refutation of "Uniformity of public opinion." May 24. Available at: www.marxists.org/reference/archive/mao/selected-works/volume-5/mswv5_42.htm

Mao Zedong (1956). Chairman Mao's talk to music workers. August 24. Available at: www.marxists.org/reference/archive/mao/selectedworks/volume-7/mswv7_469.htm

Marcussen, H. S. (1996). NGOs, the state and civil society. *Review of African Political Economy*, 23(69), 405–23.

Marinetto, M. (2003). Governing beyond the centre: A critique of the Anglo-governance school. *Political Studies*, 51(3), 592–608.

Martell, L. (2007). The third wave in globalization theory. *International Studies Review*, 9(2), 173–96.

Martin, H. P., Schumann, H. and Camiller, P. (1997). *The Global Trap: Globalization and the Assault on Prosperity and Democracy*. London: Zed Books.

Martínez, F. and Aranda, J. (2006). Abascal "invita" a López Obrador a no marginarse de las instituciones. *La Jornada*, September 17. Available at: www.jornada.unam.mx/2006/09/17/index.php?section=politica&article=012n1pol

Martinez, R. (2019). The centrist delusion. *Amass*, 24(2), 20–5.

Marx, K. (1977). *A Contribution to the Critique of Political Economy*. Moscow: Progress Publishers.

Marx, K. (1990). *Capital*, Vol. 1. London: Penguin.

Marx, K. (1992). *Early Writings* (trans. R. Livingstone and G. Benton). London: Penguin.

Mattick, P. (1981). *Economic Crisis and Crisis Theory*. London: Merlin Press.

McCaffrey, J. M. (1994). *Army of Manifest Destiny: The American Soldier in the Mexican War, 1846–1848*. New York: New York University Press.

McFaul, M. (2002). The fourth wave of democracy and dictatorship: Noncooperative transitions in the postcommunist world. *World Politics*, 54(2), 212–44.

McFaul, M. (2004). Democracy promotion as a world value. *The Washington Quarterly*, 28(1), 147–63.

McGoey, L. (2021). Philanthrocapitalism and the separation of powers. *Annual Review of Law and Social Science*, 17, 391–409.

McGoey, L., Thiel, D. and West, R. (2018). Philanthrocapitalism and crimes of the powerful. *Politix*, 1, 29–54.

McGregor, Jr., E. B. (1993). Toward a theory of public management success. In B. Bozeman (ed.), *Public Management: The State of the Art*. Hoboken, NJ: Jossey-Bass, 173–85.

McLeod, A. M. (2018). Envisioning abolition democracy. *Harvard Law Review*, 132, 1613.

McNair, B. (2000). Power, profit, corruption, and lies. *De-Westernizing Media Studies*, 69–84.

Mead, W. R. (2011). The Tea Party and American foreign policy: What populism means for globalism. *Foreign Affairs*, 90(2), 28–44.

Means, G. P. (1996). Soft authoritarianism in Malaysia and Singapore. *Journal of Democracy*, 7(4), 103–17.

Mediavilla, J. and Garcia-Arias, J. (2019). Philanthrocapitalism as a neoliberal (development agenda) artefact: Philanthropic discourse and hegemony in (financing for) international development. *Globalizations*, 16(6), 857–75.

Mendes, A. E. (2016). Digital demagogue: The critical candidacy of Donald J. Trump. *Journal of Contemporary Rhetoric*, 6(3–4), 62–73.

Mensah, J. (2008). *Neoliberalism and Globalization in Africa*. London: Palgrave Macmillan.

Mercer, C. (2002). NGOs, civil society and democratization: A critical review of the literature. *Progress in Development Studies*, 2(1), 5–22.

Merkel, W. (2004). Embedded and defective democracies. *Democratization*, 11(5), 33–58.

Middlebrook, K. (2003). *Confronting Development: Assessing Mexico's Economic and Social Policy Changes*. San Diego, CA: Stanford University Press.

Mikell, S. (2021). *A Unified Panopticon: Insights from a Study on Workplace Surveillance at Amazon and Uber*. Doctoral dissertation.

Miliband, R. (1969). *The State in Capitalist Society*. New York: Basic Books.

Miller, D. (2019). The populist fantasy: American ethno-nationalism and the dysphoria of the body politic. *Soundings: An Interdisciplinary Journal*, 102(2–3), 226–52.

Milner, H. V. (2021). Is global capitalism compatible with democracy? Inequality, insecurity, and interdependence. *International Studies Quarterly*, 65(4), 1097–110.

Ministry of Justice (2013). *Story of the Prison Population: 1993–2012*. London: Ministry of Justice. Available at: www.gov.uk/government/uploads/system/uploads/attachment_data/file/218185/storyprison-population.pdf

Mirowski, P. and Plehwe, D. (2009). *The Road from Mont Pelerin*. Boston, MA: Harvard University Press.

Mishra, R. (1999). *Globalization and the Welfare State*. Cheltenham, UK and Northampton, MA, USA: Edward Elgar Publishing.

Miyamoto, I. (2020). Surveillance technology challenges political culture of democratic states. In A. Vuving (ed.), *Hindsight, Insight, Foresight: Thinking about Security in the Indo-Pacific* (pp. 49–66). Honolulu, HI: Asia-Pacific Center for Security Studies.

Mobrand, E. (2019). *Top-Down Democracy in South Korea*. Seattle, WA: University of Washington Press.

Montaño, E. A. and Bloom, P. (2014). The closed promise: The authoritarian "grip" of democracy. *Theory and Event*, 17(3).

Montemayor, C. (2009). *Guerra en el paraíso*. Mexico: Debolsillo.

Monticelli, L. (2018). Embodying alternatives to capitalism in the 21st century. *tripleC: Communication, Capitalism and Critique*, 16(2), 501–17.

Moore, B. (1967). *Social Origins of Dictatorship and Democracy: Lord and Peasant in the Making of the Modern World*. London: Lane.

Moss, D. (2014). Repression, response, and contained escalation under "liberalized" authoritarianism in Jordan. *Mobilization: An International Quarterly*, 19(3), 261–86.

Mosse, D. (1994). Authority, gender and knowledge: Theoretical reflections on the practice of participatory rural appraisal. *Development and Change*, 25(3), 497–526.

Mosse, D. (2001). "People's knowledge," participation and patronage: Operations and representations in rural development. In B. Cooke and U. Kothari (eds), *Participation: The New Tyranny?* (pp. 16–35). London: Zed Books.

Mountz, A. and Curran, W. (2009). Policing in drag: Giuliani goes global with the illusion of control. *Geoforum*, 40(6), 1033–40.

Muller, E. N. (1995). Economic determinants of democracy. *American Sociological Review*, 60(6), 966–82.

Mulrooney, D. (2014). Rethinking national security: China's new security commission. Policy Brief No. 152, May 6. Stockholm: Institute for Security and Development Policy. Available at: www.isdp.eu/publications/policy-briefs.html?task=showbib&id=6377&return=

Mundi Index (2011). Indicators of GINI Index, Mexico. Available at: www.indexmundi.com/facts/indicators/SI.POV.GINI/compare#country=mx

Murray, R. (1971). The internationalization of capital and the nation state. *New Left Review*, 67, 84–109.

Mutalib, H. (2000). Illiberal democracy and the future of opposition in Singapore. *Third World Quarterly*, 21(2), 313–42.

Mutz, D. C. (2018). Status threat, not economic hardship, explains the 2016 presidential vote. *Proceedings of the National Academy of Sciences*, 115(19), E4330–E4339.

Mu Xuequan (2015). Xi calls for more anti-corruption measures despite achievements. *Xinhua*, January 14.

Nair, C. (ed.) (1976). *Socialism That Works: The Singapore Way*. Singapore: Federal Publications.

Naisbitt, J. (1994). *Global Paradox: The Bigger the World Economy, the More Powerful Its Smallest Players*. New York: William Morrow and Company.

Nanda, V. P. (2006). The "good governance" concept revisited. *Annals of the American Academy of Political and Social Science*, 603(1), 269–83.

Nardin, T. (2005). Humanitarian imperialism. *Ethics and International Affairs*, 19(2), 21–6.

Nasir, K. and Turner, B. S. (2013). Governing as gardening: Reflections on soft authoritarianism in Singapore. *Citizenship Studies*, 17(3–4), 339–52.

Ndegwa, S. N. (1996). *Two Faces of Civil Society*. West Hartford, CT: Kumarian Press.

Nelson, J. M. (1984). The political economy of stabilization: Commitment, capacity, and public response. In R. H. Bates (ed.), *Toward a Political Economy of Development: A Rational Choice Perspective*. Los Angeles, CA: University of California Press.

New York Times (2013). Mr. Putin's war on gays. *New York Times*, July 27.

Neyra, R. (2019). Constructing the people: Left populism and degrowth movements. *The European Legacy*, 24(5), 563–9.

Ng, T. (2014). Xi Jinping attacks concept of global hegemony, in dig at United States. *South China Morning Post*, June 29. Available at: www.scmp.com/news/china/article/1542702/xi-jinping-attacks-concept-global-hegemony-dig-united-states?page=all

Nieto, E. P. (2012). Detrás de la Transición. *El liderazgo que México requiere*, September.

Noland, M. (2020). Protectionism under Trump: The China shock, deplorables, and the first white President. *Asian Economic Policy Review*, 15(1), 31–50.

Norrie, A. and Adelman, S. (1988). "Consensual authoritarianism" and criminal justice in Thatcher's Britain. *Journal of Law and Society*, 16(1), 112–28.

Norris, P. (2011). *Democratic Deficit: Critical Citizens Revisited*. Cambridge: Cambridge University Press.

O'Hehir, A. (2014). Dick Cheney's dark victory: Torture and the demise of American democracy. *Salon*, December 13. Available at: www.salon.com/2014/12/13/dick_cheneys_dark_victory_torture_and_the_demise_of_american_democracy/

O'Neal, J. R. (1994). The affinity of foreign investors for authoritarian regimes. *Political Research Quarterly*, 47(3), 565–88.

Obama, B. (2009). News conference for London Summit. London, April 2. Available at: www.whitehouse.gov/the-press-office/news-conference-president-obama-40209

Ohmae, K. (1990). *The Borderless World*. New York: Harper Collins.

Ohmae, K. (1995). *The End of the Nation State*. New York: Free Press.

Olney, P. (2012). Globalization, transition, and insecurity in Mexico. In M. Nilsson and J. Gustafsson (eds), *Latin American Responses to Globalization in the 21st Century* (pp. 149–70). London: Palgrave Macmillan.

Olukoshi, A. O. (1998). *The Elusive Prince of Denmark: Structural Adjustment and the Crisis of Governance in Africa*. Uppsala: Nordic Africa Institute.

Ong, A. (2006). *Neoliberalism as Exception: Mutations in Citizenship and Sovereignty*. Durham, NC: Duke University Press.

Ong, A. (2007). Neoliberalism as a mobile technology. *Transactions of the Institute of British Geographers*, 32(1), 3–8.

Ordoñez, M. D. and Borja, A. L. (2018). Philippine liberal democracy under siege: The ideological underpinnings of Duterte's populist challenge. *Philippine Political Science Journal*, 39(2), 139–53.

Ortmann, S. (2011). Singapore: Authoritarian but newly competitive. *Journal of Democracy*, 22(4), 153–64.

Orwin, C. (1986). Justifying empire: The speech of the Athenians at Sparta and the problem of justice in Thucydides. *Journal of Politics*, 48(1), 72–85.

Ottaway, M. (2003). Promoting democracy after conflict: The difficult choices. *International Studies Perspectives*, 4(3), 314–22.

Ottaway, M. (2013). *Democracy Challenged: The Rise of Semiauthoritarianism*. Washington, DC: Carnegie Endowment.

Pabst, A. (2021). *Postliberal Politics: The Coming Era of Renewal*. Chichester: John Wiley & Sons.

Palley, T. (2022). Theorizing varieties of capitalism: Economics and the fallacy that "there is no alternative (TINA)." *Review of Keynesian Economics*, 10(2), 129–66.

Papadimitropoulos, E. (2017). From the crisis of democracy to the commons. *Socialism and Democracy*, 31(3), 110–22.

Paredes (1988). Existe falta de credibilidad en el proceso electoral, dice Coparmex. *El Universal*, July 21.

Parker, C. S. and Barreto, M. A. (2014). *Change They Can't Believe In: The Tea Party and Reactionary Politics in America*. Princeton, NJ: Princeton University Press.

Parker, M. (2009). Angelic organization: Hierarchy and the tyranny of heaven. *Organization Studies*, 30(11), 1281–99.

Partido Acción Nacional, Plataforma Electoral (2006). Los avances del cambio. Available at: www.ife.org.mx/portal/site/ifev2/Plataformas_electorales

Passas, N. (2000). Global anomie, dysnomie, and economic crime: Hidden consequences of globalization and neo-liberalism in Russia and around the world. *Social Justice*, 27(2), 16–44.

Pastor, M. (1987). The effects of IMF programs in the third world: Debate and evidence from Latin America. *World Development*, 15(2), 249–62.

Pastor, M. (1989). Latin America, the debt crisis, and the International Monetary Fund. *Latin American Perspectives*, 16(1), 79–110.

Pee, R. (2018). Containing revolution: democracy promotion, the Cold War and US national security. *International Politics*, 55(5), 693–711.

Pee, R. and Schmidli, W. M. (eds) (2018). *The Reagan Administration, the Cold War, and the Transition to Democracy Promotion*. New York: Springer.

Peh Shing Hui and Goh Chin Lian (2007). Framing the Singapore story with many different voices. *Straits Times*, August 4.

Pei, M. (2000). China's evolution toward soft authoritarianism. In E. Friedman and B. L. McCormick (eds), *What if China Doesn't Democratize? Implications for War and Peace* (pp. 74–98). New York: M. E. Sharpe.

Peng, X. (1987). Demographic consequences of the Great Leap Forward in China's provinces. *Population and Development Review*, 13(4), 639–70.

People's Daily (2005a). The "Washington Consensus" and "Beijing Consensus." *The People's Daily*, June 18. Available at: http://en.people.cn/200506/18/print20050618_190947.html

People's Daily (2005b). Interview: China will not dream an "American dream" but a "Chinese" one. *The People's Daily*, September 2.

Perkmann, M. and Sum, N. L. (2002). *Globalization, Regionalization and Cross-Border Regions: Scales, Discourses and Governance*. London: Palgrave Macmillan.

Persky, J. (1998). Wage slavery. *History of Political Economy*, 30(4), 627.

Peters, M. A. (2020). "The fascism in our heads": Reich, Fromm, Foucault, Deleuze and Guattari – the social pathology of fascism in the 21st century. *Educational Philosophy and Theory*, 1–9.

Phelps, M. S., Ward, A. and Frazier, D. (2021). From police reform to police abolition? How Minneapolis activists fought to make Black Lives Matter. *Mobilization: An International Quarterly*, 26(4), 421–41.

Philip, G. (1988). The lawless presidency: Economic crisis and democratic accountability in Mexico 1970–94. *Democratization*, 5(1), 23–41.

Phillips, L. (2009). Merkel and Sarkozy call for global "Economic Security" council. *EU Observer*, January 9.

Piazza, J. A. (2005). Globalizing quiescence: Globalization, union density and strikes in 15 industrialized countries. *Economic and Industrial Democracy*, 26(2), 289–314.

Pickel, A. (1993). Authoritarianism or democracy? Marketization as a political problem. *Policy Sciences*, 26(3), 139–63.

Piketty, T. (2014). *Capital in the 21st Century*. Boston, MA: Harvard University Press.

Pitlik, H. (2002). The path of liberalization and economic growth. *Kyklos*, 55(1), 57–80.

Plamenatz, J. (1992). *Man and Society: Political and Social Theory from Machiavelli to Marx*, Vol. 3. London: Longman.

Plattner, M. F. (1998). Liberalism and democracy: Can't have one without the other. *Foreign Affairs*, 77(2), 171–80.

Plattner, M. F. (2019). Illiberal democracy and the struggle on the right. *Journal of Democracy*, 30(1), 5–19.

Poe, M. (1998). What did Russians mean when they called themselves "Slaves of the Tsar"? *Slavic Review*, 57(3), 585–608.

Portes, A. (1997). Neoliberalism and the sociology of development: Emerging trends and unanticipated facts. *Population and Development Review*, 23(2), 229–59.

Poulantzas, N. A. (1978). *State, Power, Socialism*. London: Sheed and Ward.

Poulantzas, N. A. (2000). *State, Power, Socialism*. London: Verso Press.

PRI (Partido Revolucionario Institucional) (1979). *La ideología del partido de la revolución*. Mexico, DF: Comisión Nacional para la Conmemoración del Cincuetenario de la Fundación del Partido Revolucionario Institucional.

PRI (Partido Revolucionario Institucional) (1988). Julio 88. Lo que verdaderamente pasó en las elecciones VI. *La Jornada*, August 9.

Pritchett, L. and Woolcock, M. (2004). Solutions when the solution is the problem: Arraying the disarray in development. *World Development*, 32(2), 191–212.

Prizel, I. (1997). Ukraine between proto-democracy and "soft" authoritarianism. In K. Dawisha and B. Parrott (eds), *Democratic Changes and Authoritarian Reactions in Russia, Ukraine, Belarus and Moldova* (Vol. 3; pp. 330–69). Cambridge: Cambridge University Press.

Przeworski, A. and Limongi, F. (1997). Modernization: Theories and facts. *World Politics*, 49(2), 155–83.

Qureshi, E., and Sells, M. A. (2013). *The New Crusades: Constructing the Muslim Enemy*. New York: Columbia University Press.

Rajaratnam, S. (1972). Singapore: Global city. Speech to the Singapore Press Club, February 6. Available at: www.nas.gov.sg/archivesonline/speeches/record-details/fd2918de-3270-11e4-859c-0050568939ad

Rammelt, C. F. and Gupta, J. (2021). Inclusive is not an adjective, it transforms development: A post-growth interpretation of inclusive development. *Environmental Science and Policy*, 124, 144–55.

Ramo, J. C. (2004). *The Beijing Consensus*. London: Foreign Policy Centre.

Rana, J. and Rosas, G. (2006). Managing crisis post-9/11: Policing and empire. *Cultural Dynamics*, 18(3), 219–34.

Ravallion, M. and Lokshin, M. (2000). Who wants to redistribute? The tunnel effect in 1990s Russia. *Journal of Public Economics*, 76(1), 87–104.

Rawlinson, K. (2015). Singapore's Lee Kuan Yew, "a true giant of history," dies aged 91. *The Guardian*, March 13.

Reed, D. (2020). *The Digital Manufacturing Commons*. Chicago, IL: MxD.

Reid, H. and Taylor, B. (2010). *Recovering the Commons: Democracy, Place, and Global Justice*. Chicago, IL: University of Illinois Press.

Remmer, K. L. (1986). The politics of economic stabilization: IMF standby programs in Latin America, 1954–1984. *Comparative Politics*, 19(1), 1–24.

Reynolds, M. (2008). The war on drugs, prison building, and globalization: Catalysts for the global incarceration of women. *NWSA Journal*, 20(2), 72–95.

Rhodes, C. and Bloom, P. (2012). The cultural fantasy of hierarchy: Sovereignty and the desire for spiritual purity. *Research in the Sociology of Organizations*, 35, 141–69.

Rice-Oxley, M. and Cross, C. (2012). Putin's political policies: From centrist to autocratic in 12 years. *The Guardian*, March 5. Available at: www.theguardian.com/world/interactive/2012/mar/05/russian-presidential-election-2012-russia

Richards, D. and Smith, M. J. (2002). *Governance and Public Policy in the United Kingdom*. Oxford: Oxford University Press.

Roberts, A. (2010). *The Logic of Discipline*. Oxford: Oxford University Press.

Roberts, J. (2005). The power of the "imaginary" in disciplinary processes. *Organization*, 12(5), 619–42.

Roberts, S. M., Jones, J. P. and Fröhling, O. (2005). NGOs and the globalization of managerialism: A research framework. *World Development*, 33(11), 1845–64.

Robertson, G. B. (2007). Strikes and labor organization in hybrid regimes. *American Political Science Review*, 101(4), 781–98.

Robertson, R. and Khondker, H. H. (1998). Discourses of globalization: Preliminary considerations. *International Sociology*, 13(1), 25–40.

Robins, K. (1991). Tradition and translation: National culture in its global context. In J. Corner and S. Harvey (eds), *Enterprise and Heritage* (pp. 29–52). London: Routledge.

Robinson, M. and White, G. (1998). *The Democratic Developmental State: Political and Institutional Design*. Oxford: Oxford University Press.

Robinson, W. I. (1996). Globalization, the world system, and "democracy promotion" in US foreign policy. *Theory and Society*, 25(5), 615–65.

Robinson, W. I. (2019). Global capitalist crisis and twenty-first century fascism: Beyond the Trump hype. *Science and Society*, 83(2), 155–83.

Robison, R. (1988). Authoritarian states, capital-owning classes, and the politics of newly industrializing countries: The case of Indonesia. *World Politics*, 41(1), 52–74.

Robison, R. and Rosser, A. (2003). Surviving the meltdown: Liberal reform and political oligarchy in Indonesia. In M. Beeson, K. Jayasuriya, H. R. Kim and R. Robison (eds), *Politics and Markets in the Wake of the Asian Crisis* (pp. 171–91). London: Routledge.

Rodan, G. (1989). *The Political Economy of Singapore's Industrialization: National State and International Capital*. London: Palgrave Macmillan.

Rodan, G. (2004). *Transparency and Authoritarian Rule in Southeast Asia: Singapore and Malaysia*. London: Routledge Press.

Rodan, G. and Jayasuriya, K. (2009). Capitalist development, regime transitions and new forms of authoritarianism in Asia. *The Pacific Review*, 22(1), 23–47.

Rodríguez, L. and Tejada, P. (1988). La oposición no debe alterar la paz social, señalan Gobernadores. *La Jornada*, August 8.

Rodrik, D. (2011). *The Globalization Paradox: Democracy and the Future of the World Economy*. New York: W. W. Norton.

Romano, O. (2012). How to rebuild democracy, re-thinking degrowth. *Futures*, 44(6), 582–9.

Romero, J. (2003). Crecimiento y comercio. In I. Bizberg and L. Meyer (eds), *Una historia contemporánea de México: Transformaciones y permanencias*. Mexico, DF: Editorial Océano de México.

Rosamond, B. (1999). Discourses of globalization and the social construction of European identities. *Journal of European Public Policy*, 6(4), 652–68.

Rosamond, B. (2003). Babylon and on? Globalization and international political economy. *Review of International Political Economy*, 10(4), 661–71.

Rose, N. (1996). Governing "advanced" liberal democracies. In A. Sharma and A. Gupta (eds), *The Anthropology of the State: A Reader* (pp. 144–62). Hoboken, NJ: John Wiley & Sons.

Rose, N., O'Malley, P. and Valverde, M. (2006). Governmentality. *Annual Review of Law and Social Science*, 2, 83–104.

Rosenau, J. N. (2000). Change, complexity and governance in a globalizing space. In J. Pierre (ed.), *Debating Governance: Authority, Steering, and Democracy* (pp. 169–200). Oxford: Oxford University Press.

Ross, E. W. (2019). The problem of democracy in the time of Trump. *Educazione aperta*, 6, 139–51.

Roy, D. (1994). Singapore, China, and the "soft authoritarian" challenge. *Asian Survey*, 34(3), 231–42.

Royer, C. (2022). When democracies perish democratically – then what? *Comparative Political Theory*, 2(1), 69–76.

Rudra, N. (2002). Globalization and the decline of the welfare state in less-developed countries. *International Organization*, 56(2), 411–45.

Rueda, D. and Pontusson, J. (2000). Wage inequality and varieties of capitalism. *World Politics*, 52(3), 350–83.

Ruggie, J. G. (1982). International regimes, transactions and change: Embedded liberalism in the postwar economic order." *International Organisation*, 36(2), 379–415.

Safa, H. (1985). President's corner. *Latin American Studies Association*, 15(4), 1–3.

Sakwa, R. (2008). Putin's leadership: Character and consequences. *Europe-Asia Studies*, 60(6), 879–97.

Salamé, G. (1994). *Democracy without Democrats? The Renewal of Politics in the Muslim World*. London: IB Tauris.

Sandoval, M. (2020). Entrepreneurial activism? Platform cooperativism between subversion and co-optation. *Critical Sociology*, 46(6), 801–17.

Santiso, C. (2001). Good governance and aid effectiveness: The World Bank and conditionality. *Georgetown Public Policy Review*, 7(1), 1–137.

Sarfaty, J. (2012). Civil society and education advocacy in Ecuador. In A. Verger and M. Novelli (eds), *Campaigning for "Education for All": Histories, Strategies and Outcomes of Transnational Advocacy Coalitions in Education* (pp. 51–64). Rotterdam: Sense Publishers.

Sassen, S. (1996). *Losing Control? Sovereignty in the Age of Globalization*. New York: Columbia University Press.

Sautman, B. (1995). The devil to pay: The 1989 debate and the intellectual origins of Yeltsin's "soft authoritarianism." *Communist and Post-Communist Studies*, 28(1), 131–51.

Savini, F., Ferreira, A. and von Schönfeld, K. C. (eds) (2022). *Post-Growth Planning: Cities Beyond the Market Economy*. New York: Routledge.

Savvides, L. (2019). *3D Printing: Politics, Material Hacking and Grassroots*. Doctoral dissertation, University of Leicester.

Schamis, H. E. (1991). Reconceptualizing Latin American authoritarianism in the 1970s: From bureaucratic-authoritarianism to neoconservatism. *Comparative Politics*, 23(2), 201–20.

Schatz, E. (2009). The soft authoritarian tool kit: Agenda-setting power in Kazakhstan and Kyrgyzstan. *Comparative Politics*, 41(2), 203–22.

Schedler, A. (2002). The menu of manipulation. *Journal of Democracy*, 13(2), 36–50.

Schedler, A., Diamond, L. and Plattner, M. F. (1999). Restraining the state: conflicts and agents of accountability. In A. Schedler (ed.), *The Self-Restraining State: Power and Accountability in New Democracies* (pp. 333–50). Boulder, CO: Lynne Rienner.

Scheiring, G. (2020). *The Retreat of Liberal Democracy: Authoritarian Capitalism and the Accumulative State in Hungary*. Berlin: Springer Nature.

Schept, J. (2013). A lockdown facility … with the feel of a small "private college": Liberal politics, jail expansion, and the carceral habitus. *Theoretical Criminology*, 17(1), 71–88.

Schimmelfennig, F. and Scholtz, H. (2008). EU democracy promotion in the European neighbourhood: Political conditionality, economic development and transnational exchange. *European Union Politics*, 9(2), 187–215.

Schlesinger, A. M. (2004). *The Imperial Presidency*. Boston, MA: Houghton Mifflin Harcourt.

Schmitz, G. (1995). Democratization and demystification: Deconstructing "governance" as development paradigm. In D. Moore and G. Schmitz (eds), *Debating Development Discourse* (pp. 54–90). London: Macmillan.

Scholte, J. A. (1997). Global capitalism and the state. *International Affairs*, 73(3), 427–52.

Scholte, J. A. (2000). *Globalization*. London: Palgrave Macmillan.

Scholte, J. A. (2005). *Globalization: A Critical Introduction*. London: Palgrave Macmillan.

Scholte, J. A. (2008). Defining globalisation. *The World Economy*, 31(11), 1471–502.

Schröter, J. (2020). Imaginary economies: The case of the 3D printer. *Review of Evolutionary Political Economy*, 1(3), 357–70.

Schultz, S. (2012). Profiting from pain: Europe's crisis is Germany's blessing. *Der Spiegel*, January 10. Available at: www.spiegel.de/international/europe/profiting-from-pain-europe-s-crisis-is-germany-sblessing-a-808248.html

Seah, C. M. (1999). The administrative state: Quo vadis? In L. Low (ed.), *Singapore: Towards a Developed Status* (pp. 250–70). Singapore: Oxford University Press.

Sempijja, N. and Nkosi, B. (2019). National counter-terrorism (CT) policies and challenges to human rights and civil liberties: Case study of Kenya. *International Human Rights and Counter-Terrorism*, 431–48.

Serra, J. (1979). Three mistaken theses regarding the connection between industrialization and authoritarian regimes. In D. Collier (ed.), *The New Authoritarianism in Latin America* (pp. 99–163). Princeton, NJ: Princeton University Press.

Shapiro, S. A. and Tomain, J. P. (2014). *Achieving Democracy: The Future of Progressive Regulation*. Oxford: Oxford University Press.

Sheahan, J. (1980). Market-oriented economic policies and political repression in Latin America. *Economic Development and Cultural Change*, 28(2), 267–91.

Sheppard, E. and Leitner, H. (2010). Quo vadis neoliberalism? The remaking of global capitalist governance after the Washington Consensus. *Geoforum*, 41(2), 185–94.

Shonkwiler, A. and La Berge, L. C. (eds) (2014). *Reading Capitalist Realism*. Iowa City, IA: University of Iowa Press.

Shuster, S. (2010). Russia's war on terror: A crackdown by popular demand. *Time Magazine*, April 15.

Signer, M. (2009). *Demagogue: The Fight to Save Democracy from Its Worst Enemies*. New York: St Martin's Press.

Sim, J. B. Y. (2012). The burden of responsibility: Elite students' understandings of civic participation in Singapore. *Educational Review*, 64(2), 195–210.

Sim, S. F. (2001). Asian values, authoritarianism and capitalism in Singapore. *Javnost – The Public*, 8(2), 45–66.

Singh, J. T. N. (2012a). Extraction as a space of social justice? Commodity production and labor rights in Brazil and Chile. In H. Haarstad (ed.), *New Political Spaces in Latin American Natural Resource Governance* (pp. 217–38). London: Palgrave Macmillan.

Singh, J. T. N. (2012b). Who owns the minerals? Repoliticizing neoliberal governance in Brazil and Chile. *Journal of Developing Societies*, 28(2), 229–56.

Sintomer, Y., Herzberg, C. and Röcke, A. (2008). Participatory budgeting in Europe: Potentials and challenges. *International Journal of Urban and Regional Research*, 32(1), 164–78.

Skeggs, B. and Wood, H. (2012). *Reacting to Reality Television: Performance, Audience and Value*. London: Routledge Press.

Sklair, L. (1999). Competing conceptions of globalization. *Journal of World-Systems Research*, 5(2), 143–63.

Sklair, J. and Glucksberg, L. (2021). Philanthrocapitalism as wealth management strategy: Philanthropy, inheritance and succession planning among the global elite. *The Sociological Review*, 69(2), 314–29.

Skocpol, T. (2013). *Diminished Democracy: From Membership to Management in American Civic Life*. Norman, OK: University of Oklahoma Press.

Skocpol, T. and Finegold, K. (1982). State capacity and economic intervention in the early New Deal. *Political Science Quarterly*, 97(2), 255–78.

Skocpol, T. and Williamson, V. (2012). *The Tea Party and the Remaking of Republican Conservatism*. Oxford: Oxford University Press.

Slater, D. (2003). Iron cage in an iron fist: Authoritarian institutions and the personalization of power in Malaysia. *Comparative Politics*, 36(1), 81–101.

Smith, A. (1990). Towards a global culture? In M. Featherstone (ed.), *Global Culture: Nationalism, Globalization and Modernity* (pp. 171–93). London: Sage.

Smith, T. (1994). In defense of intervention. *Foreign Affairs*, 73(6), 34–46.

Smith, T. (2012). *America's Mission: The United States and the Worldwide Struggle for Democracy*. Princeton, NJ: Princeton University Press.

Smith, T. (2020). "Stand back and watch us": Post-capitalist practices in the maker movement. *Environment and Planning A: Economy and Space*, 52(3), 593–610.

So, A. Y. (2002). Social protests, legitimacy crisis, and the impetus toward soft authoritarianism in the Hong Kong SAR. In S. K. Lau (ed.), *The Tung Group: The First Five Years of the Hong Kong Special Administrative Region* (pp. 363–418). Hong Kong: Chinese University Press.

So, A. Y. and Chan, M. K. (2002). Toward soft authoritarian developmentalism? In M. K. Chan and A. So (eds), *Crisis and Transformation in China's Hong Kong* (pp. 363–84). Armonk, NY: M. E. Sharpe.

Söderbaum, F. (2004). Modes of regional governance in Africa: Neoliberalism, sovereignty boosting, and shadow networks. *Global Governance*, 10(4), 419–36.

Söderberg, J. and Netzén, A. (2010). When all that is theory melts into (hot) air: Contrasts and parallels between Actor Network Theory, autonomist Marxism and open Marxism. *Ephemera: Theory and Politics in Organization*, 10(2), 95–118.

Somma, N. (2012). The Chilean student movement of 2011–2012: Challenging the marketization of education. *Interface: A Journal for and about Social Movements*, 4(2), 296–309.

Spagnoli, F. (2004). *Democratic Imperialism: A Practical Guide*. Cambridge: Cambridge Scholars Press.

Spicer, A. and Fleming, P. (2007). Intervening in the inevitable: Contesting globalization in a public sector organization. *Organization*, 14(4), 517–41.

Spich, R. S. (1995). Globalization folklore problems of myth and ideology in the discourse on globalization. *Journal of Organizational Change Management*, 8(4), 6–29.

Springer, S. (2010). Neoliberal discursive formations: On the contours of subjectivation, good governance, and symbolic violence in posttransitional Cambodia. *Environment and Planning. D, Society and Space*, 28(5), 931.

Stavrakakis, Y. (1999). *Lacan and the Political*. London: Routledge Press.

Stavrakakis, Y. (2008). Peripheral vision subjectivity and the organized other: Between symbolic authority and fantasmatic enjoyment. *Organization Studies*, 29(7), 1037–59.

Steger, M. B. (2005). Ideologies of globalization. *Journal of Political Ideologies*, 10(1), 11–30.

Steger, M. B. (2008). *The Rise of the Global Imaginary: Political Ideologies from the French Revolution to the Global War on Terror*. Oxford: Oxford University Press.

Stenson, K. (2001). The new politics of crime control. In K. Stenson and R. R. Sullivan (eds), *Crime, Risk and Justice: The Politics of Crime Control in Liberal Democracies* (pp. 15–29). London: Willan Publishing.

Stern, A. M. (2019). *Proud Boys and the White Ethnostate: How the Alt-Right Is Warping the American Imagination*. Boston, MA: Beacon Press.

Sternthal, S. (2012). Putin's anti-American campaign. *openDemocracy*, March 2. Available at: www.opendemocracy.net/od-russia/susanne-sternthal/putin%E2%80%99s-anti-american-campaign

Stewart, B. (2020). The rise of far-right civilizationism. *Critical Sociology*, 46 (7–8), 1207–20.

Stewart, M. (1994). *The Age of Interdependence: Economic Policy in a Shrinking World*. Boston, MA: MIT Press.

Stirrat, R. L. (1996). The new orthodoxy and old truths: Participation, empowerment and other buzz words. In S. Bastian and N. Bastian (eds), *Assessing Participation: A Debate from South Asia* (pp. 67–92). New Delhi: Konark Publishers.

Strange, S. (1996). *The Retreat of the State: The Diffusion of Power in the World*. Cambridge: Cambridge University Press.

Stubbs, R. (2001). Performance legitimacy and "soft authoritarianism." In A. Acharya, B. M. Frolic and R. Stubbs (eds), *Democracy, Human Rights and Civil Society in Southeast Asia* (pp. 37–54). Toronto: Joint Centre for Asia Pacific Studies.

Stubbs, R. (2009). What ever happened to the East Asian developmental state? The unfolding debate. *The Pacific Review*, 22(1), 1–22.

Subramaniam, S. (2000). The Asian values debate: Implications for the spread of liberal democracy. *Asian Affairs: An American Review*, 27(1), 19–35.

Sudbury, J. (ed.) (2014). *Global Lockdown: Race, Gender, and the Prison-Industrial Complex*. London: Routledge Press.

Sutton, S. A. (2019). Cooperative cities: Municipal support for worker cooperatives in the United States. *Journal of Urban Affairs*, 41(8), 1081–102.

Svolik, M. W. (2012). *The Politics of Authoritarian Rule*. Cambridge: Cambridge University Press.

Sweeney, J. J. (2000). Sweeney among the globalists. *The Globalist*, November 15. Available at: www.theglobalist.com/sweeney-among-the-globalists/

Swenson, P. (2002). *Capitalists against Markets: The Making of Labor Markets and Welfare States in the United States and Sweden*. Oxford: Oxford University Press.

Swyngedouw, E. (2000). Authoritarian governance, power, and the politics of rescaling. *Environment and Planning D*, 18(1), 63–76.

Tagma, H. M., Kalaycioglu, E. and Akcali, E. (2013). "Taming" Arab social movements: Exporting neoliberal governmentality. *Security Dialogue*, 44(5–6), 375–92.

Tan, C. and Tan, C. S. (2014). Fostering social cohesion and cultural sustainability: Character and citizenship education in Singapore. *Diaspora, Indigenous, and Minority Education*, 8(4), 191–206.

Tan, H. H. (1976). Foreign investment and multinational corporations in developing countries. In C. D. Nair (ed.), *Socialism That Works: The Singapore Way* (pp. 86–95). Singapore: Federal Publications.

Tan, K. P. (2008). Meritocracy and elitism in a global city: Ideological shifts in Singapore. *International Political Science Review*, 29(1), 7–27.

Tan, K. P. (2012). The ideology of pragmatism: Neo-liberal globalisation and political authoritarianism in Singapore. *Journal of Contemporary Asia*, 42(1), 67–92.

Taylor, A. J. (1972). *Laissez-Faire and State Intervention in Nineteenth-Century Britain*. London: Palgrave Macmillan.

Taylor, B. (2019). Alt-Right ecology. In B. Forchtner (ed.), *The Far Right and the Environment: Politics, Discourse and Communication* (pp. 275–92). Abingdon: Routledge.

Taylor, C., Pevehouse, J. and Straus, S. (2013). Perils of pluralism: Electoral violence and competitive authoritarianism in Sub-Saharan Africa. Working Papers Series, Simon Fraser University.

Taylor, M. (2006). *From Pinochet to the "Third Way": Neoliberalism and Social Transformation in Chile*. London: Pluto Press.

Teichman, J. A. (2001). *The Politics of Freeing Markets in Latin America: Chile, Argentina, and Mexico*. Chapel Hill, NC: University of North Carolina Press.

Tey, T. H. (2008). Confining the freedom of the press in Singapore: A "pragmatic" press for "nation-building"? *Human Rights Quarterly*, 30(4), 876–905.

Thomas, C. (1999). Does the good governance policy of the international financial institutions privilege markets at the expense of democracy. *Connecticut Journal of International Law*, 14(2), 551–631.

Thompson, C. (2018). Philanthrocapitalism: rendering the public domain obsolete? *Third World Quarterly*, 39(1), 51–67.

Thompson, K. A. (2018). *Prisons, Policing, and Pollution: Toward an Abolitionist Framework within Environmental Justice*. Thesis.

Thompson, M. R. (2001). Whatever happened to "Asian values"? *Journal of Democracy*, 12(4), 154–65.

Thompson, M. R. (2004). Pacific Asia after "Asian values": Authoritarianism, democracy, and "good governance." *Third World Quarterly*, 25(6), 1079–95.

Thurston, R. W. (1998). *Life and Terror in Stalin's Russia, 1934–1941.* New Haven, CT: Yale University Press.

Tickell, A. and Peck, J. (2003). Making global rules: Globalisation or neoliberalisation. In J. Peck and H. W. C. Yeung (eds), *Remaking the Global Economy: Economic-Geographical Perspectives* (pp. 163–82). London: Sage.

Tie, W. (2004). The psychic life of governmentality. *Culture, Theory and Critique*, 45(2), 161–76.

Tilly, C. (1985). *War Making and State Making as Organized Crime.* Cambridge: Cambridge University Press.

Treuger, F. (2015). France's intelligence bill: Legalizing mass surveillance. *openDemocracy*, April 29. Available at: www.opendemocracy.net/digitaliberties/f%C3%A9lix-tr%C3%A9guer/france%E2%80%99s-intelligence-bill-legalises-mass-surveillance

Triadafilopoulos, T. (2011). Illiberal means to liberal ends? Understanding recent immigrant integration policies in Europe. *Journal of Ethnic and Migration Studies*, 37(6), 861–80.

Triandafyllidou, A. (2020). Nationalism in the 21st century: Neo-tribal or plural? *Nations and Nationalism*, 26(4), 792–806.

Troxler, P. (2019). Building open design as a commons. *The Critical Makers Reader: (Un)learning Technology*, 218.

Tsai, K. S. (2007). *Capitalism without Democracy: The Private Sector in Contemporary China.* Ithaca, NY: Cornell University Press.

Tsoukala, A. (2008). *Security, Risk and Human Rights: A Vanishing Relationship?* Brussels: Center for European Policy Studies.

Tucker, R. C. (1979). The rise of Stalin's personality cult. *American Historical Review*, 84(2), 347–66.

Uglow, S. (1988). *Policing Liberal Society.* Oxford: Oxford University Press.

United Nations (1993). Report of the regional meeting for Asia of the World Conference on Human Rights. Bangkok, March 29–April 2. A/CONF.157/ASRM/8. Available at: http://daccess-dds-ny.un.org/doc/

Uyangoda, J. (2015). Rebuilding institutions in the transition from soft authoritarianism. *The Island*, February 9. Available at: www.island.lk/index.php?page_cat=article-details&page=article-details&code_title=119250

Van Herpen, M. (2013). *Putinism: The Slow Rise of a Radical Right Regime in Russia.* London: Palgrave Macmillan.

Van Hüllen, V. (2012). Europeanisation through cooperation? EU democracy promotion in Morocco and Tunisia. *West European Politics*, 35(1), 117–34.

van Krieken, R. (2019). Menno ter braak on democracy, populism and fascism: Ressentiment and its vicissitudes. *Theory, Culture and Society*, 36(3), 87–103.

Velasco, A. (2013). Illiberal democracy in Latin America. *Project Syndicate*, August 12. Available at: www.project-syndicate.org/commentary/illiberal-democracy-in-latin-america-by-andres-velasco

Verkoren, W. and Kamphuis, B. (2013). State building in a rentier state: How development policies fail to promote democracy in Afghanistan. *Development and Change*, 44(3), 501–26.

Vesta, T. (1999). *Ethiopia: A Post-Cold War African State.* London: Greenwood.

Vgontzas, N. (2022). Toward degrowth: Worker power, surveillance abolition, and climate justice at Amazon. *New Global Studies*, 16(1), 49–67.

Viner, J. (1927). Adam Smith and laissez-faire. *Journal of Political Economy*, 35(2), 198–232.

Viner, J. (1960). The intellectual history of laissez-faire. *Journal of Law and Economics*, 3(1), 45–69.

Von Hippel, K. (2000). *Democracy by Force: US Military Intervention in the Post-Cold War World*. Cambridge: Cambridge University Press.

Wacquant, L. (2009). *Punishing the Poor: The Neoliberal Government of Social Insecurity*. Durham, NC: Duke University Press.

Wacquant, L. (2010). Class, race and hyperincarceration revanchist in America. *Daedalus*, 139(3), 74–90.

Wade, R. (1990). *Governing the Market: Economic Theory and the Role of Government in East Asian Industrialization*. Princeton, NJ: Princeton University Press.

Wade, R. (1996). Japan, the World Bank, and the art of paradigm maintenance: The East Asian miracle in political perspective. *New Left Review*, 3–37.

Wade, R. (2013). How high inequality plus neoliberal governance weakens democracy. *Challenge*, 56(6), 5–37.

Walker, M. (2002). America's virtual empire. *World Policy Journal*, 19(2), 13–20.

Walter, S. (2021). The backlash against globalization. *Annual Review of Political Science*, 24, 421–42.

Weber, M. (1998). *The Protestant Ethic and the Spirit of Capitalism*. London: Roxbury Publishing.

Wee, C. L. (2001). The end of disciplinary modernisation? The Asian economic crisis and the ongoing reinvention of Singapore. *Third World Quarterly*, 22(6), 987–1002.

Wee, C. L. (2007). *The Asian Modern: Culture, Capitalist Development, Singapore*. Hong Kong: Hong Kong University Press.

Weiss, T. G. (2000). Governance, good governance and global governance: Conceptual and actual challenges. *Third World Quarterly*, 21(5), 795–814.

Wexler, S., Engel, R. J., Laufer, T. and Steiner, E. (2020). "We're not the enemy and we're not asking for the world": Low-wage hospital service workers' advocacy for fair wages. *Journal of Sociology and Social Welfare*, 47, 123.

Weyland, K. (2001). Clarifying a contested concept: Populism in the study of Latin American politics. *Comparative Politics*, 34(1), 1–22.

Weyland, K. (2021). *Assault on Democracy*. Cambridge: Cambridge University Press.

White, L. T. (2014). *Policies of Chaos: The Organizational Causes of Violence in China's Cultural Revolution*. Princeton, NJ: Princeton University Press.

White, S. C. (1999). NGOs, civil society, and the state in Bangladesh: The politics of representing the poor. *Development and Change*, 30(2), 307–26.

Whitehead, L. (1996). Concerning international support for democracy in the South. In R. Luckham and G. White (eds), *Democratization in the South: The Jagged Wave* (pp. 243–73). Manchester: Manchester University Press.

Whitehouse, M. (2009). Crisis compels economists to reach for new paradigm. *Wall Street Journal*, November 4. Available at: www.wsj.com/articles/SB125720159912223873

Whitmore, B. (2013). Vladimir Putin, conservative icon. *The Atlantic*, December 20. Available at: www.theatlantic.com/international/archive/2013/12/vladimir-putin-conservative-icon/282572/

Wickham, J. A. (2002). September 11 and America's war on terrorism: A new manifest destiny? *American Indian Quarterly*, 26(1), 116–44.

Widner, J. A. (1994). *Economic Change and Political Liberalization in Sub-Saharan Africa*. Baltimore, MD: Johns Hopkins University Press.

Wilkinson, M. A. (2021). *Authoritarian Liberalism and the Transformation of Modern Europe*. Oxford: Oxford University Press.

Williams, R. (1973). Base and superstructure in Marxist cultural theory. In M. G. Durham and D. M. Kellner (eds), *Media and Cultural Studies: Keyworks* (pp. 130–43). Hoboken, NJ: John Wiley & Sons.

Willmott, H. (1993). Strength is ignorance; slavery is freedom: Managing culture in modern organizations. *Journal of Management Studies*, 30(4), 515–52.

Wilson, J. and Swyngedouw, E. (eds) (2014). *The Post-Political and Its Discontents: Spaces of Depoliticization, Spectres of Radical Politics*. Edinburgh: Edinburgh University Press.

Wilson, R. A. (ed.) (2005). *Human Rights in the "War on Terror."* Cambridge: Cambridge University Press.

Winfield, B. H. and Peng, Z. (2005). Market or party controls? Chinese media in transition. *Gazette*, 67(3), 255–70.

Wodak, R. (2019). The trajectory of far-right populism: A discourse-analytical perspective. In B. Forchtner (ed.), *The Far Right and the Environment: Politics, Discourse and Communication* (pp. 21–37). Abingdon: Routledge.

Wolfe, A. (1977). *The Limits of Legitimacy: Contradictions of Contemporary Capitalism*. New York: Free Press.

Wood, E. M. (1997). Modernity, postmodernity or capitalism? *Review of International Political Economy*, 4(3), 539–60.

Wood, G. (1997). States without citizens: The problem of the franchise state. In D. Hulme and M. Edwards (eds), *NGOs, States and Donors: Too Close for Comfort?* (pp. 79–92). London: Palgrave Macmillan.

Woodcock, J. (2020). The algorithmic panopticon at Deliveroo: Measurement, precarity, and the illusion of control. *Ephemera*, 20(3), 67–95.

Woodcock, J. and Cant, C. (2022). Platform worker organising at Deliveroo in the UK: From wildcat strikes to building power. *Journal of Labor and Society*, 1, 1–17.

World Bank (1989). *Sub-Saharan Africa – From Crisis to Sustainable Growth: A Long-Term Perspective Study*. Washington, DC: World Bank.

World Bank (1992). *Governance and Development*. Washington, DC: World Bank.

World Bank (1993). *Main Report: A World Bank Policy Research Report*. New York: Oxford University Press.

World Bank (2013). *World Bank Report: Ethiopia*. Washington, DC: World Bank.

Wortman, R. S. (2000). *Scenarios of Power: Myth and Ceremony in Russian Monarchy, Volume 2: From Alexander II to the Abdication of Nicholas II*. Princeton, NJ: Princeton University Press.

Wright, E. O. (1979). *Class, Crisis and the State*. London: Verso.

Wuthnow, R. (2019). *The Left Behind*. Princeton, NJ: Princeton University Press.

Wylie, R. F. (1979). Mao Tse-tung, Ch'en Po-ta and the "Sinification of Marxism," 1936–38. *The China Quarterly*, 79, 447–80.

Xenakis, D. K. (2000). Order and change in the EuroMediterranean system. *Mediterranean Quarterly*, 11(1), 75–90.

Xi Jinping (2012). China's new party chief Xi Jinping's speech. BBC News, November 15. Available at: www.bbc.co.uk/news/world-asia-china-20338586

Xi Jinping (2014). Speech by H. E. Xi Jinping President of the People's Republic of China at China International Friendship Conference in Commemoration of the 60th

Anniversary of the CPAFFC, May 15. Available at: http://en.cpaffc.org.cn/content/details25-47426.html

Xu, X. (2021). To repress or to co-opt? Authoritarian control in the age of digital surveillance. *American Journal of Political Science*, 65(2), 309–25.

Yaffe, D. S. (1973). The Marxian theory of crisis, capital and the state. *Economy and Society*, 2(2), 186–232.

Yang, D. L. (1998). *Calamity and Reform in China: State, Rural Society, and Institutional Change Since the Great Leap Famine*. Stanford, CA: Stanford University Press.

Yardley, W. (2011). The branding of the Occupy movement. *New York Times*, November 27.

Yeo, G. Y. B. (1990). Luck, leaders and institutions. *Speeches*, 14(4), 101–10.

Yom, S. L. and Al-Momani, M. H. (2008). The international dimensions of authoritarian regime stability: Jordan in the post-Cold War era. *Arab Studies Quarterly*, 30(1), 39–60.

Yue, A. (2006). Cultural governance and creative industries in Singapore. *International Journal of Cultural Policy*, 12(1), 17–33.

Yuhan, S. H. (2004). Imperial presidency strikes back: Executive Order 13,233, the National Archives, and the capture of presidential history. *New York University Law Review*, 79(4), 1570–604.

Zaidi, S. A. (1999). NGO failure and the need to bring back the state. *Journal of International Development*, 11(2), 259.

Zakaria, F. (1997). The rise of illiberal democracy. *Foreign Affairs*, 76(6), 22–43.

Zakaria, F. (2014). The rise of Putinism. *Washington Post*, July 31. Available at: www.washingtonpost.com/opinions/fareed-zakaria-the-rise-of-putinism/2014/07/31/2c9711d6-18e7-11e4-9e3b-7f2f110c6 265_story.html

Zelnick, J. R., Goodkind, S. and Kim, M. E. (2022). "It would be foolish to pretend that our jobs aren't political": Social workers organizing for power in the nonprofit sector. *Affilia*, 37(1), 5–12.

Zernike, K. (2010). *Boiling Mad: Inside Tea Party America*. London: Palgrave Macmillan.

Zhang, J. (2012). From Hong Kong's capitalist fundamentals to Singapore's authoritarian governance: The policy mobility of neoliberalising Shenzhen, China. *Urban Studies*, 49(13), 2853–71.

Zimmerer, J. (2007). Colonialism and the Holocaust: Towards an archeology of genocide. *Development and Dialogue*, 50(November), 95–124.

Žižek, S. (1989). *The Sublime Object of Ideology*. London: Verso.

Žižek, S. (1993). *Tarrying with the Negative*. Durham, NC: Duke University Press.

Žižek, S. (1994). *The Metastases of Enjoyment: Six Essays on Woman and Causality*. London: Verso.

Žižek, S. (1997). *The Plague of Fantasies*. London: Verso.

Žižek, S. (1998). The seven veils of fantasy. In D. Nobus (ed.), *Key Concepts of Lacanian Psychoanalysis*. London: Rebus Press.

Žižek, S. (2006). *The Universal Exception*. London: Continuum.

Žižek, S. (2013). Zero Dark Thirty: Hollywood's gift to American power. *The Guardian*, January 25.

Zuboff, S. (2019). *The Age of Surveillance Capitalism: The Fight for a Human Future at the New Frontier of Power*. London: Profile Books.

Zygmuntowski, J. J. (2018). Commoning in the digital era: Platform cooperativism as a counter to cognitive capitalism. *Praktyka teoretyczna*, 27, 168–92.

Index

Printed and bound by CPI Group (UK) Ltd, Croydon, CR0 4YY

16/04/2025

14658488-0001